SHIPS OF THE CIVIL WAR
1861–1865

SHIPS OF THE CIVIL WAR
1861–1865

AN ILLUSTRATED GUIDE TO THE FIGHTING VESSELS
OF THE UNION AND THE CONFEDERACY

KEVIN J. DOUGHERTY

METRO BOOKS
NEW YORK

METRO BOOKS
New York

An Imprint of Sterling Publishing
387 Park Avenue South
New York, NY 10016

Editorial and design by
Amber Books Ltd
74–77 White Lion Street
London N1 9PF
www.amberbooks.co.uk

Project Editor: Michael Spilling
Designer: Andrew Easton
Picture Research: Terry Forshaw

All artworks courtesy of Tony Gibbons © Amber Books
All photographs courtesy of Library of Congress

ISBN: 978-1-4351-4592-4

For information about custom editions, special sales, and premium and corporate purchases, please
contact Sterling Special Sales at 800-805-5489 or specialsales@sterlingpublishing.com.

Manufactured in China

2 4 6 8 10 9 7 5 3 1

www.sterlingpublishing.com

Contents

Introduction

ON APRIL 19, 1861, SIX DAYS AFTER THE FIRST BATTLE OF FORT SUMTER, PRESIDENT ABRAHAM LINCOLN ISSUED A PROCLAMATION DECLARING THE BLOCKADE OF THE SOUTHERN STATES FROM SOUTH CAROLINA TO TEXAS. ON APRIL 27, THE BLOCKADE WAS EXTENDED TO VIRGINIA AND NORTH CAROLINA. THE PURPOSE OF THE BLOCKADE WAS TO ISOLATE THE CONFEDERACY FROM EUROPEAN TRADE. DECLARING A BLOCKADE AND MAKING IT EFFECTIVE, HOWEVER, WERE TWO DIFFERENT THINGS.

THE FEDERAL NAVY

When Lincoln came to office, the U.S. Navy consisted of a total of 90 warships. Of these, 22 were unserviceable and 27 out of commission. That left only 41 warships in commission. With such scant resources and 189 harbor and river openings along the 3,549 miles (5,711 km) of Confederate shoreline between the Potomac and the Rio Grande, clearly some focus was needed.

Responsibility for the Federal (also commonly referred to as the Union) blockade strategy rested with the Blockade Board that Secretary of the Navy Gideon Welles created in June 1861 to study the conduct of the blockade and to devise ways of improving its efficiency. Captain Samuel Du Pont presided over the Board and used it as an effective forum to plan the Federal naval strategy.

If Welles now had a strategy, he still faced the daunting task of building the infrastructure to implement it. First he purchased every merchant craft that could be convert to a transport or fighting vessel. He entered into contracts for eight additional sloops of war. He contracted for "90-day gunboats" to be ready for commissioning in three months. Thirty-nine double-ended side-wheel steamers for river service were hurried to completion and ironclads were built. As a result of these efforts, by the end of the war, the U.S. Navy was among the most powerful in the world, with 671 commissioned ships.

Between 1861 and 1865 its officer population had increased from 1,300 to 6,700 while the enlisted ranks had swollen from 7,500 to 51,500. Over the course of the war, naval expenditures jumped tenfold from $12 million to $123 million. The production of this fleet was one of the more obvious demonstrations of the size, industrial, and financial advantages the North enjoyed over the South.

ABOVE: *The Civil War saw the introduction of several novel technologies. This torpedo boat was part of the Confederate effort to resist the tightening Federal blockade at Charleston.*

OPPOSITE: *The Battle of Hampton Roads in March 1862 featured the first clash of the ironclads, the Federal* Monitor *and the Confederate* Virginia.

THE BOMBARDMENT AND CAPTURE OF FORT HINDMAN, ARKANSAS POST, ARK. JANY 11TH 1863.

By the Gun boats, commanded by Rear Admiral D.D. Porter, and the Union troops under Maj'Gen' M'Clernand, the number of Prisoners taken was 7000 being...

OPPOSITE: *Steampower freed ships from the vagaries of winds and currents and allowed the Federal Navy to penetrate into the interior of the Confederacy by patrolling its rivers with gunboats like this one.*

The Navy's growth was fueled by its eight navy yards. The ones in Washington, D.C., Philadelphia, Pennsylvania, New York, New York, Boston, Massachusetts, Portsmouth, New Hampshire, and Mare Island, California remained in Union hands at the outbreak of the war. The ones in Norfolk, Virginia and Pensacola, Florida were briefly controlled by the Confederacy, but quickly recovered.

The Union also had a naval depot in Cairo, Illinois and a repair and supply station in Baltimore, Maryland. Soon these facilities were operating at full capacity, and captured ports such as New Orleans, Louisiana and Port Royal, South Carolina were added to the Federal resources. While the government facilities experienced moderate expansion during the war, most of the new Union warships were built in civilian locations. These combined resources dwarfed the South's meager capabilities.

Welles also oversaw organizational innovations that helped build his Navy. In addition to the Blockade Board, he

LEFT: *Although lacking formal doctrine, the Army and Navy conducted joint operations such as this attack on Fort Hindman (or Arkansas Post) on the Arkansas River.*

made liberal use of other such forums like an Ironclad Board. He created the position of Assistant Secretary of the Navy, which was ably filled by Gustavus Fox. Welles obtained Congressional approval to increase the number of Navy bureaus to eight, which handled matters related to Yards and Docks, Equipment and Recruiting, Navigation, Ordnance, Construction and Repair, Steam Engineering, Provisions and Clothing, and Medicine and Surgery. Examining boards helped force ineffective officers into retirement and promote promising talent based on merit.

The officer ranks were systematized, including adding the ranks of ensign, lieutenant commander, captain, rear admiral and vice admiral. Many of Welles' administrative changes remained in place long after he left his post in 1869. Of no small note is the fact that the Navy under Welles accomplished this growth and change largely without accompanying graft or corruption.

Some 118,044 sailors served in the Union Navy during the war. According to one study, their average age was 26, considerably older than their Army counterparts. Most were easterners,

with New York, Massachusetts, and Pennsylvania being the leading providers. They tended to come from the poor, urban classes and were a rougher group of individuals, and not as idealistically committed to the war effort as soldiers.

The promise of regular pay and food often was more of a motivation to join the Navy than patriotism. About 45 percent of sailors were foreign born with most of these coming from Ireland.

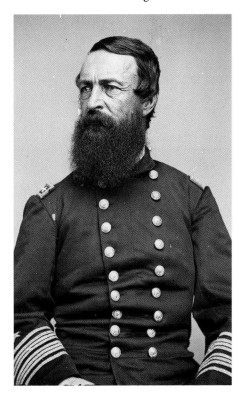

ABOVE: *Admiral David Porter was among the younger naval officers who rose to lead the Federal Navy during the Civil War.*

OPPOSITE: *Sailors in the Federal Navy were an eclectic group. Those who served on monitors, such as the* Saugus *shown here, labored under physically difficult conditions. Often, up to 150 crew would be crammed onto a single vessel.*

About 16 percent of the Navy's total strength during the war was black, and ship crews were integrated.

Welles was fortunate to inherit a distinguished pre-war officer corps. Du Pont brought with him valuable experience with blockade duty gained from the Mexican War. David Farragut, who would be the first to hold the new rank of vice admiral, had joined the Navy at the age of nine in 1810 and had served in the War of 1812. Others like David Porter had less pre-war experience but would, nevertheless, go on to rise to greatness.

The Navy made a host of contributions to the Federal war effort. Its powerful fleet allowed joint forces to descend almost anywhere along the Confederacy's vast coastline, stretching thin the South's limited defenses. An ever-tightening blockade isolated the Confederacy from foreign goods and a market for its cotton. Steam power allowed the Union to project its military might up rivers and into the interior of the Confederacy, ultimately dividing it in two when the Federals gained control of the Mississippi. Although the war was ultimately decided by the battles fought by the great land armies, the contribution of the Navy to the Union victory was one of North's more important advantages.

THE CONFEDERATE NAVY

Secretary of the Navy Stephen Mallory faced an almost impossible task in building a Confederate Navy. The Confederate Navy started out with no ships, inherited five from the seceded states, and grew to about 130. Still the Confederacy simply lacked the industrial shipbuilding capacity to keep up with the North. The Federal Navy's superior strength allowed it not just to control the coastline but to use steam power to penetrate into the heart of the Confederacy via large rivers like the Mississippi. There was little the Confederate Navy could do to counter this threat.

RIGHT, TOP: *One of the early Federal victories that showed the Confederacy's vulnerability to river operations was the capture of Fort Henry in February 1862.*

RIGHT, BELOW: *The Sinking of the* Cumberland *by the Ironclad* Merrimack *off Newport News, Virginia, March 8, 1862. Unable to match the large Federal wooden fleet, the Confederacy hoped to even the score with ironclads. The ironclad's sinking of of a large sail ship showed the potential of this new weapon.*

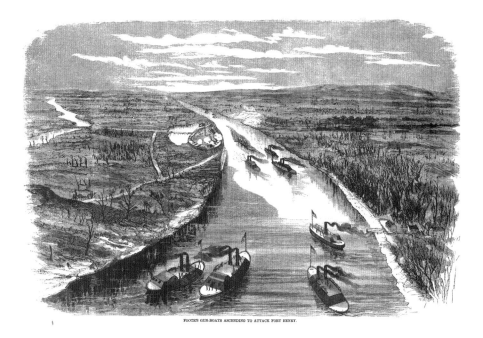

FOOTE'S GUN-BOATS ASCENDING TO ATTACK FORT HENRY.

ABOVE: *The* CSS Stonewall *was part of the Confederacy's effort to augment its limited domestic ship production capability.*

The Navy Mallory envisioned was designed almost entirely for the purpose of defeating the Federal blockade. To this end, Mallory developed a two-pronged approach. First he would confront the blockade directly by building domestically or buying abroad a few powerful ships that by quality would outmatch the Federal advantage in quantity. As he explained to his wife, "Knowing that the enemy could build one hundred ships to one of our own, my policy has been to make ships so strong and invulnerable as would compensate for the inequality of numbers."

Because of the South's limited industrial capacity, Mallory relied on James Bulloch to leverage British sympathies and shipyards. These efforts succeeded in obtaining four vessels for the Confederacy: the *Shenandoah*, *Florida*, and *Alabama*, all built in Britain, and the CSS *Stonewall*, which was built in France. Overseas ship production, however, was a lengthy and uncertain process, so Mallory also did what he could to build domestically. His principal hope lay in ironclads, which offered the promise of wreaking havoc with the Federal wooden fleet. Throughout the war the Confederacy initiated construction of 52 ironclads and completed almost 30 of them. Although this was an impressive achievement given the Confederacy's limited resources, the fact remained that the ironclads produced in Southern shipyards were little more than armored, floating artillery batteries, capable of little more than harbor defense.

Institutionally, Mallory modeled the Confederate Navy on the customs and regulations of the U.S. Navy. This included the creation of "offices" such as the "Office of Provisions and Clothing" or the "Office of Orders and Detail." Pay tables also followed a Federal pattern. The Confederate Navy even continued the Federal practice of allocating each enlisted man a ration of a half-pint of spirits or wine a day.

Mallory found himself short of almost everything but officers. There he had the opposite problem—too many experienced officers for the few available command operations. Men like Josiah Tattnall and Franklin Buchanan had commanded squadrons at sea in the "Old Navy" and now were competing for a handful of converted tugboats and river steamers. While promotion was rapid in the Confederate Army, Confederate Navy

OPPOSITE: *The massive Federal industrial base cranked out a seemingly countless number of new vessels, such as the ironclad* St. Louis.

officers usually ended the war at the rank they had entered it or at best received one promotion.

In May 1863, Mallory ingeniously created an entirely new naval service called the "Provisional Navy of the Confederate States." All enlisted men were automatically transferred to this new organization, but commissioned officer billets would be filled only by presidential appointment. This technique allowed Mallory to select those younger officers that showed promise and advance men based on talent rather than strictly on seniority.

Mallory had no such embarrassment of riches in the enlisted ranks. The Confederate Navy's enlisted strength peaked at 4,500, at least 25 percent below requirements, and its average enlisted strength was probably around 3,000. Without an indigenous seafaring population, the South simply had a smaller natural pool of personnel. Free

blacks could enlist with the approval of the local squadron commander or the Navy Department, and slaves could serve with their master's permission. Although accurate figures are not known, a fair number of blacks served in the Confederate Navy as coal heavers, stewards, and, in some select cases, highly skilled tidewater pilots.

Outside the Navy, hundreds of enterprising individuals took their chances running the blockade in order to bring cargoes in and out of the Confederacy. Their efforts helped satiate the South's dependence on overseas goods and also produced handsome profits for the blockade runners.

Blockade runners possessed several advantages. Blockade duty was monotonous and dreary, and it was hard for the Federals to be constantly vigilant. Blockade runners could exploit this weakness using the element of surprise to take advantage of a momentary Federal lapse in attention. Blockade runners also often had local knowledge of the intricacies of the Confederate coast and knew how to use the geography to their advantage. The Federal ships

OPPOSITE: *Steampower and improved munitions reversed the old assumption that one gun on land was equal to four on the water. Here, Federal ships bypass Fort Morgan on Mobile Bay.*

could obviously not be everywhere, and the blockade runner needed to find just one seam to avoid detection. These opportunities for success and the potential for huge profits attracted a wide variety of blockade runners.

The Confederacy also sought to counter the Federal naval superiority by the use of naval mines, "torpedoes" in the lexicon of the day. They were detonated either by contact with a ship or by an electric current initiated by an operator on shore. Torpedoes were systematically incorporated into the Confederate defenses of Mobile Bay and Charleston Harbor and used less formally in the river defenses, particularly of the Mississippi's tributaries.

In the final analysis, the creation of a Confederate Navy was a remarkable achievement against overwhelming odds, but still a woeful counter to its powerful Federal opponent. With the Confederacy's lengthy coast and numerous rivers, the Federal Navy could strike anywhere, and the small Confederate Navy could defend only a few isolated locations. In spite of its Herculean efforts, the Confederate Navy showed little in the way of tangible results.

RIGHT: *Among the older generation of the war's great naval heroes was Admiral David Farragut, shown here atop the* Hartford's *mainmast at Mobile Bay.*

PRANG'S
American Chromos.
LASHED TO THE SHROUDS.

L. PRANG & CO.

CSS *Manassas* (1861)

THE *MANASSAS* BEGAN HER CAREER AS A PRIVATEER. BUSINESSMAN JOHN STEVENSON RAISED FUNDS BY SUBSCRIPTIONS TO BUY THE *ENOCH TRAIN*, A NEW ENGLAND ICEBREAKER, WITH THE INTENTION OF USING HER FOR THIS PURPOSE. SHE WAS ORIGINALLY BUILT IN 1855 AS A TWIN-SCREW TOWBOAT AT MEDFORD, MASSACHUSETTS, BY JAMES O. CURTIS.

New Orleans boatbuilders expanded the *Enoch Train's* length from 128 to 143 feet (39–43.5 m), beam from 26 to 33 feet (7.9–10 m), and depth from 12.6 ft to 17 feet (3.8–5.2 m). They then rebuilt the ship with massive 17 inch (432 mm) beams to make a solid bow of 20 feet (6 m). Over this lumber, workers laid a covering of thin iron plates, rendering the exposed part of the vessel shot-proof. The result was a strange-looking turtle- or egg-shaped vessel. Locals informally called it "The Turtle" until it was officially renamed the *Manassas* in honor of the Confederate victory there.

The *Manassas* carried a crew of 33, but only one gun, a stationary 32 pounder carronade. In many ways the gun was a nuisance because the main weapon of the *Manassas* was an underwater iron ram designed to tear holes in the sides of the Federal wooden fleet. Admiral David Porter called her "the boat with the iron horn."

First Use of a Ram

With the Federal fleet gathering around New Orleans, Commodore George Hollins seized the *Manassas* from Stevenson and pressed it into Confederate service on October 11, 1861. Manned by soldiers commanded by Lieutenant Alexander Warley and volunteers from the fleet, the *Manassas* was joined by six lightly armed riverboats to form a small flotilla that Hollins launched against Captain John Pope's unsuspecting Federal fleet assembled at Head of Passes.

There, in the early morning hours of October 12, the *Manassas* drove a 5 inch (127 mm) hole into the hull of the *USS Richmond*, marking the first wartime use of an ironclad ram. The collision disabled one of the *Manassas'* engines, rendering her unable to attack other prey, and

Warley was forced to ground her in a mudbank.

Panic and confusion swept the Federal fleet and by 8.00 a.m. Pope gave the order "to get underway." Somehow the order was interrupted as "abandon ship," and the ensuing inglorious retreat became known as "Pope's Run." Porter declared it "the most ridiculous affair that ever took place in the American Navy." Indeed, *Manassas'* attack on the Richmond created fear in the hearts of many Federal commanders and began a syndrome of "ram fever." Nonetheless, the *Manassas* was little help to the defenders of New Orleans when Admiral David Farragut launched a determined attack on April 24, 1862 that captured the city.

SPECIFICATIONS

DISPLACEMENT: 387 tons (351 tonnes)

DIMENSIONS: 143 ft x 33 ft x 17 ft (44 m x 10 m x 5.2 m)

ARMAMENT: One 64 pounder gun

ARMOR: 1.5 inches (38 mm) iron plate. The bow was filled in with timber.

MACHINERY: Steam engine

SPEED: Unknown

CREW: 36

CSS *Manassas*

GUN
Manassas carried only one gun.
When the gun was run in, the
hatch automatically closed.

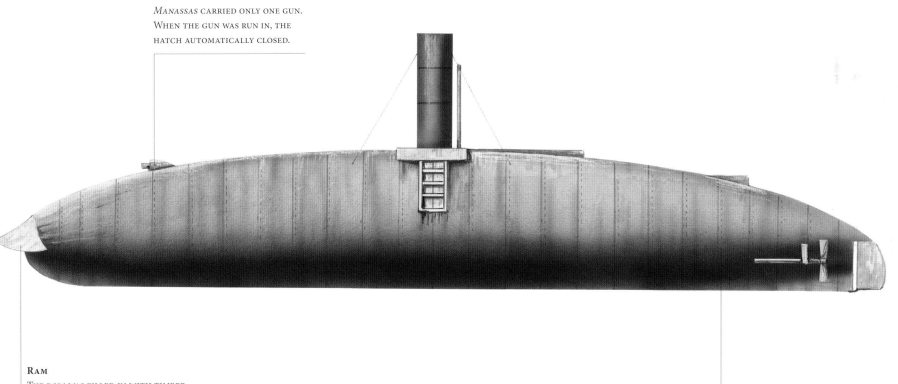

RAM
The bow was filled in with timber
to form a 20 ft (6 m) long ram.

IRON
The oak deck was sheathed with
1.5 in (38 mm) of iron plate.

CSS *Arkansas* (1862)

THE CSS *ARKANSAS* WAS AN IRONCLAD RAM THAT WAS STILL UNDER CONSTRUCTION IN MEMPHIS, TENNESSEE AS FEDERAL FORCES CLOSED IN ON THE CITY IN MAY 1862. TO ESCAPE CAPTURE, THE *ARKANSAS* WAS TOWED UP THE YAZOO RIVER TO YAZOO CITY, MISSISSIPPI, WHERE WORK WAS RESUMED. USING MUCH INGENUITY AND IMAGINATION, LIEUTENANT ISAAC BROWN GOT THE VESSEL READY FOR ACTION IN ABOUT FIVE WEEKS.

On July 15, Brown took the *Arkansas* down the Yazoo River towards Vicksburg. Time was critical as the ship drew 13 feet (4 m) and the river was going down. To make matters worse, on the trip downriver, the ship's boiler sprang a leak and soaked one of the powder magazines. By this time the Federals had learned of the *Arkansas* and dispatched the gunboats *Carondelet* and *Tyler* and the ram *Queen of the West* to investigate. In the ensuing battle, the *Arkansas* badly damaged the two gunboats and continued on into the Mississippi River, where she fought her way through the Federal fleet around Vicksburg. In that encounter, Brown reported being able to fire "to every point of the circumference without fear of hitting a friend or missing an enemy."

The Confederates did not escape unharmed, however, with Brown receiving two head wounds and the *Arkansas* taking a debilitating shot to the pipe connecting the furnace to the smokestack and several shots that penetrated her armor. In the final tally, the Confederates had lost 12 men killed and 18 wounded. The Federals lost 17 killed and 42 wounded. One Federal ship had been disabled and every wooden ship in the Federal fleet had been hit at least once. It was a dramatic victory for a lone Confederate ironclad. Admiral David Farragut was furious, condemning his fleet's performance as "the most disreputable naval affair of the war."

Attack in Vicksburg

While in Vicksburg, the *Arkansas* was attacked by the Queen of the West and the ironclad *Essex* on July 22. Swinging his vessel away from the bank, prow out, Brown presented as small a target as possible and the *Arkansas* was not seriously damaged. The Confederates did, however, lose seven killed and six wounded. Both Federal ships remained intact, but had taken a beating before Commander David Porter called off the attack. The *Essex* had been hit 42 times.

The *Arkansas* was then ordered to assist Confederate forces under Major General John Breckinridge that were attempting to retake Baton Rouge, Louisiana. In the process, the *Arkansas* suffered a severe machinery breakdown on August 6 while battling the *Essex*. Brown ran the *Arkansas* ashore and blew her up to prevent capture. The wreck remains unrecovered, according to one theory on the west bank of the Mississippi River near Sunrise, Louisiana.

SPECIFICATIONS

DISPLACEMENT: 800 tons (725 tonnes)

DIMENSIONS: 165 ft x 35 ft x 11.5 ft (50 m x 11 m x 3.5 m)

ARMAMENT: Two 8 in (203 mm) Columbiads in bow ports; two 6.4 in (163 mm) Brooke rifles in stern ports; two 6.4 in (163 mm) Brooke rifles; four 8 in (203 mm) Dahlgren smoothbore guns in broadside ports

ARMOR: Casemate: railroad iron over wood and compressed cotton; pilothouse: 2 in (51 mm); top: 1 in (25 mm)

MACHINERY: Twin screw

SPEED: 8 knots

CREW: 232

CSS *Arkansas*

PAINT
A COAT OF BROWN PAINT WAS APPLIED TO HELP HIDE *ARKANSAS* AGAINST THE RIVERBANKS OF THE YAZOO RIVER.

STERN
ARKANSAS WAS QUITE FAST: THE TAPERED STERN ALLOWED THE WATER TO CLOSE UP QUICKLY BEHIND HER.

HULL
THE MIDDLE 8 FT (2.4 M) SECTION OF HER HULL WAS FLAT-BOTTOMED.

CSS *Atlanta* (1862)

THE CSS *ATLANTA* WAS ORIGINALLY BUILT IN GLASGOW, SCOTLAND AND LAUNCHED IN MAY 1861 AS THE MERCHANT STEAMSHIP *FINGAL*. THE ENTERPRISING CONFEDERATE AGENT IN ENGLAND JAMES BULLOCH PURCHASED HER, LOADED HER WITH SUPPLIES AND TOOK HER TO BERMUDA ON OCTOBER 15, 1861.

CSS *TEXAS*

From there she ran the Federal blockade and reached Savannah, Georgia on November 22. She brought with her an immensely valuable cargo of 14,000 Enfield rifles; one million cartridges; two million percussion caps; thousands of sabers, bayonets, rifles and revolvers; 10 rifled cannons and their ammunition; and assorted medical supplies.

The tightening blockade prevented the *Fingal* from returning to England, so she was cut down to the waterline by Asa and Nelson Tift and rebuilt as a 1,006 ton (912 tonne) ironclad ram. She was 206 feet (62 m) in length, had three screws and a crew of 145 men. She boasted two 7 inch (178 mm) Brooke rifles and two 6.4 inch (162 mm) Parrott rifles, along with a bow-mounted spar torpedo.

On June 17, 1863, Commander William Webb led the *Atlanta* out of the Wilmington River and into battle with the Federal ironclads *Nahant* and *Weehawken*. In a brief and lopsided battle, the *Atlanta* was able to get off only seven shots before running ashore and surrendering. One of her crew was killed and 16 others were wounded.

The U.S. Navy sent the captured ship to the Philadelphia Navy Yard, where she was repaired and recommissioned as the USS *Atlanta* in February 1864. She went on to serve in both the South and North Atlantic Blockading Squadrons and engaged Confederate cavalry attacking Fort Powhatan, Virginia on May 21, 1864. She was decommissioned in Philadelphia in June 1865 and ultimately became the Haitian warship *Triumph*.

CSS *Texas* (1865)

The CSS *Texas* was one of the two Columbia class ships designed by Naval Constructor John Porter. These ships were 1,520 ton (1,378 tonne) displacements and mounted six guns. At a length of 21 feet (66 m), it was slightly longer than her sister the *Columbia*, but had a shorter casemate. She was launched in Richmond, Virginia, in January 1865, and was still fitting out when Federal forces captured the Confederate capital city in April. The incomplete twin-screw ironclad was taken to the Norfolk Navy Yard, where she was sold in October 1867.

SPECIFICATIONS

DISPLACEMENT: 1,006 tons (912 tonnes)

DIMENSIONS: 204 ft x 41 ft x 15 ft 9 in (62.2 m x 12.5 m x 4.8 m)

ARMAMENT: Two 7 in (178 mm) Brooke rifles; two 6.4 in (163 mm) Brooke rifles

ARMOR: Casemate: 4 in (102 mm); hull: 2 in (51 mm)

MACHINERY: 1 shaft; steam engine; 1 boiler

SPEED: 10 knots

CREW: 145

CSS *Atlanta*

CASEMATE
THE CASEMATE WAS MADE OF THE RAILROAD IRON THE SHIP HAD BEEN CARRYING WHEN IT WAS TRAPPED AS A CARGO SHIP AT SAVANNAH.

DECK
THE WOODEN MAIN DECK WAS 3 FT (0.91 M) THICK.

ARMORED DECK
THE ARMORED DECK PROJECTED 6 FT (1.83 M) BEYOND THE ORIGINAL CARGO SHIP HULL.

CSS *Baltic* (1862)

THE CSS *BALTIC* WAS ONE OF SIX CONFEDERATE IRONCLADS CONVERTED FROM EXISTING VESSELS. THIS 624 TON (566 TONNE) SIDE-WHEEL IRONCLAD RAM WAS ORIGINALLY A RIVER TOWBOAT BUILT IN PHILADELPHIA, PENNSYLVANIA IN 1860.

CSS COLUMBIA

She was purchased by the state of Alabama, converted to a warship, and turned over to the Confederate States Navy for operation in Mobile Bay and nearby rivers in mid-1862. She was 186 feet (56 m) in overall length, 3 feet (91 cm) in beam and had a depth of 6 feet 4 inches (1.93 m). She carried an 86-man crew and had iron plating forward and probably cotton bales aft for protection.

The *Baltic* was first commanded by Lieutenant James Johnston and then Lieutenant Charles Simms, who declared her "as rotten as punk and as fit to go into action as a mud scow." Nonetheless she was the only ironclad operating in Mobile Bay until the *Tennessee* was completed in 1864. In the meantime the *Baltic* busied herself emplacing obstacles and torpedoes in the bay. She took no part in the climactic battle there on August 5, 1864.

Indeed the *Baltic* was in poor condition by early 1863 and had been stripped of

her armor and otherwise dismantled in July 1864. Her armor was used to protect the CSS *Nashville*. The *Baltic's* hulk was captured by Union forces at Hubba Bluff on the Tombigbee River, Alabama on May 10, 1865. She was sold on December 31, 1865.

CSS *Columbia* (1865)

The CSS *Columbia* was part of a Tennessee class of ironclads that sought to continue improvements from the Richmond and Charleston classes. Other than the characteristic "diamond-hull," each vessel in the class was unique. The *Columbia* was constructed under contract in Charleston, South Carolina in 1864 of yellow pine and white oak with iron fastenings. Her hull work was done by F.M. Jones according to plans developed by John Porter. James Eason was responsible for the plating and machinery. She was 189 feet (57 m) in length and had the distinctively

shortened casemate of her class that was intended to conserve precious metal. She was clad with 6 inches (152 mm) of iron and declared "uncommonly strong." She carried a crew of fifty and was designed to mount six or eight guns.

Unfortunately for the Confederacy, the *Columbia* struck either some rocks or a sunken wreck near Fort Moultrie shortly after she was launched on January 12, 1865. With her back broken, she was never commissioned. The Confederates were able to salvage some guns and armor, but the Federals took possession of the wreck when Charleston fell on February 18. They raised and repaired her on April 26. The *Vanderbilt* towed her to Hampton Roads, Virginia on May 25 and she was subsequently sold.

SPECIFICATIONS

DISPLACEMENT: 642 tons (582 tonnes)

DIMENSIONS: 186 ft x 38 ft x 6 ft 5 in (57 m x 12 m x 1.96 m)

ARMAMENT: Two 12 pounder Dahlgren howitzers; two 32 pounder guns; one 42 pounder gun

ARMOR: 2.5 in (63.5 mm)

MACHINERY: Side-wheel steamer

SPEED: 5 knots

CREW: 86

CSS *Baltic*

DECK
BUNKS WERE PROVIDED FOR THE
OFFICERS BELOW DECK, BUT THE REST OF
THE 86-MAN CREW SLEPT ON DECK.

ARMOR
ONCE DECOMMISSIONED, HER
RAILROAD IRON ARMOR WAS USED TO
PLATE THE *NASHVILLE*.

HULL
HER HULL ABOVE THE WATER LINE LEAKED.

USS *Benton* (1862)

THE USS *BENTON* WAS A 1,033 TON (937 TONNE) IRONCLAD RIVER GUNBOAT MEASURING OVER 300 FEET (91 M) LONG. JAMES EADS CONVERTED HER FROM ONE OF HIS SALVAGE SHIPS, A SNAGBOAT, IN ST. LOUIS, MISSOURI FOR THE ARMY'S WESTERN GUNBOAT FLOTILLA. THIS UNUSUAL ORGANIZATION BEGAN IN 1861 AS AN ARMY RESPONSE TO THE NAVY'S LIMITED INTEREST IN RIVERINE OPERATIONS.

The Army began procuring combat vessels both by converting commercial boats such as the *Benton* and building new ones. The first three commanders of the Western Gunboat Flotilla were Navy officers, but they took orders from the Army department commander. On October 1, 1862, the flotilla transferred to the Navy and then became the Mississippi River Squadron under the command of Flag Officer David Porter.

The *Benton* was unique among the early ironclads because her casemate was completely iron armored. Her armor was 2½ inches (63.5 mm) at its thickest and was backed by 20 to 34 inches (508–863 mm) of wood. She was commissioned in February 1862 and was active in the Federal operations to open the Mississippi River and its tributaries. One authority declared her "the most powerful craft on the river." Indeed, her 16-gun battery was the heaviest battery of any vessel during the war. On the other hand, her hybrid stern and side-wheel propulsion mechanism failed to produce the hoped for maneuverability, and it required a sluggish 8 to 12 minutes to bring her around.

Blockade

In March 1862, Major General John Pope captured New Madrid, Missouri, a Confederate position blocking Federal navigation of the Mississippi. He then crossed the river and turned the defenses of Island No. 10, another Confederate position blocking Mississippi traffic. During the operation he was supported by Flag Officer Andrew Foote. The *Benton* served as Foote's flagship for the operation. Later that spring, she participated in the captures of Fort Pillow and Memphis. During the summer, the *Benton* battled the Confederate ironclad *Arkansas* near Vicksburg, Mississippi, deftly avoiding the *Arkansas'* clumsy attempt to ram her. She participated in an expedition up the Yazoo River before being transferred to the Navy in October 1862, and becoming Porter's flagship in the Mississippi River Squadron.

In December 1862, the *Benton* was damaged by Confederate gunfire during another operation on the Yazoo. Perhaps most famously, she was one of the ships that ran past Vicksburg on April 16, 1863. The *Benton* then participated in the unsuccessful bombardment of Grand Gulf, which Porter declared "the strongest place on the Mississippi." She supported the siege of Vicksburg with naval gunfire until the Confederates surrendered there on July 4. Her last significant Civil War action was the frustrating Red River Campaign in Louisiana between March and May 1864. She was decommissioned in July 1865.

SPECIFICATIONS

DISPLACEMENT: 1,033 tons (937 tonnes)

DIMENSIONS: 202 ft x 72 ft x 9 ft (62 m x 22 m x 2.7 m)

ARMAMENT: Eight 9 in (228 mm) Dahlgren smoothbores; two 100 pounder Parrott rifles; two 50 pounder Dahlgren rifles; four 32 pounder Dahlgren rifles

ARMOR: Forward casemate: 2.5 in (64 mm) backed by 2.5 ft (76 cm) of wood; lateral casemate: .625 in (15.9 mm); pilot house: 2.5 in (64 mm)

MACHINERY: Steam-driven stern paddlewheel; two inclined engines

SPEED: 5.5 knots

CREW: 176

USS *Benton*

PILOT HOUSE
THE ARMOR OVER THE PILOT HOUSE
WAS 2.5 IN (63.5 MM) THICK.

WHEEL
BENTON HAD A SINGLE STERN WHEEL.

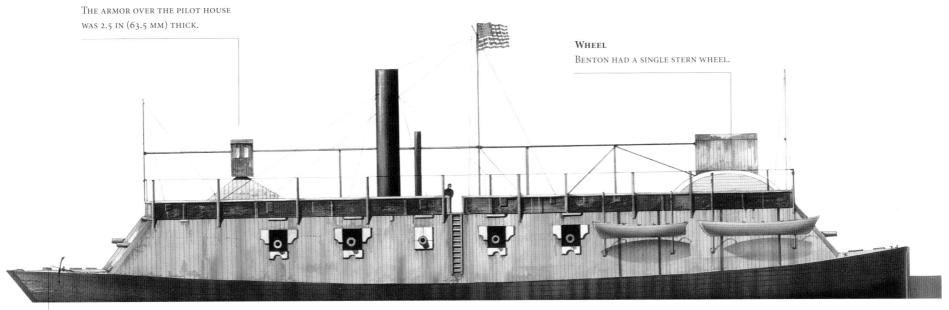

BOW
IN BEING CONVERTED FROM A
CATAMARAN-HULLED SALVAGE
VESSEL, A NEW BOW WAS ADDED.

USS *Cairo* *(1862)*

THE *CAIRO* WAS A STATE OF THE ART GUNBOAT DESIGNED SPECIFICALLY FOR COMBAT ON THE WATERS OF THE WESTERN THEATER. SHE WAS BUILT TO HAVE A SHALLOW DRAFT OF JUST 6 FEET (1.8 M), AND AT 175 FEET (53 M) LONG AND 51 FEET (15.5 M) WIDE, SHE WAS BROADER FOR HER LENGTH THAN AN OCEANGOING VESSEL.

She had two steam engines that drove a center-mounted paddle wheel, and her engines had a vociferous appetite for coal, burning over 1 ton an hour; but with them, the *Cairo* could reach a top speed of approximately 6 knots.

The *Cairo* had a varied assortment of weapons, including three 7 inch (178 mm) rifles, three 8 inch (203 mm) smoothbores, six 32 pounder smoothbores and one 30 pounder Parrott rifle. The guns were located in a slope-sided casemate with three ports facing forward, four to each side, and two to the stern. The casemate was protected by 2½ inches (63 mm) of armor fixed over timbers 2 feet (600 mm) thick. It had rounded corners with railroad rails providing additional protection. The octagonal pilothouse was protected by 1½ inches (38 mm) of iron over timbers. The *Cairo*'s weak areas were in her rear

and under the surface, which were both essentially unarmored.

Obviously, the Confederates had no ability to go toe-to-toe against such a formidable weapon. Instead, they adopted a form of guerrilla warfare in which bushwhackers harassed Federal boats working the rivers, to include using naval mines (called "torpedoes" in the lexicon of the day).

Torpedo Attack

On December 12, 1862 a five-vessel Federal flotilla consisting of the *Marmora*, *Signal*, *Queen of the West*, *Pittsburgh*, and *Cairo* was patrolling the Yazoo River. The *Marmora* and the *Signal* had patrolled the Yazoo the day before and seen numerous scows and floats that indicated torpedoes. The situation on the Yazoo was no doubt dangerous, and the *Pittsburgh* and the *Cairo*, both ironclads, had been added to the force to provide extra support

to the December 12 operation. When the tin-clad *Marmora* found evidence of torpedoes, Commander Thomas Selfridge impetuously ordered the *Cairo* to push ahead.

Almost immediately the *Cairo* was rocked by two explosions in quick succession. According to the most likely account that the torpedo was detonated by a friction primer, Selfridge had run into a trigger line that exploded one torpedo under the port bow and the linked torpedo just off the port side. In just 12 minutes, the *Cairo* sank with only her smokestacks and flagstaff visible above the water. It was the first naval vessel in history to be sunk by a mine. The wreck of the *Cairo* was recovered in 1964 and is now on display at the Vicksburg National Military Park.

SPECIFICATIONS

DISPLACEMENT: 512 tons (464 tonnes)

DIMENSIONS: 175 ft x 51 ft 2 in x 6 ft (53 m x 15.6 m x 1.8 m)

ARMAMENT: Three 8 in (203 mm) smoothbore guns; three 42 pdr rifles; six 32 pdr rifles; one 30 pdr rifle

ARMOR: Forward casemate: 2.5 in (64 mm); pilot house: 2.5 in (64 mm); side covering the machinery: 2.5 in (64 mm); forward casemate: 3.5 in (89 mm)

MACHINERY: Paddle wheel-propelled five-boiler steam engine with 22 in (560 mm) cylinder; 6 ft (1.8 m) stroke

SPEED: 4 knots

CREW: 251

USS *Cairo*

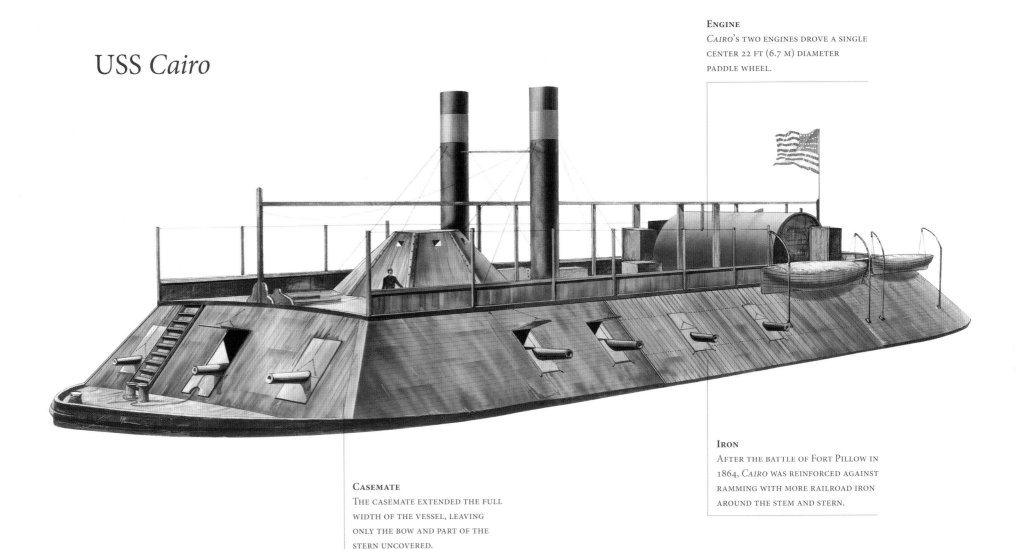

ENGINE
CAIRO'S TWO ENGINES DROVE A SINGLE
CENTER 22 FT (6.7 M) DIAMETER
PADDLE WHEEL.

CASEMATE
THE CASEMATE EXTENDED THE FULL
WIDTH OF THE VESSEL, LEAVING
ONLY THE BOW AND PART OF THE
STERN UNCOVERED.

IRON
AFTER THE BATTLE OF FORT PILLOW IN
1864, *CAIRO* WAS REINFORCED AGAINST
RAMMING WITH MORE RAILROAD IRON
AROUND THE STEM AND STERN.

USS *Eastport* (1862)

THE USS *EASTPORT* HAS THE DISTINCTION OF HAVING SERVED IN A CIVILIAN CAPACITY AND FOR BOTH THE CONFEDERATE AND FEDERAL CAUSES. SHE BEGAN HER CAREER AS A CIVILIAN SIDE-WHEEL STEAMER BUILT IN NEW ALBANY, INDIANA. SHE WAS USED BY THE UNION NAVY AS A CONVOY AND PATROL VESSEL ON CONFEDERATE WATERWAYS.

The Confederates were in the process of converting her into an ironclad when she was captured by Flag Officer Andrew Foote's gunboats at Cerro Gordo, Tennessee after the victory at Fort Henry in February 1862. Although Union forces captured several Confederate gunboats during the war, the *Eastport* was the only one that was still under construction when it was captured and was, ultimately, completed by the Union. She entered U.S. service in August as a 570 ton (517 tonne) ironclad river gunboat and ram, and was transferred to the Navy in October 1862.

The *Eastport* had a relatively undistinguished war career. Her large size and weight made maneuvering difficult, and she repeatedly ran aground. Such mishaps required numerous repairs that kept her out of service for long periods of time. After repairs from a February 1863 grounding near Vicksburg, Mississippi,

the *Eastport* participated in the Red River Campaign in the spring of 1864. The *Eastport* had increasingly been manned by black crewmen, and by this time some 28 percent of her crew were black. Most of these men were recently freed slaves.

After grounding twice while guarding the line of communications at Grand Ecore, Louisiana, on April 15 the *Eastport* was struck by a Confederate torpedo. The damage was slight, but a small leak developed. As the *Eastport* moved forward, she grounded eight times in the shallow water before ultimately becoming entangled on a bed of sunken logs.

Scuttled

With Major General Nathaniel Banks' army in retreat to Alexandria, Confederates controlled both sides of the river and surrounded the stranded *Eastport* near Montgomery, Louisiana. Admiral David Porter ordered the

Eastport, which by now was receiving regular fire from Confederate snipers, destroyed. On April 26, after one abortive effort, Commander Sam Phelps succeeded in igniting a charge of 3,000 pounds (1,360 kg) of black powder in a powerful explosion that destroyed the ship.

Even so, the wreck remained a navigational hazard and on June 23, 1865, the steamer *Ed. F. Dix* struck her and sank. An archaeological examination of the site of the wreck was conducted in 1995. The vessels were examined in-place and after the survey was completed they were reburied.

SPECIFICATIONS

DISPLACEMENT: 700 tons (635 tonnes)

DIMENSIONS: Length: 280 ft (85 m); Beam: not known; Draught: 6 ft 3 in (1.91 m)

ARMAMENT: Two 12 pounder guns; four 32 pounder guns; two 30 pounder guns

ARMOR: Unknown

MACHINERY: Steam engine

SPEED: Unknown

CREW: 150

USS *Eastport*

USS EASTPORT

TOWER

THE CONNING TOWER WAS ADDED AFTER *EASTPORT*'S CAPTURE BY UNION FORCES.

DECK

ORIGINALLY A STEAMER, *EASTPORT* WAS CUT DOWN TO MAIN DECK LEVEL, HAD BOILERS INSTALLED, AND A SLANTING CASEMATE FRAME ADDED.

CREW

EASTPORT CARRIED A CREW OF 150.

USS *Essex* (1862)

THE USS *ESSEX* WAS ORIGINALLY BUILT IN 1856 IN NEW ALBANY, INDIANA AS THE STEAM FERRY *NEW ERA*. SHE WAS PURCHASED IN SEPTEMBER 1861 BY THE U.S. ARMY FOR ITS WESTERN GUNBOAT FLOTILLA AND CONVERTED INTO A 355 TON (322 TONNE) "TIMBERCLAD" GUNBOAT. STILL USING THE NAME *NEW ERA*, SHE TOOK PART IN AN EXPEDITION UP THE CUMBERLAND RIVER IN NOVEMBER 1861.

After being renamed the *Essex*, she received iron armor and other modifications and was active in an engagement with Confederate gunboats near Lucas Bend, Missouri on January 11, 1862. Commanded by Admiral David Porter's brother Bill, she participated in the attack on Fort Henry, Tennessee in February and was badly damaged. She first came under fire while Major General Ulysses Grant was on board conducting reconnaissance. The exchange convinced Grant his troops would have to disembark some distance from Fort Henry. On February 6 she came under more serious fire that caused 30 casualties and left the *Essex* drifting slowly downriver out of the battle.

Porter, albeit without official authorization, spared little expense in repairing his ship. Lengthened, widened, re-engined, re-armored and completely altered in appearance, the *Essex* emerged as a 1,000 ton (907 tonne) ironclad river gunboat, one of the most powerful on the western rivers.

Fight with the *Arkansas*

She was back in service in time for operations against Vicksburg, Mississippi, and on July 22 she joined the ram *Queen of the West* in running past the enemy stronghold and engaging the Confederate ironclad *Arkansas*. Porter brought his vessel to within 5 feet (1.5 m) of the *Arkansas*, and was close enough to take the ram by boarding had he not been driven off by fire from Confederate artillery and infantry on the banks. The Federals broke off the engagement.

Although struck by 42 shots, the *Essex* somehow escaped major damage. She proceeded downriver and joined Admiral David Farragut's squadron as the only Federal ironclad on the lower Mississippi. In that capacity, she helped repel a Confederate attack on Baton Rouge, Louisiana on August 5. As a result of that failed effort, the Confederates destroyed the *Arkansas* to prevent her from falling into Federal hands.

Formally transferred to the Navy in October 1862, the *Essex* remained active on the rivers through the rest of the Civil War. She helped with the occupation of Baton Rouge in December 1862, and she participated in the capture of Port Hudson, Louisiana between May and July 1863. She also took part in the ill-fated Red River Expedition in March–May 1864. Decommissioned in July 1865, the *Essex* was later sold to private interests who returned her name to the *New Era*. She was scrapped in 1870.

SPECIFICATIONS

DISPLACEMENT: 640 tons (581 tonnes)

DIMENSIONS: 250 ft x 60 ft x 6 ft (76 m x 18 m x 1.8 m)

ARMAMENT: One 32 pounder gun; three 11 in (279 mm) Dahlgren smoothbore guns; one 10 in (254 mm) Dahlgren smoothbore; one 12 pounder howitzer

ARMOR: Forward casemate: 1.75 in (44 mm); sides 0.75 in (19 mm)

MACHINERY: Two single cylinder engines; four boilers

SPEED: 5.5 knots

CREW: 124

USS *Essex*

CASEMATE
THE HIGH CASEMATE HOUSED TWO
DECKS: THE UPPER ONE FOR OFFICERS'
QUARTERS.

PILOT HOUSE
THE PILOT HOUSE WAS ONLY PROJECTED
3.5 FEET (1 M) ABOVE DECK.

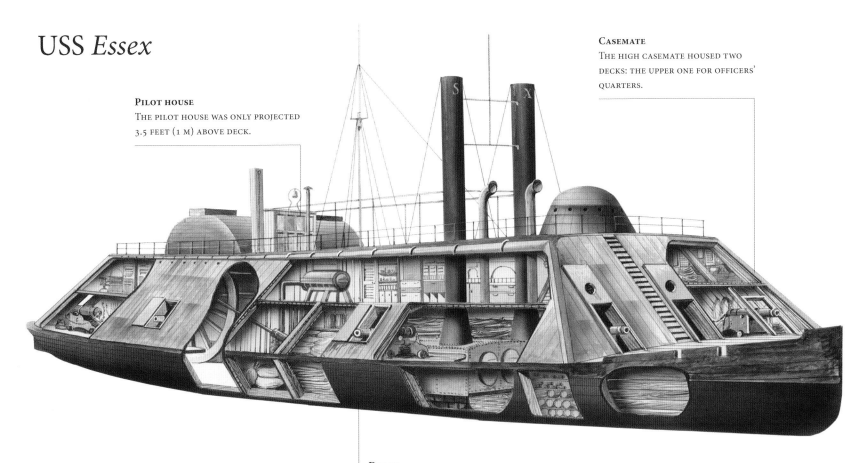

DRAFT
BOAT BUILDERS WERE MASTERS AT CONSTRUCTING
VESSELS THAT COULD CARRY A HEAVY LOAD ON A
DRAFT OF ONLY A FEW FEET.

USS *Galena* (1862)

THE USS *GALENA* WAS A 950 TON (862 TONNE) IRONCLAD GUNBOAT DESIGNED BY SAMUEL H. POOK FOR C.H. BUSHNELL & COMPANY AND BUILT IN MYSTIC, CONNECTICUT. COMMISSIONED ON APRIL 21, 1862 AS THE SECOND OF THE U.S. NAVY'S FIRST THREE ARMORED WARSHIPS, SHE WAS IMMEDIATELY SENT TO HAMPTON ROADS, VIRGINIA TO JOIN THE *MONITOR* IN CONTAINING THE CSS *VIRGINIA*.

The *Galena* figured prominently in Major General George McClellan's 1862 Peninsula Campaign. On May 15, Commander John Rodgers and a Federal squadron of five vessels— the ironclads *Monitor* and *Galena,* as well as the *Aroostook, Port Royal,* and *Naugatuck*—advanced on Drewry's Bluff, a Confederate strongpoint on the James River less than 8 miles (13 km) south of Richmond.

In a four-hour engagement, this small Federal fleet proved no match for the defenders, with the astutely positioned Confederate artillery carrying the day. The *Galena* alone was hit 44 times. This fire was especially effective because from Drewry's Bluff's position 90 feet (27 m) above the river, the Confederates were able to deliver plunging fire down on the *Galena*, penetrating the ironclad's thin deck armor, while the Federal shells were unable to reach the Confederates high on the bluff. Twelve members of the *Galena's* crew were killed in the engagement.

However, this pounding did not deter Corporal John Mackee, a member of the U.S. Marine contingent aboard the *Galena*. Mackee delivered a steady stream of fire against the Confederates and became the first Marine to win the Medal of Honor.

The *Galena* remained in the James River area through the next four months, shelling enemy shore positions on several occasions. When McClellan decided to call off his offensive and withdraw to Harrison's Landing, he established a comfortable headquarters aboard the *Galena* on the James.

Mobile Bay

With the end of the Peninsula Campaign, the *Galena* was stationed in Hampton Roads until May 1863, when she went to Philadelphia for repairs and alterations.

There, the *Galena* was stripped of her iron plating, given a heavier gun battery and enlarged sail rig. She was recommissioned in February 1864 as a conventional unarmored steam warship.

In May she joined the West Gulf Blockading Squadron's pending assault on Mobile Bay, Alabama. When Admiral David Farragut launched his attack on August 5, 1864, the stronger lead ships easily suppressed fires from Fort Morgan, but once they passed the position, the Confederates were able to concentrate on the weaker ones such as the *Galena*, which brought up the rear.

The *Galena* served in the East Gulf Blockading Squadron from September to November 1864 and ended the war serving on the James and Nansemond Rivers in Virginia. She was decommissioned in June 1865 and was eventually broken up in 1872 at the Norfolk Navy Yard.

SPECIFICATIONS

DISPLACEMENT: 950 tons (862 tonnes)

DIMENSIONS: 210 ft x 36 ft x 11 ft (64 m x 11 m x 3.4 m)

ARMAMENT: Eight 9 in (230 mm) Dahlgren guns; two 100 pounder Parrott rifles

ARMOR: 3.75–4 in (95–102 mm) made up of interlocking bars

MACHINERY: Two vibrating lever engines driving a single screw

SPEED: 8 knots

CREW: 164

USS *Galena*

TUMBLE HOME
Galena HAD A PRONOUNCED 45-DEGREE
TUMBLE HOME (THE NARROWING OF THE
SHIP'S HULL ABOVE THE WATER-LINE).

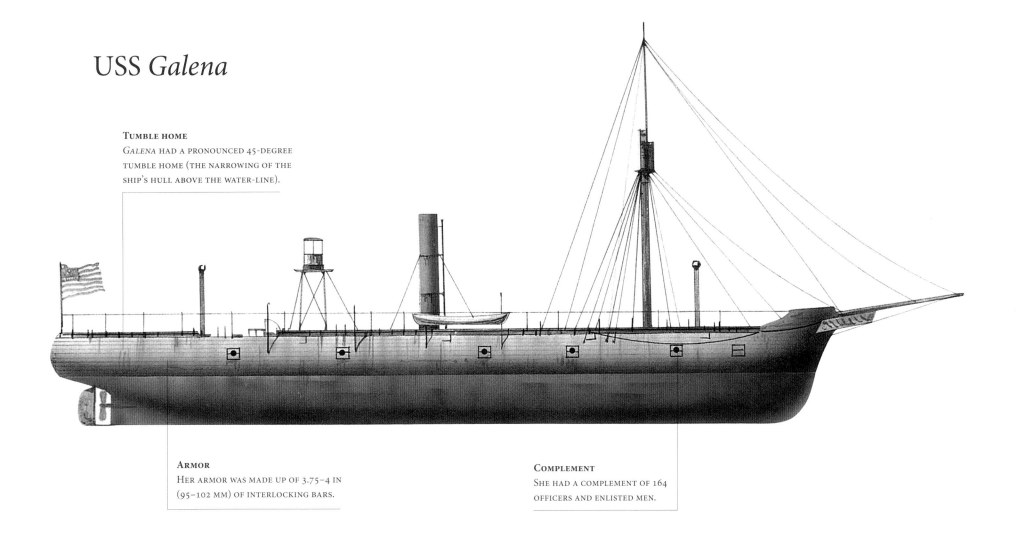

ARMOR
HER ARMOR WAS MADE UP OF 3.75–4 IN
(95–102 MM) OF INTERLOCKING BARS.

COMPLEMENT
SHE HAD A COMPLEMENT OF 164
OFFICERS AND ENLISTED MEN.

USS *Lafayette* (1862)

THE USS *LAFAYETTE* BEGAN ITS SERVICE AS A SIDE-WHEEL STEAMER BUILT IN ST. LOUIS, MISSOURI IN 1848 AS THE *ALECK SCOTT*. SHE WAS AMONG THE VESSELS PURCHASED BY THE U.S. GOVERNMENT FOR THE WESTERN GUNBOAT FLOTILLA AND RENAMED *FORT HENRY* ON MAY 18, 1862. SHE WAS CONVERTED TO AN IRONCLAD RAM AT ST. LOUIS AND RENAMED *LAFAYETTE* ON SEPTEMBER 8, 1862.

Unlike the unusual casemate configuration of her sister ship *Choctaw*, the *Lafayette* had one long casemate stretching from her paddle wheels almost all the way to her bow. She was over 300 feet (91 m) long and her great weight mounted on a conventional riverboat hull with a conventional Western riverboat power plant resulted in inevitably slow speed.

The *Lafayette* was fitted with the same experimental India rubber protection as the *Choctaw*. Commodore William Porter claimed this combination of rubber and 2½ inches (63 mm) of iron would provide the equivalent protection of 5 inches (127 mm) of iron. His brother, Admiral David Porter disagreed, thinking it was a useless configuration that contributed only to rot in the backing of the armor. With the rest of the flotilla she was transferred to the Navy on October 1 and soon joined Admiral Porter's Mississippi

River Squadron. Captain Henry Walke was her commander.

The *Lafayette* followed the Porter's flagship the Benton when he ran past the Confederate batteries at Vicksburg, Mississippi on April 16, 1863. With the ram *General Sterling Price* lashed to her starboard side, the *Lafayette* drew her share of fire. Ensign Elias Smith reported "New York conflagrations and Fourth of July pyrotechnics—they were nothing to it!" The *Lafayette* received nine "effective" shots through her casemate and had her coal barge sunk as she ran the gauntlet. The *Tuscumbia* took her in tow and helped her complete the passage.

Mission at Grand Gulf

Five days later, Porter used the *Lafayette* to reconnoiter the Confederate works at Grand Gulf, which he was unable to shell into submission on April 29. The *Lafayette* presented a big target, and during that

bombardment she was struck 17 times. Five of these hits penetrated her iron casemate, casting further doubt on the promise of William Porter's rubber and iron composite design. None of these shots did serious damage, however.

The *Lafayette* then patrolled the Red River, joining the Pittsburgh in shelling Simmesport, Louisiana on June 4, 1863. From March to May 1864, the *Lafayette* participated in the Red River Campaign. She spent the remainder of the war stationed on the lower Mississippi, safeguarding river transportation from attack, monitoring the cotton trade and interdicting the movement of Confederate forces. The *Lafayette* was decommissioned on July 23, 1865 and sold in New Orleans on March 12, 1866.

SPECIFICATIONS

DISPLACEMENT: 1,000 tons (907 tonnes)

DIMENSIONS: 280 ft x 45 ft x 8 ft (85 m x 14 m x 2.4 m)

ARMAMENT: Two 11 in (280 mm) Dahlgren smoothbore guns; four 9 in (230 mm) Dahlgren smoothbore guns; two 100 pounder Parrott rifles

ARMOR: 1 in (25.4 mm) plate over 1 in (25.4 mm) India rubber

MACHINERY: Two engines with an 8 ft (2.4 m) stroke driving two steel wheels

SPEED: 4 knots against river

CREW: 106

USS *Lafayette*

GUNS
TWO 11 IN (279 MM) GUNS FACED
FORWARD THROUGH THE ROUNDED
FRONT SECTION.

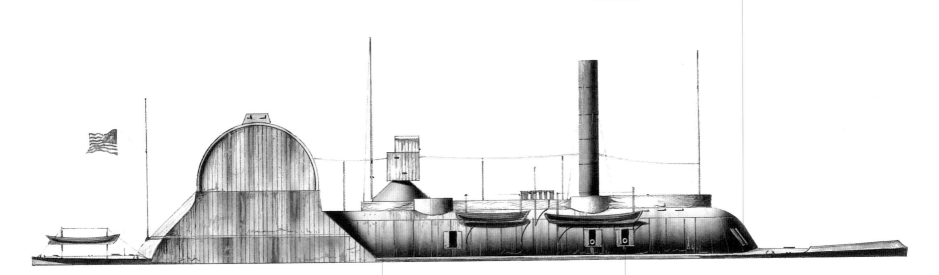

CASEMATE
LAFAYETTE WAS VERY SIMILAR TO *CHOCTAW*,
EXCEPT THAT ITS LONG, ONE-PIECE CASEMATE
WAS CONTINUED BACK TO THE WHEELS.

BROADSIDE
THE 9 IN (228 MM) GUNS WERE
IN THE BROADSIDE.

CSS *Louisiana* (1862)

As part of his plan to use ironclads to defeat the vastly larger Federal fleet, in September 1861 Confederate Secretary of the Navy Stephen Mallory authorized two ironclads be built in New Orleans. One was the *Mississippi*, and the other, to be built by E.C. Murray, was the *Louisiana*. Murray had a solid 20-year reputation during which he had built more than 120 vessels.

Still, ironclad construction was something new, and Murray was besieged by a host of resource and bureaucratic problems. He had promised to deliver the *Louisiana* by January 25, 1862, but it was not until April 19 that she was placed into service. By then Admiral David Farragut was making his final preparations to attack New Orleans.

The *Louisiana* was commanded by Commander Charles McIntosh. She carried 16 guns, including two rifled 7 inch (178 mm) guns, three 9 inch (228 mm) shell-guns, four 8 inch (203 mm) shell-guns, and seven 32 pounders. Of these, however, only 10 were in serviceable condition. The rest had been mismounted or were being manned by crews with no experience in the use of heavy naval guns. The ship had no motive power and had generally been poorly designed and constructed. Lieutenant William Ward declared it "a total failure."

The ship's shortcomings became readily apparent during the battle. The *Louisiana* had been rushed into service for which she was unprepared, and McIntosh found her engines "lamentably deficient." Given these limitations, McIntosh and Commander John Mitchell, who was in charge of the Confederate naval defenses, decided the best use of the *Louisiana* was to tie her to the east bank as a floating battery.

"Infamous Act"

As Farragut's fleet dashed passed Forts Jackson and St. Philip on the morning of April 24, the *Louisiana* fired just 12 shots. Mitchell then proposed turning the *Louisiana*'s guns against Major General Benjamin Butler's Army forces as they advanced overland to cut off the forts, but was unable to get the vessel in action. As Brigadier General Johnson Duncan and Admiral Porter were signing the surrender articles aboard the USS *Harriet Lane*, the *Louisiana* was cast adrift towards Farragut's fleet and burst into flames as her 4 tons (4.5 tonnes) of powder ignited. Both Federal and Confederates blamed Mitchell for instigating this "infamous act."

SPECIFICATIONS

DISPLACEMENT: 1,400 tons (1,270 tonnes)

DIMENSIONS: 264 ft x 62 ft x 12–13 ft (80 m x 19 m x 3.66–3.96 m)

ARMAMENT: Two 7 in (178 mm) Brooke rifles; four 8 in (203 mm) Dahlgren smoothbore guns; three 9 in (228 mm) guns; seven 32 pounder guns

ARMOR: Unknown

MACHINERY: Four engines, plus two huge paddle wheels in a center well; two screws and twin rudders

SPEED: Unknown

CREW: 300

CSS *Louisiana*

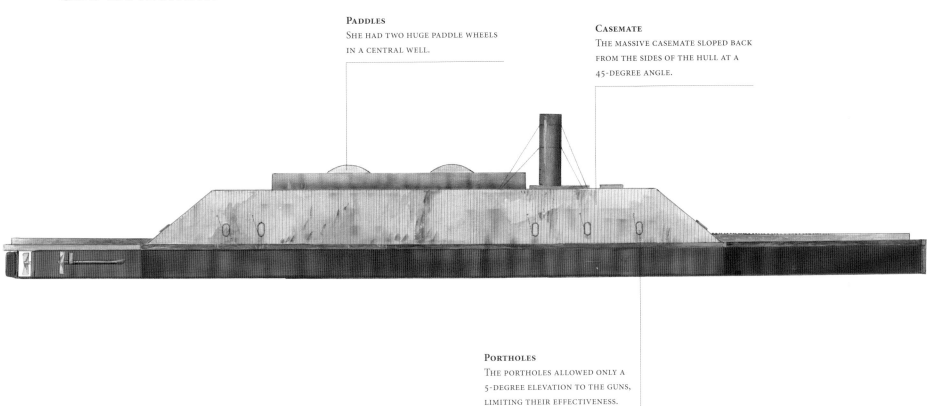

PADDLES
SHE HAD TWO HUGE PADDLE WHEELS
IN A CENTRAL WELL.

CASEMATE
THE MASSIVE CASEMATE SLOPED BACK
FROM THE SIDES OF THE HULL AT A
45-DEGREE ANGLE.

PORTHOLES
THE PORTHOLES ALLOWED ONLY A
5-DEGREE ELEVATION TO THE GUNS,
LIMITING THEIR EFFECTIVENESS.

CSS *Mississippi* (1862)

IN ADDITION TO THE *LOUISIANA*, THE *MISSISSIPPI* WAS THE OTHER IRONCLAD FOR WHICH
CONFEDERATE SECRETARY OF THE NAVY STEPHEN MALLORY CONTRACTED AT NEW ORLEANS IN
SEPTEMBER 1861. THE *MISSISSIPPI* WAS TO BE BUILT BY NELSON AND ASA TIFT. THE TIFT BROTHERS
HAD NO SHIPBUILDING EXPERIENCE, BUT WERE POLITICALLY WELL CONNECTED.

They briefed Mallory on an ambitious plan to build a vessel 260 feet (79 m) in length with a 58 foot (17 m) beam and a depth from the surface of 15 feet (4.5 m). There would be two sets of boilers, each 42 inches (1.06 m) in diameter and 30 feet (9 m) long. These would power three engines that the Tifts expected to allow speeds of up to 14 knots. After later analysis, the Tifts realized the vessel would have to be widened by 20 feet (6 m) to allow more boiler and furnace space.

Design miscalculations such as these drove up costs and lengthened production time. The Confederacy's limited industrial capacity to produce the *Mississippi*'s 44 foot (13.5 m) center shaft also slowed the process. The Tifts had promised Mallory delivery by December 15, 1861. The *Mississippi* did not enter service until April 20, 1862.

Even then, the ship was ill-prepared for the task that lay ahead. She was still a partially finished hulk without an engine. It had been designed to carry 18 guns, but none had arrived and her iron cladding was not yet in place. With Admiral David Farragut poised to attack New Orleans, the *Mississippi* was useless in such a condition. Captain William Whittle, who had been sent by Mallory to New Orleans on March 29, received orders to send the hulk upriver where it could be completed.

Whittle instructed Commander Arthur Sinclair, who was scheduled to take command of the *Mississippi* whenever the Tifts finished her, to "use every exertion in his power to get her upriver, and failing to do so, to destroy her."

Fiery End

After much effort, Sinclair found two steamers to tow the *Mississippi* to safety, but they were unable to stem the current. After receiving orders from Whittle to "not let her fall into the hands of the enemy," Sinclair destroyed the *Mississippi*. The Confederates would have to try to defend New Orleans without her. As Farragut advanced upriver, the vessel that was once intended to "be the terror of the seas" floated helplessly by, engulfed in flames.

SPECIFICATIONS

DISPLACEMENT: 1,400 tons (1,270 tonnes)

DIMENSIONS: 250 ft x 58 ft x 15 ft (79.2 m x 17.7 m x 4.6 m)

ARMAMENT: More than 20 guns, including four 7 in (178 mm) guns at the bow and stern

ARMOR: 4.5 in (115 mm) iron

MACHINERY: 3-screw steamer

SPEED: 14 knots (estimated)

CREW: Unknown

CSS *Mississippi*

ARMAMENT
MISSISSIPPI CARRIED 20 GUNS,
INCLUDING FOUR 7 IN (178 MM)
WEAPONS AT THE BOW AND STERN.

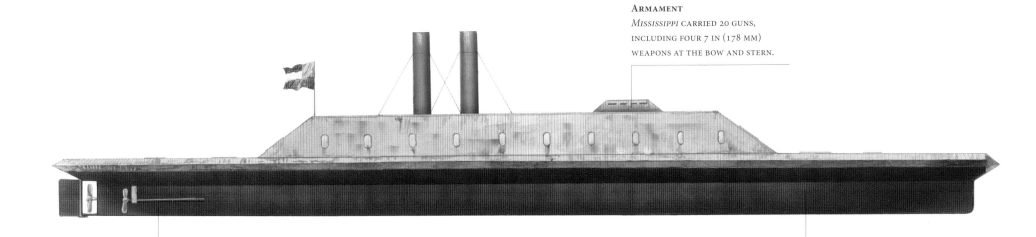

HULL
THE HULL WAS 2 FT (0.6 M) THICK AT
THE SIDES AND 3 FT (0.91 M) THICK AT
THE BOW.

ENGINES
THE THREE-SCREW ENGINES ALLOWED
THE *MISSISSIPPI* TO REACH AN
ESTIMATED 14 KNOTS.

USS *Monitor* (1862)

BY THE TIME JOHN ERICSSON BEGAN WORK ON THE FEDERAL'S FIRST IRONCLAD, THE CONFEDERATES HAD A THREE-MONTH HEAD START ON THE *VIRGINIA*. NONETHELESS, ERICSSON BUILT THE *MONITOR* IN LESS THAN 100 DAYS, JUST IN TIME TO CHECK THE RAMPAGE THE *VIRGINIA* HAD BEGUN AT HAMPTON ROADS ON MARCH 8, 1862.

The *Monitor* had a 172 foot (52 m) long, flat hull with no more than a foot or two of freeboard. The heavy oak beams of her raft deck supported a strake of 7 inch (179 mm) oak, which was then plated with 1 inch (25 mm) of iron. In the midship section, a revolving iron turret rose nine feet (2.75 m) above the deck and mounted two 11 inch (279 mm) Dahlgren guns, which could throw a 165 pound (75 kg) solid shot 1 mile (1.6 km) every seven minutes. Aft of the turret was the smoke pipe and forward was a stubby iron pilothouse. This claustrophobic structure of less than 12 square feet (1.1 sq. m) housed the pilot, helmsman, and commanding officer during battle.

The most significant advantage the *Monitor* had over the *Virginia* was her 12 foot (3.6 m) draft and high maneuverability. She had a 59-man crew, all of whom had volunteered directly from the Navy. Her captain was Lieutenant John Worden, a 28-year Navy veteran recently released after spending seven months in a Confederate prison. Nine days after she was commissioned, the *Monitor* was towed from New York to the Chesapeake by tugboat and steamed past the Virginia capes late in the afternoon of March 8. By then the first day of the Battle of Hampton Roads had concluded, with the *Virginia* wreaking havoc on the Federal fleet and eager to finish the job the next day.

"Gigantic Cheese Box"

The arrival of the *Monitor* evened the score. Lieutenant James Rochelle of the CSS *Patrick Henry* described the new vessel as "such a craft as the eyes of a seaman never looked upon before—an immense shingle floating on the water, with a gigantic cheese box rising from its center; no sails, no [paddle] wheels, no smokestack, no guns." After what amounted to two two-hour engagements, separated by a 30-minute intermission, the two ironclads battled to a draw. Both ships had taken a beating and several men were wounded, but there were no fatalities.

In spite of the tactical stalemate, strategically the Battle of Hampton Roads must be counted as a Federal victory, because although the *Virginia* was still a threat, anxiety over her potential to destroy the Federal fleet single-handedly was abated. The Federal blockade would stand, and a major obstacle had been removed from the path of what would become Major General George McClellan's Peninsula Campaign.

SPECIFICATIONS

DISPLACEMENT: 987 tons (895 tonnes)

DIMENSIONS: 172 ft x 41 ft 6 in x 10 ft 6 in (52 m x 12.65 m x 3.2 m)

ARMAMENT: Two 11 in (280 mm) smoothbore Dahlgren guns in the turret

ARMOR: Iron plates (each 1 in/25 mm thick); turret: 8 in (203 mm); belt around hull (with 18 in/457 mm freeboard): 5 in (127 mm)

MACHINERY: Double-trunk cylinders with two-in-one casting, plus two large return box boilers

SPEED: 6 knots

CREW: 59

USS *Monitor*

DECK
WITH A LOW FREEBOARD, THE SEA
COULD WASH FREELY OVER THE DECK
AND THUS REDUCE ROLL.

HULL
MONITOR HAD AN UNUSUALLY SHAPED
HULL WITH A FLAT FLOOR.

SHELF
THE SHELF FORMED BY THE OVERLAPPING
RAFT OVER THE HULL WAS INTENDED TO
KEEP THE VESSEL STEADY.

USS *New Ironsides* *(1862)*

In July 1861, Secretary of the Navy Gideon Welles asked Congress to authorize a committee to study the emerging ironclad technology. The resulting Ironclad Board was comprised of Commodore Joseph Smith, Captain Hiram Paulding, and Commander C.H. Davis. In September, the Board selected three of 17 proposed vessels for contract. One was to become the USS *New Ironsides*.

At 4,120 tons (3,737 tonnes), the New Ironsides was the largest of this initial group of three "saltwater" armored warships. Along with the *Galena*, it became one of just two oceangoing broadside armored vessels that saw wartime service. The *New Ironsides* was built in Philadelphia, Pennsylvania and commissioned in August 1862.

The *New Ironsides* joined the South Atlantic Blockading Squadron in January 1863. For the next year, she operated in support of the blockade of Charleston, South Carolina, and took part in several attacks on the Confederate fortifications defending that city. Though underpowered and leeward at sea, her heavy broadside battery of eight heavy guns on each side, coupled with her 4½ inches (114 mm) of iron protection laid over some 15 inches (381 mm) of wood, made her particularly well suited for the protracted Federal operations against Charleston.

Charleston Action

The first of these actions took place on April 7, 1863, when Admiral Samuel Du Pont sent the *New Ironsides* and eight other ironclads into Charleston Harbor to subject Fort Sumter to a prolonged bombardment. As the flagship, the *New Ironsides* took a position in the center of the line to facilitate command and control. The Confederate fire was massive beyond description. The *New Ironsides* alone took 93 hits, but, unlike several of her sister vessels, was not seriously damaged. The stiff Confederate resistance led the conservative Du Pont to call off the attack.

In other action outside Charleston, the *New Ironsides* was damaged in a spar torpedo attack by the CSS *David* during the night of October 5, 1863. Nonetheless, the *New Ironsides* remained on station for six months before going to Philadelphia in May 1864 for repairs and a general overhaul.

Upon completion of this work in August, the *New Ironsides* joined the North Atlantic Blockading Squadron under the command of Commodore William Radford. She had the honor of opening the battle in the unsuccessful first Federal attack against Fort Fisher, North Carolina. During the successful second attack on January 13, 1865, the *New Ironsides* delivered deadly and accurate fire and contributed to the Federal victory that closed Wilmington, the Confederacy's last open port.

The *New Ironsides* closed out the Civil War supporting Union activities in the Hampton Roads area. She was decommissioned in April 1865 and laid up in Philadelphia. On December 16, 1866, she was accidentally destroyed by fire.

SPECIFICATIONS

DISPLACEMENT: 4,120 tons (3,734 tonnes)

DIMENSIONS: 230 ft x 57 ft 6 in x 15 ft 8 in (70.1 m x 17.5 m x 4. 8 m)

ARMAMENT: Fourteen 11 in (279 mm) smoothbore Dahlgren guns; two 150 pounder Parrott rifles; two 50 pounder Dahlgren guns

ARMOR: Belt: 4.5 in (114 mm); Battery: 4.5 in (114 mm); Deck: 1 in (25 mm); Bulkheads: 2.5 in (64 mm)

MACHINERY: Not known

SPEED: 7 knots

CREW: 449

USS *New Ironsides*

SPEED
THE CONTRACT SPEED OF 9.4 KNOTS WAS
NEVER REACHED. IT COULD REACH ONLY
6.5 KNOTS.

HULL
THE MASSIVE HULL WAS 12 IN (304 MM)
THICK AT THE WATERLINE.

GUNPORTS
THE GUNPORTS WERE 7 FT (2.14 M) ABOVE
WATER BUT HAD A LIMITED ARC OF FIRE.

CSS *Palmetto State* (1862)

THE CSS *PALMETTO STATE* WAS PART OF THE SIX-SHIP RICHMOND CLASS BUILT AFTER THE REALIZATION THAT SECRETARY OF THE NAVY STEPHEN MALLORY'S PLAN TO USE HEAVY IRONCLADS LIKE THE *VIRGINIA* IN OFFENSIVE OPERATIONS WAS A FAILURE. THIS NEW CLASS OF IRONCLAD RAMS SHARED THE *VIRGINIA*'S CONVENTIONAL HULL AND SIMILARLY INCLINED AND THICK CASEMATE, BUT WAS DESIGNED TO CARRY ONLY FOUR GUNS.

The *Palmetto State* was built in Charleston, South Carolina under the supervision of Lieutenant Commander Duncan Ingraham and was commissioned in September 1862. Like other ships in her class she was propelled by a single screw and suffered from being underpowered. She was commanded by Commander John Rutledge. Some of her crew later volunteered for service aboard the CSS *Hunley*.

Harbor Attack

On January 31, 1863, the *Palmetto State* joined the *Chicora* in attacking the Federal wooden steamers blockading Charleston Harbor, inflicting significant damage to the *Mercedita* with her ram and 7 inch (178 mm) Brooke rifle. The shot hit the *Mercedita*'s boiler, filling her with steam, and then exploding against the ship's inner hull. With water pouring into the 5 foot (1.5 m) hole, the *Mercedita* had to surrender.

The Confederates would have liked to take the *Mercedita* as a prize, but lacking a crew for that purpose, Ingraham demanded the *Mercedita*'s executive officer, Lieutenant Commander Trevett Abbot, "give his word of honor, for his captain, officers and crew" that they would not serve against the Confederacy "until regularly exchanged." Abbot gave his verbal promise and the *Mercedita* was released. The *Chicora* also crippled the *Keystone State* before the *Housatonic* arrived to drive the Confederates back to the protection of Fort Moultrie's guns.

Although General Pierre Gustave Toutant Beauregard, commander of Charleston's defenses, clearly indulged himself in a hyperbole in declaring the blockade had thus been lifted, this effort did mark one of the few successful Confederate attacks on the Federal fleet.

For the remainder of the war, the *Palmetto State* remained in the Charleston area, helping repulse several Federal attacks. She was destroyed with the *Chicora* and the *Charleston* on February 18, 1865, when the city was evacuated. The U.S. Army Corps of Engineers located the three wrecks in 1929 during the dredging of Town Creek, and any remnants of the ship were probably removed during the dredging operation.

SPECIFICATIONS

DISPLACEMENT: Approx 850 tons (771 tonnes)

DIMENSIONS: 150 ft x 34 ft x 12 ft (46 m x 10 m x 3.7 m)

ARMAMENT: Two 7 in (178 mm) Brooke rifles; two 9 in (228 mm) Dahlgren smoothbore cannons

ARMOR: Sides: 4 in (102 mm) with 22 in (559 mm) oakwood backing and 2 in (51 mm) at each end of the battery

MACHINERY: Steam engine

SPEED: 5 knots

CREW: 150

CSS *Palmetto State*

ENGINE
WITH AN ENGINE TAKEN FROM A SMALL STEAMER, *PALMETTO STATE* WAS NOT POWERFUL ENOUGH TO MAKE MORE THAN 5 KNOTS.

ARMAMENT
THE IRONCLAD WAS ARMED WITH TWO 9 IN (228 MM) SMOOTHORE GUNS AND TWO 7 IN (178 MM) BROOKE RIFLES.

SIDE ARMOR
THE IRONCLAD'S SIDE ARMOR INCLUDED 22 IN (559 MM) OAKWOOD BACKING.

CSS *Richmond* (1862)

CSS *Richmond*, first of a class of six ironclad rams, was built at the Norfolk Navy Yard in Virginia. With the Federal Peninsula Campaign in progress, the *Richmond* was hastily launched in early May 1862, as the Confederates prepared to evacuate the Norfolk area.

USS *CAMANCHE*

She was towed up the James River to Richmond and completed there in July. She was commissioned in November and joined the James River Squadron in protecting Richmond from waterborne assault.

Considered too valuable to risk against the growing number of Union gunboats patrolling the area, the *Richmond* made only occasional appearances downriver in 1862 and 1863. By mid-1864, however, two additional ironclads had joined the James River Squadron, allowing Commander John Mitchell to act more aggressively as Major General Ulysses Grant pushed the Federal Army south.

The *Richmond* participated in actions at Dutch Gap on August 13, 1864, Fort Harrison on September 29 to October 1, Chaffin's Bluff on October 22, and Fort Brady on December 7. Under command of John McIntosh Kell she grounded on January 23, 1864 on the first day of the Battle of James River while trying to negotiate river obstructions at Trent's Reach and received heavy fire. She sustained further damage on January 24 from the Union monitor *Onondaga* before she could be refloated and withdrawn upriver.

USS *Camanche* (1862)

Mare Island Navy Yard, California was the Navy's first navy yard on the west coast. Although far from the main action of the Civil War, rumors of raids by Confederate commerce raiders like the *Alabama* created local fears.

Congress responded by authorizing a modern ironclad to provide security. The result was the USS *Camanche*, a 1,335 ton (1,211 tonne) Passaic-class monitor.

Realizing it was impossible for the vessel to journey safely from the east coast all the way to California, the Navy had the *Camanche* manufactured in Jersey City, New Jersey, and the pieces were then sent around Cape Horn in the sailing ship *Aquila* to San Francisco, California, where *Aquila* sank in November 1863. The monitor's parts were salvaged and assembled in San Francisco. The *Camanche* went into commission in May 1865, just after the end of the Civil War. Until the arrival of the larger twin-turret monitor *Monadnock* over a year later, the *Camanche* was the Navy's only ironclad warship on the Pacific coast, although her career was a quiet one.

As Federal forces closed in on Richmond, Rear Admiral Raphael Semmes ordered the *Richmond* and other vessels of the James River Squadron destroyed on April 3, 1865.

SPECIFICATIONS

DISPLACEMENT: 1,356 tons (1230 tonnes)

DIMENSIONS: 172 ft 6 in x 34 ft x 12 ft (52.5 m x 10 m x 3.7 m)

ARMAMENT: Four rifled guns; two shell guns; one spar torpedo

ARMOR: Side: 4 in (102 mm)

MACHINERY: Twin engines

SPEED: 6 knots

CREW: 150

USS *Richmond*

STEAM ENGINE
THE *RICHMOND*'S STEAM ENGINE COULD
MANAGE AN AVERAGE SPEED OF 5–6
KNOTS—SLOWER THAN MANY IRONCLADS.

GUNS
THE IRONCLAD INCLUDED SIX GUNS:
FOUR RIFLED GUNS (TWO ON EACH SIDE)
AND TWO SHELL GUNS.

TORPEDO
THE *RICHMOND* LATER INCLUDED
A SINGLE SPAR TORPEDO.

CSS *Virginia* (Merrimack; 1862)

THE CSS *VIRGINIA* BEGAN HER LIFE AS THE *MERRIMACK*, A 350 TON (317 TONNE), 40-GUN STEAM
FRIGATE THAT THE FEDERALS BURNED AND SCUTTLED WHEN THEY ABANDONED GOSPORT NAVY YARD
ON APRIL 20, 1861. CONFEDERATE ENGINEERS RAISED THE HULK AND FOUND IT TO BE IN GOOD SHAPE,
EXCEPT FOR THE UPPER WORKS, WHICH HAD BEEN DESTROYED BY THE FIRE.

Confederate Secretary of the Navy Stephen Mallory proposed equipping the *Merrimack* with armor and using it to break the ever-tightening Federal blockade. Naval Constructor John Luke Porter and Lieutenant John Mercer Brooke then designed an ironclad ram that completely changed the face of the Civil War on the water. Workers cut the hull down to the berth deck and built a casemate with slanting sides and ports for 10 guns. The casemate walls contained 24 inches (609 mm) of oak and pine timber with 4 inches (101 mm) of armor plating.

Hampton Roads

On March 8, 1862, the *Merrimack*, which had by now been rechristened the *Virginia*, sailed into Hampton Roads, where Commodore Franklin Buchanan saw five Federal blockade ships lying in anchor. First the *Virginia* went after the *Congress* and the *Cumberland*, engaging them both in battle. Shells from the *Congress* as well as from Federal coastal batteries bounced off the *Virginia*'s sloped armor with little effect. When he was as close as he wanted, Buchanan opened the *Virginia*'s ports and delivered a starboard broadside against the *Congress*. Then he rammed the *Cumberland*, leaving a hole one of her officers said was large enough to accommodate "a horse and cart."

As the *Cumberland* was sinking, the wounded *Congress* slipped her cable and had run aground trying to escape. The *Virginia*'s deeper draft forced her to remain 200 yards (183 m) away, but she nonetheless mercilessly raked the helpless *Congress* from end to end. After confusion between Federal naval and land forces over surrender, the *Virginia* dropped back and set the wooden *Congress* on fire with red-hot cannonballs.

By now the other three frigates from Fort Monroe had entered the fray, but the *Virginia* caused them to run aground as they rushed to the battle. The tide, however, was beginning to ebb, and Executive Officer Lieutenant Catesby Roger Jones, who had assumed command after Buchanan was wounded, broke off the *Virginia*'s attack against the *Minnesota* and withdrew towards the deeper waters of the Elizabeth River.

The next day the Federal ironclad *Monitor* arrived on the scene, and the two ironclads battled to a tactical draw during the Battle of Hampton Roads. Later, when the Confederates evacuated Yorktown and withdrew up the Peninsula towards Richmond, Norfolk fell into Federal hands. The *Virginia*'s draft was too deep for her to withdraw up the James River, and on May 11, she was abandoned and blown up.

SPECIFICATIONS

DISPLACEMENT: 4,000 tons (3,629 tonnes)

DIMENSIONS: 275 ft x 51 ft 2 in x 21 ft (83.8 m x 15.6 m x 6.4 m)

ARMAMENT: Two 7 in (178 mm) Brooke rifles; two 6.4 in (160 mm) Brooke rifles; six 9 in (228 mm) Dahlgren smoothbores; two 12 pdr howitzers

ARMOR: Belt: 1–3 in (25–76 mm); Deck: 1 in (25 mm); Casemate: 4 in (102 mm)

MACHINERY: Two horizontal back-acting steam engines

SPEED: 10 knots

CREW: 150

CSS *Virginia*

CASEMATE
THE CASEMATE WAS 170 FOOT (52 M) LONG. ITS SIDE SLOPED AT 36 DEGREES.

RUDDER
VIRGINIA STEERED BADLY, NEEDING ABOUT 40 MINUTES TO TURN 180 DEGREES.

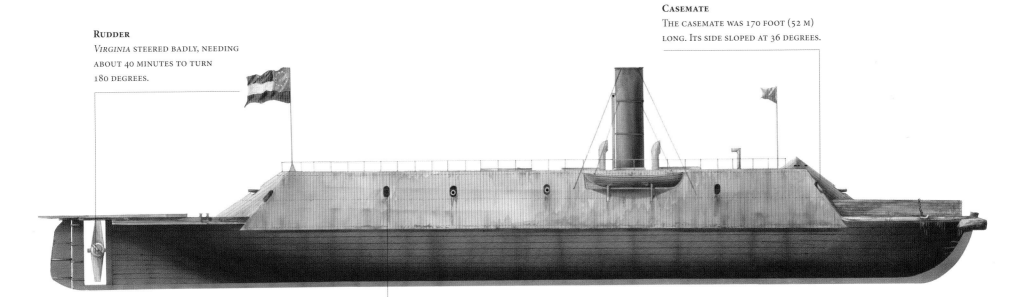

GUN PORTS
THERE WERE 14 ELLIPTICAL GUN PORTS CUT INTO THE SHIP'S STRUCTURE.

CSS *Albemarle* (1863)

THE CSS *ALBEMARLE* WAS A RELATIVELY SMALL IRONCLAD RAM BUILT ON THE ROANOKE RIVER AT EDWARDS FERRY, NORTH CAROLINA. SHE WAS LAID DOWN IN APRIL 1863, LAUNCHED IN JULY AND COMMISSIONED IN APRIL 1864 UNDER THE COMMAND OF COMMANDER JAMES COOKE. SHE HAD A CREW OF 150 MEN, BUT MOUNTED JUST TWO 6.4 INCH (160 MM) RIFLED GUNS.

Her greatest advantage was her shallow draft, which allowed her to operate in the sounds where the deeper-draft Union monitors could not go.

The *Albemarle* saw her first action on April 19 as part of a joint Army–Navy operation against Plymouth, North Carolina. She sank the USS *Southfield* and drove off the USS *Miami* and two other gunboats, isolating the Federal garrison from its waterborne communications. A Confederate brigade commanded by Brigadier General Robert Hoke then surrounded the town and used infantry attacks as well as fire from his artillery and the *Albemarle* to compel the Federals to surrender. The stunning victory earned Hoke a promotion to major general.

The *Albemarle* was back in action on May 5, joining the *Cotton Plant* and the *Bombshell* in an attack against seven Federal blockade ships in the mouth of the Roanoke. The *Albemarle* and the USS *Sassacus* fought a close-in battle that included ramming, shot, hand grenades and rifle fire. The three-and-a-half hour battle was finally halted by darkness, and the *Albemarle* withdrew up the Roanoke. Although this exchange ended in a draw, the *Albemarle*'s presence was rapidly becoming a threat to the Federal position on North Carolina's coastal rivers. Hoping to end this danger, the Federals launched a five-man raid on May 25. The objective was to destroy the Confederate menace with two 100 pound (45.3 kg) torpedoes, but an alert sentry discovered the attack and the Federals were driven off.

Lieutenant William Cushing finally silenced the *Albemarle* in a daring raid on the night of October 27–28. Cushing took the torpedo boat *Picket Boat Number One* upriver to Plymouth. The Confederates had placed a protective boom of logs around the *Albemarle*, but Cushing struck the obstacle at high speed in a launch, road up and over the logs, and came to rest near his target. Amid a hail of bullets, Cushing somehow managed to position the spar under the ram. The explosion tore a 6 foot (1.8 m) hole in the *Albemarle* and she quickly sank. To escape, Cushing rowed a skiff 8 miles (13 km) to Albemarle Sound, where he was picked up by the *Valley City*. Of the 14 men who had accompanied Cushing on the launch, only one other escaped. Two drowned and the other 11 were captured.

The destruction of the *Albemarle* allowed the Federals to recapture Plymouth. When they did, they refloated the *Albemarle* and took her to the Norfolk Navy Yard in April 1865, where she remained until she was eventually sold in October 1867. A partial reconstruction of the *Albemarle* is on display at the National Civil War Naval Museum in Columbus, Georgia.

SPECIFICATIONS

DISPLACEMENT: 376 tons (341 tonnes)

DIMENSIONS: 158 ft x 35.4 ft x 9 ft (48 m x 10.8 m x 2.7 m)

ARMAMENT: Two 6.4 in (162 mm) Brooke double-banded rifles

ARMOR: 2 in (51 mm) iron plating

MACHINERY: Two horizontal non-condensing engines geared to the propeller by four gear wheels

SPEED: 4 knots

CREW: 150

CSS *Albermarle*

SHIELD
SHE HAD AN OCTAGONAL SHIELD 60 FT (18.3 M) LONG.

INTERIOR
WATER CONSTANTLY TRICKLED DOWN THE INSIDE WALLS. THE CREW USUALLY SLEPT ASHORE.

HULL
WITH A FLAT BOTTOM, *ALBEMARLE* COULD FLOAT IN ONLY 6 FT (1.8 M) OF WATER.

USS *Choctaw* (1863)

THE USS *CHOCTAW* WAS ORIGINALLY BUILT IN 1856 IN NEW ALBANY, INDIANA AS A SIDE-WHEEL MERCHANT STEAMER. SHE WAS ACQUIRED BY THE U.S. GOVERNMENT IN SEPTEMBER 1862 AND BEGAN TO BE CONVERTED TO A WARSHIP USING PLANS DEVELOPED BY COMMODORE WILLIAM PORTER. THE *CHOCTAW* WAS COMMISSIONED IN MARCH 1863 AS A 1,004-TON (911 TONNE) IRONCLAD RIVER GUNBOAT AND RAM, AND WAS ASSIGNED TO THE MISSISSIPPI RIVER SQUADRON.

Porter's original design was altered during the conversion process, and the *Choctaw*'s transformation was a radical one. Her length was extended from 245 to 280 feet (74 m to 85 m). Instead of building one long casemate as was common in previous vessels, the *Choctaw*'s constructors erected three. The first was a small one forward towards the bow with sides slanting towards the deck in all directions. It mounted three 9 inch (228 mm) smoothbores and a massive 100 pounder. Just forward of the paddle wheels, another casemate was equipped with two 24 pounders. Astern of the wheels was a third casemate with two 30 pounder rifles to protect the stern. This casemate was wooden, but the other two had the novel design of 1 inch (25 mm) of armor plating covering 1 inch (25 mm) of India rubber. The idea behind this technique was that the rubber would cushion the blow and cause enemy projectiles to bounce away from the *Choctaw*. Even her wheels were covered in a protective box. In spite of her imposing appearance, the *Choctaw* was very slow, able to make only 2 knots against the current, and her experimental protection did not live up to expectations.

Running the Gauntlet

When Major General Ulysses Grant succeeded in running the gauntlet at Vicksburg, Mississippi on April 16 and 26 of 1863, he suggested to Major General William Sherman that a diversion near Chickasaw Bluffs might be useful. Promising to "make as strong a demonstration as possible," Sherman began this move on April 29 with 10 regiments loaded aboard Admiral David Porter's transports. As part of this operation, Sherman's force came under heavy Confederate fire near Hayne's Bluff on April 30. Sherman reported

the *Choctaw* was struck 59 times in this exchange, "but her injuries were not in any vital part" and "strange to say, no one was hurt." Sherman's attack succeeded in causing Confederate Lieutenant General John Pemberton to redirect some forces he had sent south to oppose Grant towards Hayne's Bluff. Then in May, the *Choctaw* helped with the capture of Yazoo City and the destruction of the Confederate Navy Yard there.

On June 7, the *Choctaw* helped repulse a Confederate attack at Milliken's Bend, Louisiana. In the spring of 1864, the *Choctaw* participated in the Red River Campaign and finally was decommissioned in July 1865. She was sold in March 1866.

SPECIFICATIONS

DISPLACEMENT: 1,004 tons (911 tonnes)

DIMENSIONS: 260 ft x 45 ft x 8 ft (79 m x 14 m x 2.4 m)

ARMAMENT: Ram; one 100 pounder rifle; three 9 in (228 mm) smoothbore cannons; two 30 pounder rifles

ARMOR: 1 in (25.4 mm) iron plus 1 in (25.4 mm) rubber on the casemate

MACHINERY: Two engines with 8 ft (2.4 m) strokes, each driving a wheel

SPEED: 9 knots

CREW: 106

USS *Choctaw*

SIDE-WHEEL STEAMER
Choctaw HAD INDEPENDENT WHEELS,
WHICH PROVIDED BETTER STEERING.

CASEMATES
THE TWO FORWARD CASEMATES WERE
COVERED BY IRON PLATES ON TOP OF 1 IN
(25 MM) RUBBER, WHICH SOON ROTTED.

HOWITZERS
THE GUNS IN THE SECOND CASEMATE WERE FOR
SWEEPING THE FORWARD STRUCTURE IN CASE
OF BOARDING.

USS *Keokuk* (1863)

THE USS *KEOKUK* WAS A 677 TON (614 TONNE) IRONCLAD, BUILT IN NEW YORK CITY BY CHARLES WHITNEY. SHE WAS ORIGINALLY NAMED THE *MOODNA*, BUT SHE WAS RENAMED PRIOR TO BEING LAUNCHED IN DECEMBER 1862. THE *KEOKUK* WAS AN EXPERIMENTAL IRONCLAD STEAMER WITH TWO STATIONARY, CYLINDRICAL GUN TOWERS, EACH WITH THREE GUN PORTS.

Her armor was alternating horizontal iron bars and strips of wood. Often mistaken for a double turreted monitor, the *Keokuk*'s novel and untested design made many observers skeptical. She was commissioned in early March 1863. Later that month the *Keokuk* arrived at Port Royal, South Carolina and joined the South Atlantic Blockading Squadron.

On April 7, 1863, Admiral Samuel Du Pont made an all-out attack on heavily defended Charleston. Du Pont's plan was to run past Morris Island without returning fire, steam into the harbor, and open fire on Fort Sumter at close range. After Fort Sumter had been reduced, Du Pont would then concentrate on the Morris Island forts. This plan ran afoul when the *Weehawken*, Du Pont's lead vessel, encountered obstacles strung across the channel from Fort Sumter northeastwards to Fort Moultrie. The

ensuing delay foiled Du Pont's plan of running past the point where Confederate fire was the most concentrated. By about 3.00 p.m., Du Pont's fleet was under fire from nearly 100 Confederate guns and mortars. About 15 minutes later, Du Pont ordered his ships to return fire.

Firefight

For some two hours, Confederates and Federals exchanged fire at ranges between 550 and 800 yards (500 and 730 m). The Confederate guns were especially accurate, delivering some 400 hits and heavily damaging several monitors. The volume of fire was extremely lopsided with the Confederates firing 2,229 rounds compared to just 139 for the Federals. Du Pont broke off the action at dusk, writing to his wife, "We have failed as I felt sure we would." The Confederate forts had held. During the battle, the *Keokuk* had attracted more than her share of

attention. She had advanced ahead of the other ships and lay less than 600 yards (550 m) from Fort Sumter in a narrow channel. For a half an hour she remained in that vulnerable position, receiving the "undivided attention" of the Confederate guns. The *Keokuk* was hit 90 times. Her alternating armor design proved insufficient protection, and one-fifth of the hits she received pierced her at or below the waterline. "Completely riddled," she was able to withdraw and anchor out of range, only to sink on the morning of April 8, 1863.

The *Keokuk* thus ended her short career after about one month of commissioned service. Enterprising Confederates then conducted a remarkable salvage operation that netted two valuable 11 inch (279 mm) Dahlgrens from the wreck, as well as finding the *Keokuk*'s signal book and a key to breaking the Federal code.

SPECIFICATIONS

DISPLACEMENT: 677 tons (614 tonnes)

DIMENSIONS: 159 ft 6 in x 36 ft x 8 ft 6 in (48.62 m x 11 m x 2.59 m)

ARMAMENT: Two 11 in (280 mm) smoothbore Dahlgren guns; ram bow

ARMOR: 4 in (102 mm) thick, partly covering the hull

MACHINERY: Four condensing engines driving two small screws

SPEED: 9 knots

CREW: 92

USS *Keokuk*

GUN TOWERS
GRATINGS COVERED THE TOP OF THE
GUN TOWERS THROUGH WHICH TWO
FAN BLOWERS DREW IN FRESH AIR.

GUNPORTS
EACH GUN COULD FIRE THROUGH
ONE OF THREE GUNPORTS AT A
90-DEGREE ANGLE.

SIDES
KEOKUK WAS AN UNUSUAL-SHAPED
IRONCLAD WITH HIGH SLOPING SIDES.

CSS *Missouri* (1863)

BECAUSE JOHN PORTER DESIGNED THE CSS *MISSOURI* TO USE EXISTING PADDLE-WHEEL ENGINES, SHE WAS POWERED BY A STERN-MOUNTED WHEEL PROTECTED BY A CASEMATE. SHE WAS BUILT IN SHREVEPORT, LOUISIANA AND LAUNCHED THERE ON APRIL 14, 1863 UNDER THE DIRECTION OF LIEUTENANT JONATHAN H. CARTER.

USS *SANDUSKY*

Carter had suggested the vessel be named "Caddo" after the local parish, but Secretary of the Navy Stephen Mallory rejected the idea.

The *Missouri* was 190 feet (60 m) long and her casemate was covered with 4½ inches (114 mm) of railroad iron that was laid diagonally to avoid cutting. Her machinery came from a wrecked riverboat. Although she was designed to have an armament of six heavy guns, all Carter could muster were an 11 inch (279 mm) and a 9 inch (228 mm) Dahlgren from the captured *Indianola* and an old 32 pounder siege gun from the Army.

"As ready for service as she could be," the *Missouri* was officially turned over to the Navy on September 12, 1863. Her commander, Lieutenant Commander Charles Fauntleroy, was decidedly unimpressed. He told Carter "he hoped the damned boat would sink" and "that

he never intended to serve on her if he could help it."

The *Missouri* had a rather unremarkable career, seeing no combat action, but spending the war in transportation and mining operations along the Red River between Shreveport and Alexandria. She surrendered to U.S. naval forces on June 3, 1865 at Shreveport, the last Confederate ironclad to do so in home waters. She was sold at Mound City, Illinois on November 29, 1865.

USS *Sandusky* (1865)

The *Sandusky* was a Marietta class iron-hulled riverine ironclad built by Joseph Tomlinson, Andrew Hartupee and Samuel Morrow in Pittsburgh, Pennsylvania. Broader, shorter and shallower than other versions, she featured a single turret and relatively light armor. The armor at the turret was only 6 inches (152 mm), and 1½ inches (38 mm) on the sides.

The contract for the *Sandusky* and the *Marietta* was signed on May 16, 1862, and the construction time was set at 150 days. On July 23, Naval Constructor Edward Hartt verbally directed the builders to initiate "many expensive additions, alterations, and changes in construction of the vessels, directly at variance with the requirements of the contract." Rather than the "simple and cheap river vessels they had agreed for," Hartupee argued he and his partners were now being required to build something much larger, more complicated and more costly. Numerous delays ensued, and the *Sandusky* saw no wartime service. She was finally launched in mid-January 1865, but not completed until December 26, 1865. She was accepted by the Navy on April 25, 1866 but never commissioned.

SPECIFICATIONS

DISPLACEMENT: Unknown

DIMENSIONS: 183 ft x 53 ft x 8ft 6 in (55.8 m x 16 m x 2.6 m)

ARMAMENT: One 11 in (281 mm) Dahlgren smoothbore; one 9 in (228 mm) Dahlgren smoothbore; one 32 pounder (14.5 kg) siege gun

ARMOR: 4.5 in (114 mm)

MACHINERY: Two poppet-valve engines with a 7 ft (2.1 m) 6 in (152.4 mm) stroke connected to the shaft at right angles

SPEED: 6 knots

CREW: Unknown

USS *Missouri*

WHEEL
THE SINGLE STERN WHEEL MADE
MISSOURI DIFFICULT TO STEER.

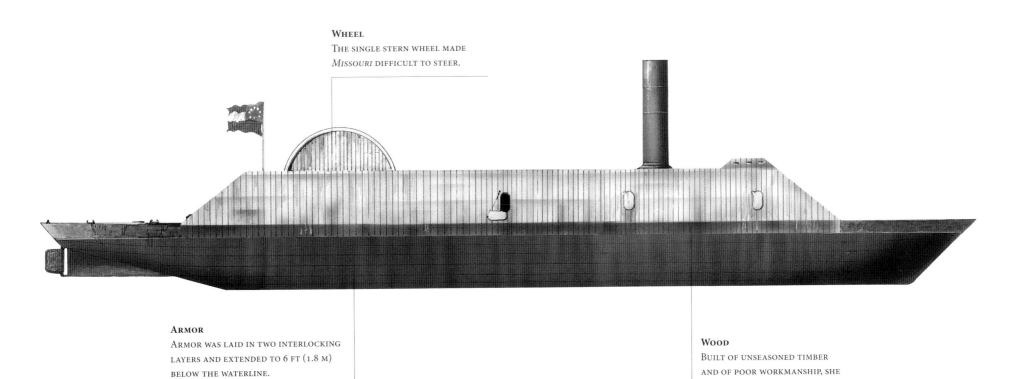

ARMOR
ARMOR WAS LAID IN TWO INTERLOCKING
LAYERS AND EXTENDED TO 6 FT (1.8 M)
BELOW THE WATERLINE.

WOOD
BUILT OF UNSEASONED TIMBER
AND OF POOR WORKMANSHIP, SHE
LEAKED BADLY.

USS *Osage* (1863)

THE USS *OSAGE* WAS BUILT BY JAMES EADS AT THE UNION IRON WORKS IN CARONDELET, MISSOURI AND COMMISSIONED IN JULY 1863. SHE WAS A 523 TON (474 TONNE), NEOSHO-CLASS, SINGLE-TURRET IRONCLAD RIVER MONITOR DESIGNED TO OPERATE ON THE SHALLOWEST OF THE RIVERS OF THE MISSISSIPPI RIVER BASIN.

USS *DUNDERBERG*

Once launched, the Neosho-class vessels were found to draw even less water than required by contract, so additional armor was added to the deck and around the boilers. The *Osage* had two 11 inch (279 mm) Dahlgren smoothbore guns in the revolving turret and one 12 pounder deck gun. However, her stern wheel propulsion would not allow full 360-degree fire from the Dahlgrens.

Under the command of Lieutenant Joseph Couthany, she operated in the Mississippi River area in 1863 and 1864. Between February and March 1864 she participated in expeditions up Louisiana's Black and Ouachita Rivers, and then the Red River Campaign between March and May with Commander Thomas Selfridge as her commander. Her main activity during this campaign was confiscating Confederate cotton. She did serve with the *Lexington* as rear guard of Admiral David Porter's withdrawal to Grand Ecore. On this mission she grounded in the shallow water opposite Blair's Landing and, once cleared, fought off a determined attack by two brigades of dismounted cavalry commanded by Brigadier General Tom Green.

In February 1865, she was transferred to the West Gulf Blockading Squadron for employment in Mobile Bay. In late March she took part in an attack on Spanish Fort, near Mobile, Alabama. While recharting the Blakely River as part of that operation, the *Osage* struck a torpedo under her bow and sank on March 29. Five of her crew were killed and 11 wounded. Her hulk was later raised and sold in November 1867.

USS *Dunderberg* (1865)

The USS *Dunderberg* was designed by John Lenthall and built by W.H. Webb inNew York. Intended to be a seagoing ironclad frigate ram, she displaced 7,060 tons (6,403 tonnes) and was brigantine rigged. Designed for broadside fire, she mounted 16 guns. She was powerfully built with a double bottom, a collision bulkhead and a massive solid oak ram. Laid down late in 1862, she was launched on March 2, 1865. By then, construction had been so delayed that the Navy refused to accept her and she was never commissioned. Instead, as part of its policy to reduce its number of vessels, the Navy returned her to her builder in 1867. Webb then sold her to France, which bought her in part to prevent Prussia from acquiring her. She served as the *Rochambeau* in the French Navy, helping to blockade Prussia in 1870.

SPECIFICATIONS

DISPLACEMENT: 523 tons (474 tonnes)

DIMENSIONS: 180 ft x 45 ft x 4 ft 6 in (55 m x 13.7 m x 1.3 m)

ARMAMENT: Two 11 in (279 mm) smoothbore Dahlgren guns

ARMOR: Sides: 2.5 in (63.5 mm); turret: 6 in (152.4 mm)

MACHINERY: Two non-condensing horizontal engines driving a stern wheel

SPEED: 7.5 knots

CREW: 100

USS *Osage*

PILOT HOUSE
AT FIRST ONLY A SINGLE WOODEN STRUCTURE WAS CARRIED JUST BEFORE THE WHEELHOUSE, BUT OVER TIME MORE STRUCTURES WERE ADDED.

TURRET
THE MODIFIED ERICSSON TYPE TURRET HAD A 300-DEGREE FIELD OF FIRE.

DRAFT
OSAGE HAD AN EXTREMELY SHALLOW DRAFT, BUT COULD SOMETIMES BE DIFFICULT TO CONTROL IN A SWIFT CURRENT.

USS *Roanoke* (1863)

THE USS *ROANOKE* WAS A 4,772 TON (4,283 TONNE) STEAM FRIGATE BUILT AT THE NORFOLK NAVY YARD IN PORTSMOUTH, VIRGINIA. SHE WAS COMMISSIONED IN MAY 1857 AND HAD AN ACTIVE CAREER BEFORE THE CIVIL WAR. HER MOST NOTEWORTHY DUTY DURING THIS PERIOD WAS RETURNING WILLIAM WALKER TO THE UNITED STATES AFTER HIS FAILED FILIBUSTER IN NICARAGUA.

She was decommissioned in 1860, only to be brought back into service in June 1861 for the Civil War.

The *Roanoke* spent much of 1861 enforcing the blockade off North and South Carolina. She was among the first blockaders to get in position, taking up her station off Cape Fear on July 12. She then moved to Hampton Roads, Virginia, and was there on March 1862 when the ironclad *Virginia* attacked. Fortunately for the *Roanoke*, the *Virginia* focused her attention on closer, more vulnerable targets, but Captain John Marston did report, "One shot went through our foresail, cutting away two of our shrouds, and several shells burst over and near the ship, scattering their fragments on the deck." The *Roanoke* fired on the *Virginia*, but Marston's pivot guns lacked sufficient range.

The *Roanoke* was then sent to New York, where she was decommissioned and work was begun to convert the steam frigate into a large triple-turret ironclad. Between late March 1862 and June 1863, she was cut down to her gun deck and rebuilt. It had been hoped the work would take less time, but problems with armor supply and fabrication slowed the process considerably. When the work was finally complete, she was sent back to Hampton Roads for blockade duty. During the voyage southwards it became obvious she was unsuited for fighting on the open ocean.

Big Gun Deterrent

The *Roanoke*'s deep draft restricted her to the main shipping channels, but as the war progressed, the Federals were able to add much more depth to their blockade than they had been able to achieve at the beginning of the war. The *Roanoke*'s six heavy guns were a useful deterrent as a final barrier in case the Confederate ironclads on the James River were able to break out. After the war, she was sent to New York, where she was decommissioned in June 1865.

SPECIFICATIONS

DISPLACEMENT: 6,300 tons (5,715 tonnes)

DIMENSIONS: 63 ft 8¼ in x 52 ft 6 in x 23 ft 6 in (80.37 m x 16 m x 7.16 m)

ARMAMENT: Two 10 in (254 mm) smoothbore guns; four 8 in (203 mm) smoothbores

ARMOR: Turret: 11 in (279 mm); sides: 4.5 in (114 mm); deck: 1.5 in (38 mm); pilot house: 9 in (228 mm)

MACHINERY: Two horizontal direct-acting trunk engines developing 997 hp (743 kW) and driving a single screw

SPEED: 6 knots

CREW: 350

USS *Roanoke*

TURRETS
ORIGINALLY, FOUR TURRETS WERE
PLANNED BUT IT WAS REALIZED THAT
THE VESSEL COULD NOT SUPPORT
SUCH WEIGHT.

KEEL
ROANOKE PROVED A POOR SEABOAT,
ROLLING HEAVILY IN A SEAWAY.

HULL
THE FINAL WEIGHT ON THE WOODEN
HULL WAS TOO HIGH AND THE VESSEL
DREW TOO MUCH WATER.

CSS *Savannah* (1863)

THE CSS *SAVANNAH* WAS ONE OF SIX RICHMOND CLASS IRONCLAD RAMS. CONSTRUCTED BY HENRY F. WILLINK AT THE SAVANNAH SHIPYARDS, GEORGIA, HER IRON PLATES WERE MANUFACTURED IN ATLANTA AND THEN BROUGHT TO SAVANNAH TO BE CUT, DRILLED, AND MOUNTED. SHE WAS PROTECTED BY 4 INCHES (101 MM) OF IRON ARMOR COVERING 22 INCHES (559 MM) OF WOOD.

She had a conventional hull and casement with single screw.

The *Savannah*'s engines were built in Columbus, Georgia but were underpowered and she could manage a top speed of only about 6 knots. It took her almost 30 minutes to complete a full turn. She was 172½ feet (52.5 m) in length and had a 34 foot (10 m) beam and a 12½ foot (3.8 m) draft. Her armament included two 7 inch (179 mm) rifled cannons and two 6.4 inch (160 mm) Brooke guns. She had a crew of 180 officers and men. She was laid down in April 1862, launched on February 4, 1863 and became operational in July. She was soon the flagship of Flag Officer Josiah Tattnall's Savannah River squadron, helping guard the water approaches to Savannah.

On April 10–11, 1863, a massive Federal bombardment forced the surrender of Fort Pulaski, which guarded the mouth of the Savannah River. The victory sealed off the Savannah Harbor, but the Confederates had built a formidable defense anchored on the Charleston & Savannah Railroad that helped thwart an advance inland. The Savannah saw limited action, but was part of this effort to deter Union offensive operations.

First Combat

Her first combat occurred in December 1864 when Major General William Sherman neared Savannah on his march across Georgia. The Confederate defenders proved no match for the advancing Federals, and the *Savannah*'s crew facilitated Lieutenant General William Hardee's withdrawal across the river by helping to build an improvised pontoon bridge.

After Sherman's men had occupied Savannah, the *Savannah* exchanged fire with Union forces there, including firing on Fort Jackson on December 20. Ironically, these were the only shots fired on the old Confederate position throughout the war. Trying to escape, the *Savannah* ran into some of the Confederacy's own torpedoes, leading Sherman to declare her a "trapped lion." On December 21 Tattnall ordered the *Savannah* to be burned to prevent capture. She was run aground on the South Carolina shore and set afire.

SPECIFICATIONS

DISPLACEMENT: 406 tons (368 tonnes)

DIMENSIONS: 172 ft 6 in x 34 ft x 12 ft 6 in (52.5 m x 10 m x 3.8 m)

ARMAMENT: Two 7 in (178 mm) rifled cannons; two 6.4 in (163 mm) Brooke rifles

ARMOR: 4 in (101 mm) of iron covering 22 in (559 mm) of wood

MACHINERY: Low pressure steam engine

SPEED: 6.5 knots

CREW: 180

CSS *Savannah*

FUNNEL
UNDER FIRE FROM UNION FORCES, ONE SHOT EVEN PLUNGED DOWN *SAVANNAH*'S FUNNEL.

ARMAMENT
HER ARMAMENT INCLUDED TWO 7 IN (179 MM) RIFLED CANNONS AND TWO 6.4 IN (160 MM) BROOKE RIFLES.

DRAFT
SAVANNAH'S DEEP 12 FT 6 IN (3.8 M) DRAFT HAD PREVENTED HER FROM GOING ABOVE THE TOWN OF SAVANNAH TO HELP IN THE DEFENSIVE LINE.

USS *Canonicus* (1864)

THE USS *CANONICUS* WAS THE NAME SHIP OF A CLASS OF NINE 2,100 TON (1,905 TONNE) MONITORS. SHE WAS BUILT IN BOSTON, MASSACHUSETTS AND COMMISSIONED IN APRIL 1864. SHE SERVED IN THE JAMES RIVER AREA OF VIRGINIA FROM MAY 1864 UNTIL LATE IN THE YEAR, TAKING PART IN SEVERAL ENGAGEMENTS WITH CONFEDERATE BATTERIES.

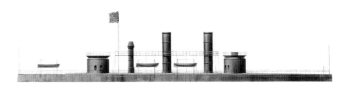

USS *KALAMAZOO*

Her most significant service came at the end of 1864 on December 24 and 25 , during the unsuccessful first attack on Fort Fisher, which guarded Wilmington, North Carolina, the last seaport still open to the Confederacy. This attempt was marred by a failure in cooperation between the Army and the Navy, a massive but inaccurate bombardment, and a tepid land assault. Managing their scant ammunition, the Confederate defenders delivered limited but accurate fire. The *Canonicus* alone was hit 36 times.

The Federals regrouped and launched a much better planned, coordinated and executed attack on January 13, 1865. Admiral David Porter committed all five of his ironclads at short range to draw Confederate fire. The enemy's positions thus revealed by the muzzle flashes, Porter delivered precise and well-measured fire that helped the Federals capture the fort. Chief Quartermaster Daniel Stevens received the Medal of Honor for three times replacing the *Canonicus*' flag when Confederate fire had shot it away.

The *Canonicus* closed out the Civil War mainly stationed off Charleston, South Carolina. She did make one excursion to Havana, Cuba, in search of the Confederate ironclad Stonewall. She was decommissioned in late June 1865, only to return to commissioned status for Atlantic coast and Gulf of Mexico cruises from 1872 until 1877. She saw no further active service, but was towed to Hampton Roads, Virginia in mid-1907 to be exhibited during the Jamestown Exposition. She was sold for scrap the next year with the distinction of being the last survivor of the Navy's once-large fleet of Civil War monitors.

USS *Kalamazoo*

The USS *Kalamazoo* was a double turreted monitor. Ship construction commenced in 1863 at New York Navy Yard. No longer needed for the Civil War, work was suspended on November 27, 1865 and was never resumed. The unfinished ship was renamed *Colossus* on June 15, 1869, but never saw service. She was broken up in 1884.

SPECIFICATIONS

DISPLACEMENT: 2,100 tons (1,905 tonnes)

DIMENSIONS: 225 ft x 43 ft 8 in x 13 ft 6 in (69 m x 13.31 m x 4.11 m)

ARMAMENT: Two 15 in (381 mm) Dahlgren smoothbore guns

ARMOR: Turret: 10 in (254 mm); sides: 5 in (127 mm); pilot house: 10 in (254 mm)

MACHINERY: Two double-trunk horizontal engines driving a single screw

SPEED: 8 knots

CREW: 85

USS *Canonicus*

ENGINES
CANONICUS HAD TWO DOUBLE-TRUNK
ENGINES DRIVING A SINGLE SCREW.

HULL
WHILE THE SMOOTHER HULL SHAPE
GREATLY IMPROVED PERFORMANCE,
NONE MADE THE ANTICIPATED SPEED
OF 13 KNOTS.

INTERIOR
MONITORS WERE UNCOMFORTABLE VESSELS
BECAUSE OF THE CONSTANT DAMPNESS CREATED
BY CONDENSATION ON THE IRON HULLS.

USS *Casco* (1864)

HOPING TO DEVELOP SHALLOW DRAFT MONITORS CAPABLE OF OPERATING IN EXTREMELY SHALLOW RIVERS, SUCH AS THE SMALLER TRIBUTARIES OF THE MISSISSIPPI, THE NAVY DEPARTMENT EMBARKED ON A RATHER ILL-CONCEIVED PROGRAM TO BUILD 20 CASCO-CLASS VESSELS.

USS *HUNTSVILLE*

The original design was reasonably sound, but Chief Engineer Alban Simers made subsequent modifications that increased the weight of the vessels without compensating for the extra stress on the hull. When the flaw became apparent, Simers was removed from the project, and John Ericsson, the famous designer of the *Monitor*, was called in to try to fix the problem.

Ericsson's solution was to raise the hulls of the monitors by nearly 2 feet (60 cm), which added still more weight to the vessels. Of the original 20 ordered, only three, the *Casco, Chimo,* and *Nabuc*, entered service during the Civil War. Even these were modified by having their turrets removed and being converted to torpedo boats. In addition to the retractable spar torpedo, each carried an 11 inch (279 mm) Dahlgren on an open mount.

The *Casco* was launched in May 1864 by Atlantic Works in Boston,

Massachusetts. After her conversion to a torpedo boat, she was commissioned on December 4, 1864 with Acting Master C.A. Crooker in command. Eventually the *Casco* was towed to Hampton Roads in March 1865. Relegated to guard duty, she supported the advance of the Federal Navy to Richmond by removing torpedoes in the James River. In mid-April, she was transferred to the Potomac Flotilla, where she served for the duration of the war. She was decommissioned on June 10, 1865 at Washington Navy Yard, where she was taken apart in April 1875.

CSS *Huntsville* (1864)

The *Huntsville* was launched on February 7, 1863 in Selma, Alabama and completed in Mobile. She was commissioned with Lieutenant Julian Myers in command. Designed to be an ironclad, in reality the *Huntsville* was only partially armored.

Her high-pressure engines are believed to have been transferred from a river steamer, although it had been intended to supply them from the Naval Iron Works in Columbus, Georgia. These engines proved defective, and the *Huntsville* also lacked a full complement of guns. Because of these deficiencies, she rendered no active service other than guarding the waters around Mobile. After the Confederate defeat at Mobile Bay on August 5, 1864, she escaped up the Spanish River. She was sunk 12 miles (19 km) from Mobile on April 12, 1865 as Federal forces under Major General Edward Canby were entering the city.

SPECIFICATIONS

DISPLACEMENT: 1,175 tons (1,066 tonnes)

DIMENSIONS: 225 ft x 45 ft x 9 ft (68.6 m x 13.7 m x 2.7 m)

ARMAMENT: One 11 in (280 mm) Dahlgren smoothbore cannon; one spar torpedo

ARMOR: Unknown

MACHINERY: Two inclined direct-acting engines driving two screws

SPEED: 9 knots

CREW: 120

USS *Casco*

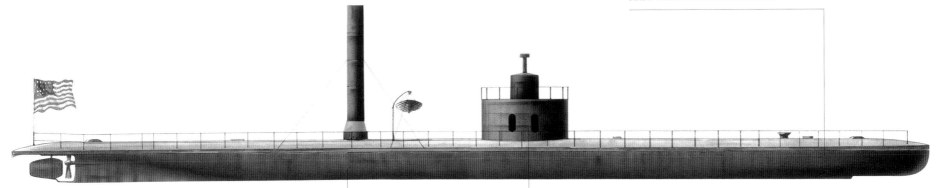

TORPEDO BOAT
CASCO AND HER SISTER SHIPS WERE
CONVERTED DURING PRODUCTION TO TORPEDO
BOATS BUT THEIR LOW SPEED OF FIVE KNOTS
MADE THEM USELESS IN THIS ROLE.

DRAFT
PLANNED WITH A SHALLOW 4 FT (1.2 M)
DRAFT SUITABLE FOR NAVIGATING THE
MISSISSIPPI, THE FINAL 9 FT (2.7 M) DRAFT
SHIP WAS FAR LESS USEFUL.

ARMAMENT
CASCO CARRIED ONE 11 IN (279 MM)
DAHLGREN SMOOTHBORE GUN.

USS *Dictator* (1864)

THE USS *DICTATOR* WAS A SINGLE-TURRETED IRONCLAD MONITOR, DESIGNED BY JOHN ERICSSON. AT ALMOST TWICE THE SIZE OF THE ORIGINAL *MONITOR*, THE *DICTATOR* REPRESENTED ERICSSON'S VISION OF A "SEA-GOING MONITOR." ALTHOUGH HER GREATER DRAFT MADE HER BETTER AT SEA, IT OBVIOUSLY REDUCED HER EFFECTIVENESS IN THE COASTAL WATERS. ERICSSON ORIGINALLY PLANNED TO NAME HER *PROTECTOR*, BUT THE NAVY DEPARTMENT FAVORED A MORE AGGRESSIVE-SOUNDING NAME.

The *Dictator* displaced 4,438 tons (4,025 tonnes), was 312 feet (95 m) in length, and mounted two 15 inch (381 mm) Dahlgren guns. Her armor protection was impressive: 15-inches (381 mm) on the turret, 12 inches (304 mm) on the pilothouse, 6 inches (152 mm) on the sides, and 1½ inches (38 mm) on the deck. A tall ventilator abaft the turret gave her a distinctive profile.

The *Dictator* differed from previous designs in ways additional to her massive size. The overhang of her upper hull was less pronounced, and at the bow the upper and lower hull sections were blended together to form a unified bow structure. The result was cleaner hull lines that made things easier on the *Dictator*'s engines. Ericsson hoped to get 16 knots from the streamlined design, but the *Dictator* disappointingly could only make nine. She was launched on December 26, 1863

by Delamater Iron Works, New York, New York. The city had been the site of bloody riots against the draft in 1863, and it was feared that such discontent might resurface during the presidential election of 1864. President Abraham Lincoln's challenger, George McClellan, had a sizable following in New York and authorities were in no mood to let trouble start. The *Dictator*'s guns were loaded, and she was positioned to discourage any rioting.

Blockade Duty

She was commissioned on November 11, 1864 with the venerable Commander John Rodgers in command of a 174-man crew. She was assigned to duty with North Atlantic Blockading Squadron in anticipation of her supporting the attack on Fort Fisher, North Carolina, but problems with engine overheating prevented her participation. Instead,

the *Dictator* cruised on the Atlantic coast from December 15, 1864 until she was placed out of commission on September 5, 1865 at League Island Navy Yard. After the war, she was placed in and out of commission several times until being sold for scrap on September 27, 1883.

SPECIFICATIONS

DISPLACEMENT: 4,438 tons (4,026 tonnes)

DIMENSIONS: 312 ft x 50 ft x 20 ft 6 in (95 m x 15 m x 6.25 m)

ARMAMENT: Two 15 in (380 mm) Dahlgren smoothbores

ARMOR: Turret: 15 in (381 mm); hull sides: 6 in (152 mm); pilot house: 12 in (305 mm)

MACHINERY: Two vibrating lever engines driving a single 21 ft 6 in (6.5 m) screw, developing about 1,000 hp (746 kW)

SPEED: 9 knots, but usually 6 knots

CREW: 174

USS *Dictator*

TURRET
TWO TURRETS HAD BEEN PLANNED, BUT
ULTIMATELY ONLY ONE MASSIVE TURRET
WAS FITTED.

AIR TRUNKS
AIR WAS DRAWN IN THROUGH THE
AIR TRUNK AFT AND THE TOP OF
THE TURRET.

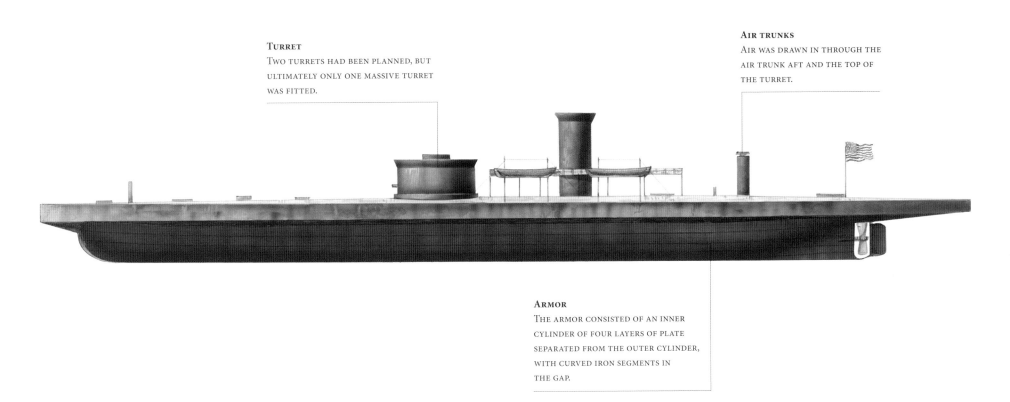

ARMOR
THE ARMOR CONSISTED OF AN INNER
CYLINDER OF FOUR LAYERS OF PLATE
SEPARATED FROM THE OUTER CYLINDER,
WITH CURVED IRON SEGMENTS IN
THE GAP.

CSS *Fredericksburg* (1864)

THE IRONCLAD CSS *FREDERICKSBURG* WAS A LENGTHENED FOUR-GUN VERSION OF THE ALBEMARLE CLASS. SHE WAS BUILT IN RICHMOND, VIRGINIA, IN PART FROM CONTRIBUTIONS RAISED BY THE CONFEDERATE WOMEN. ON MARCH 17, 1862, THE RICHMOND *DISPATCH* APPEALED FOR FUNDS TO BUILD AN IRONCLAD TO HELP DEFEND VIRGINIA. THE ARTICLE MENTIONED THAT THE WOMEN OF SOUTH CAROLINA AND GEORGIA WERE TRYING TO RAISE MONEY FOR A SIMILAR PROJECT.

As a result of this initiative, on April 4 the Ladies Defense Association of Richmond was formed. Similar organizations sprang up in other Southern cities. The Richmond association raised at least $30,000 for the cause, and the *Fredericksburg*, *Charleston,* and *Georgia* are known as the "Ladies' Gunboats" in honor of their funding sources.

The *Fredericksburg* was reported to have been completed and waiting armament on November 30, 1863 and was commissioned in March 1864. The 188-foot (57 m) vessel was commanded by Commander Thomas Rootes, who took her to join the James River Squadron where she was active until the end of the war.

Shore Engagement

On September 29, 1864, the Union army launched a massive attack that captured Confederate Fort Harrison and threatened Chaffin's Bluff. General Robert E. Lee requested support from the James River Squadron and Rootes moved the *Richmond* and the *Fredericksburg* downriver to Kingsland Ranch where they engaged Union forces north of the river near Fort Harrison. A marine officer went ashore to judge the effectiveness of the fires and found they were landing short and endangering friendly troops. Rootes then ordered an increase in the charges from 12–14 pounds (5–6 kg) of powder for the rifled guns and a shift in position of the vessels to just above Chaffin's Bluff.

These adjustments allowed the fires to reach Fort Harrison, scattering the Federals there. The ships continued to provide effective fires and suffered little damage from the enemy. Some casualties did occur, however, when a shell burst inside one of the *Fredericksburg*'s 7 inch (179 mm) Brooke rifled guns.

On January 23, 1865, the *Fredericksburg* descended the James River with fellow ironclads the *Virginia II* and the *Richmond*, and five smaller vessels to attack the Federal supply depot in City Point. The crew of the *Fredericksburg* cleared an obstruction the Federals had placed to block the river. Although this action allowed the Confederate vessels to move forward, the USS *Onondaga* soon arrived in time to repulse the attack.

With the evacuation of Richmond and Petersburg, Rear Admiral Raphael Semmes ordered the *Fredericksburg* and other ships in the vicinity destroyed on April 3, 1865.

SPECIFICATIONS

DISPLACEMENT: 700 tons (635 tonnes)

DIMENSIONS: 188 ft x 40 ft 3 in x 9 ft 6 in (57 m x 12.27 m x 2.90 m)

ARMAMENT: One 11 in (280 mm) smoothbore cannon; one 8 in (204 mm) rifled cannon; two 6.4 in (164 mm) rifled cannons

ARMOR: 4 in (102 mm)

MACHINERY: Steam engine

SPEED: 5 knots

CREW: 150

CSS *Fredericksburg*

ROOF
AT FIRST, HER ROOF WAS A FIRE HAZARD,
BEING MADE OF WOOD. IT WAS LATER
REPLACED BY IRON BARS.

ARMOR
FREDERICKSBURG'S ARMOR WAS 4 IN
(107 MM) THICK.

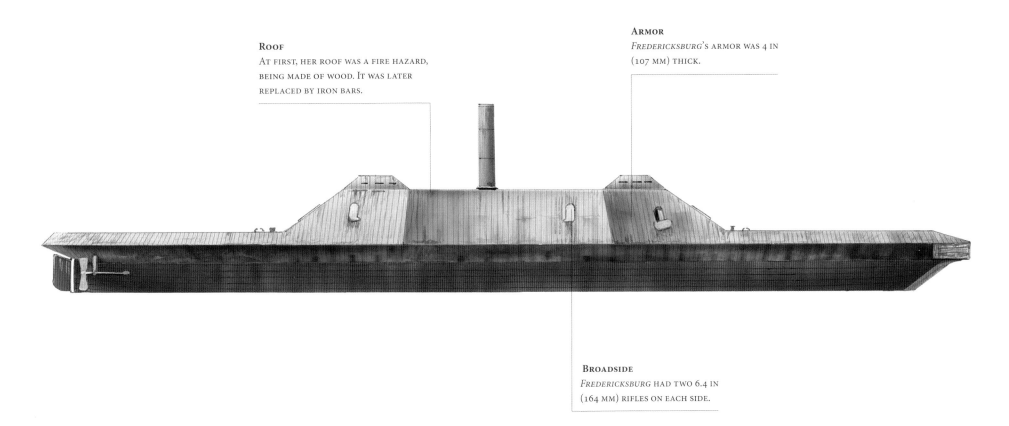

BROADSIDE
FREDERICKSBURG HAD TWO 6.4 IN
(164 MM) RIFLES ON EACH SIDE.

CSS *Jackson* (1864)

THE CSS *JACKSON* WAS ALSO COMMONLY KNOWN AS THE CSS *MUSCOGEE*. SHE WAS LAUNCHED ON DECEMBER 22, 1864 AND WAS NEARING COMPLETION WHEN THE FEDERALS ATTACKED COLUMBUS, GEORGIA IN THE LAST DAYS OF THE CIVIL WAR. COLUMBUS WAS ONE OF THE SOUTH'S FEW INDUSTRIAL CENTERS, PERHAPS SECOND ONLY TO RICHMOND, VIRGINIA IN FURNISHING SUPPLIES AND PROVISIONS TO THE CONFEDERATE QUARTERMASTER DEPARTMENT.

Of particular importance to the *Jackson* was the Columbus Iron Works, which had been established in 1853 to manufacture farm implements, but, with the coming of the Civil War, had become a significant producer of cannon, weapons, munitions and ship machinery. Also in Columbus was the important Navy Yard commanded by Lieutenant Augustus McLaughlin that had supplied engine machinery for many of the Confederacy's ironclads. It was also where the CSS *Chattahoochee* had gone for repairs and installation of engines and a new boiler in June 1864.

Columbus was also important as the site of a major railroad and shipping network made possible by the Chattahoochee River. Hoping that she would descend the Chattahoochee to open seas and break the blockade, the Jackson was contracted by the Confederate government in 1862, but she experienced numerous delays during production.

Dock-bound

Finally in early 1865 the *Jackson* was tied up dockside for final fitting. She was nearly 225 feet (68 m) long and 54 feet (16 m) wide and weighed 2,000 tons (1,814 tonnes), making her the largest ironclad built from the hull up by the Confederacy. By now, however, Major General William Sherman had captured Atlanta, and the citizens of Columbus were bracing for an attack from the east.

Although Sherman instead headed for Savannah, Columbus did not escape. On March 22, 1865, Brigadier General James Wilson began a cavalry raid from the extreme northwest corner of Alabama, captured Selma on April 2, Montgomery on April 12 and then set his sights on Columbus.

Wilson swept aside the weak Confederate defenses on April 16, and his troops begun laying waste to Columbus's industrial capabilities, including the Iron Works. The Federals set the *Jackson* aflame and adrift on the river. The fire lasted for nearly two weeks, burning the ship to the waterline. She sank into the mud on the bottom of the river about 30 miles (48 km) south of Columbus. The *Jackson* was raised in a Herculean effort in 1961, and her remains are now on display at the National Civil War Naval Museum in Columbus. One of the Brooke rifles intended for her is even fired from time to time there.

SPECIFICATIONS

DISPLACEMENT: 2,000 tons (1,814 tonnes)

DIMENSIONS: 175 ft x 35 ft (53 m x 11 m)

ARMAMENT: Two 32 pounder guns

ARMOR: 4 in (102 mm) of plate iron over 20 in (508 mm) of White Oak

MACHINERY: Stern wheel steam engine

SPEED: Unknown

CREW: 75

CSS *Jackson*

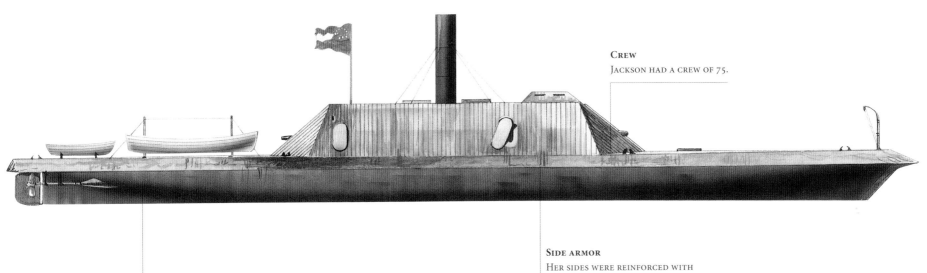

CREW
JACKSON HAD A CREW OF 75.

SIDE ARMOR
HER SIDES WERE REINFORCED WITH
20 IN (508 MM) OF WHITE OAK.

WEIGHT
WEIGHING 2,000 TONS (1,814 TONNES),
SHE WAS THE LARGEST IRONCLAD
BUILT FROM THE HULL UP BY THE
CONFEDERACY.

CSS *Nashville* *(1864)*

ON SEPTEMBER 16, 1862, SECRETARY OF THE NAVY STEPHEN MALLORY CONTRACTED WITH TWO BUILDERS TO CONSTRUCT THE IRONCLAD *NASHVILLE* IN MONTGOMERY, ALABAMA FOR THE SIZABLE SUM OF NEARLY $670,000. SHE WAS BUILT AT AN IMPROVISED SHIPYARD IN CYPRESS CREEK INLET, JUST ABOVE THE CITY WHARF.

The Naval Iron Works at Columbus, Georgia, supervised the construction and supplied two steam engines for the Nashville's side paddle wheels. She was launched in the Alabama River on May 20, 1863. At 271 feet (82 m) in length and 62 feet 6 inches (19 m) in beam, the *Nashville* was a large vessel for the Alabama. She displaced 1,100 tons (997 tonnes).

The *Nashville* then moved downriver to the Navy Yard in Selma for further outfitting, and was then towed to Mobile. With a depth of 13 feet (3.9 m) and a draft of 10 feet 9 inches (3.27 m) , crossing the shallow Dog River Bar with its mere 10 ft (3 m) of water required ingenuity, and to make the passage, the Nashville had to be equipped with flotation devices called "camels." This problem solved, she arrived in Mobile Bay on June 16, 1863, where she was scheduled to be completely clad in iron plating. Because of plating shortages,

however, she was never fully outfitted with armor and much of what she did receive was from the decommissioned CSS *Baltic*.

Shortcomings

The *Nashville* also had problems receiving its armament. Scheduled to be fitted with an array of one 24 pounder howitzer and seven Brooke rifled guns cast in Selma, the slope of the ship's armor ended up requiring longer guns. The iron works in Selma was able to complete only three of these pieces. Other weaknesses included exposed side-wheels and slow speed. Nonetheless, the Federal Navy was very concerned about the threat the *Nashville* and the *Tennessee* potentially posed to an attack on Mobile Bay. When the battle finally came on August 5, 1864, however, the *Nashville* was still unprepared, and stayed out of the fight, moored to a wharf in upper Mobile Bay.

The *Nashville* saw brief action at the very end of the war and was the last major Confederate warship to engage Union forces. In early 1865, as the Federals advanced up the eastern shore of Mobile Bay, the *Nashville* provided effective supporting fire to the Confederate defenders until April 9 when the Confederates evacuated Spanish Fort. The *Nashville* then withdrew up the Tombigbee River with a small flotilla commanded by Captain Ebenezer Farrand, who surrendered the Nashville and the rest of his small command on May 10. The U.S. Government sold the *Nashville* at auction on November 22, 1867, and she was broken up for scrap.

CSS *Nashville*

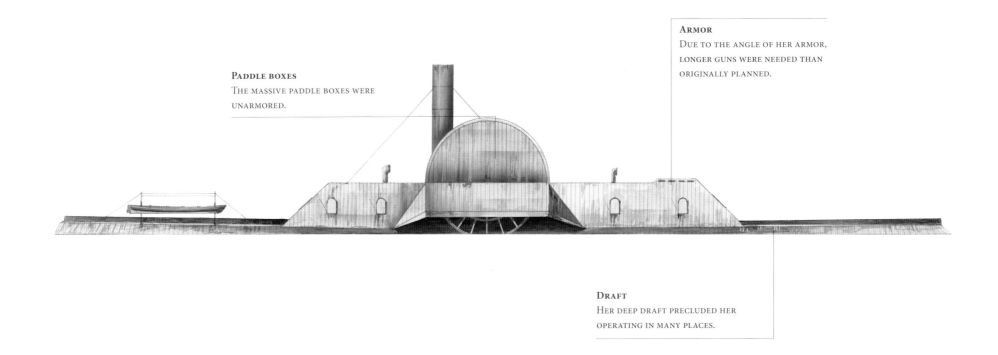

PADDLE BOXES
THE MASSIVE PADDLE BOXES WERE
UNARMORED.

ARMOR
DUE TO THE ANGLE OF HER ARMOR,
LONGER GUNS WERE NEEDED THAN
ORIGINALLY PLANNED.

DRAFT
HER DEEP DRAFT PRECLUDED HER
OPERATING IN MANY PLACES.

CSS *Neuse* (1864)

THE CONSTRUCTION OF THE CSS *NEUSE* HAS BEEN CALLED "A MICROCOSM OF THE SOUTH'S PROBLEMS IN FASHIONING A WARTIME NAVY." THE PROCESS BEGAN AT WHITE HALL, NORTH CAROLINA ON THE BANKS OF THE NEUSE RIVER. THE FACT THAT UNION FORCES WERE MAKING PERIODIC RAIDS IN THE AREA WAS ONE OF THE EARLY PROBLEMS THAT WORRIED LIEUTENANT COMMANDER JAMES COOKE, WHO HAD BEEN SENT TO SUPERINTEND THE CONSTRUCTION EFFORT.

Cooke's fears were realized on December 14, 1862 when forces under Brigadier General John Foster routed the Confederates at Kinston and moved up the south bank of the Neuse River, following the retreating enemy to White Hall. Foster's men caught sight of the *Neuse* in her early stages of construction and hoped to destroy it but were prevented from doing so by Confederate resistance. The *Neuse* was, however, struck several times by Federal fire. Although the vessel was not severely damaged, construction was delayed.

After Foster's troops left the White Hall vicinity, work was resumed, and in mid-March 1863 the *Neuse* was set free to drift downriver to Kinston, where it would receive its fittings, machinery and iron plating. Once the *Neuse* arrived in Kinston, however, administrative problems and a lack of equipment caused additional delays. Machinery from Richmond, Virginia did not begin to arrive until January 1864. In the meantime, the Confederates had failed in an effort to recapture New Bern, making completion of the *Neuse* even more important. In February 1864, Secretary of the Navy Stephen Mallory dispatched Lieutenant Robert Minor to Kinston "to hasten the completion of the gunboat."

Grounded

Although construction was not yet complete, the battlefield situation prompted the Navy to order the *Neuse* to combine with its sister ship the *Albemarle* in an effort to recapture part of New Bern. On April 22, 1864, the *Neuse* steamed out of her "cat hole," but barely moved half a mile downriver before grounding on a sandbar. When the river rose in mid-May, the *Neuse* was freed, but, rather than attacking New Bern, she returned to Kinston. By the time her construction was finished in June, troops were no longer available to support offensive operations and the *Neuse* remained idle.

As Confederate fortunes steadily evaporated, advancing Federals descended on Kinston in the spring of 1865. Defense was largely futile, but on March 12 the *Neuse* fired her only shots in anger at advancing enemy cavalry units. Captain Joseph Price then ordered the *Neuse* be scuttled. The crew set fire to the vessel, and a massive explosion on her port bow finally sank the ill-fated ship. After a two-year effort, the hulk of the *Neuse* was raised in 1963 and is now displayed in Kinston.

SPECIFICATIONS

DISPLACEMENT: About 376 tons (341 tonnes)

DIMENSIONS: 152 ft x 34 ft x 9 ft (46 m x 10 m x 2.7 m)

ARMAMENT: Two 6.4 in (160 mm) Brooke rifles

ARMOR: 4 in (100 mm) of iron backed with 4 in (100 mm) of oak

MACHINERY: Steam

SPEED: 4 knots (estimated)

CREW: 150

CSS *Neuse*

ARMOR
THE ARMOR WAS ROLLED RAILROAD IRON BUT THERE WERE PROBLEMS GETTING IT TO THE VESSEL BECAUSE THE ARMY VIRTUALLY MONOPOLIZED THE RAILROAD.

ARMAMENT
NEUSE CARRIED TWO 6.4 IN (163 MM) BROOKE RIFLES.

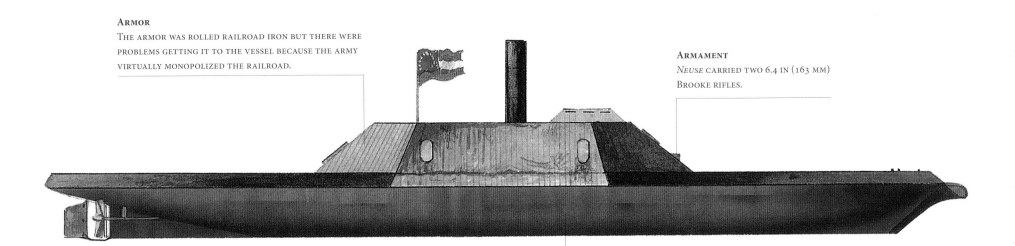

HULL
INTENDED TO OPERATE ON RIVERS, *NEUSE* AND HER SISTER SHIPS WERE GIVEN FLAT FLOORS AND SHALLOW DRAFTS.

USS *Onondaga* (1864)

THE USS *ONONDAGA* WAS BUILT IN GREENPOINT, NEW YORK, LAUNCHED IN 1863 AND COMMISSIONED IN MARCH 1864. SHE WAS 2,592 TONS (2,351 TONNES) AND 226 FEET (69 M) LONG, AND WAS THE FIRST IRONCLAD INTRODUCED DURING THE WAR WITH TWO REVOLVING TURRETS, MOUNTING FOUR GUNS INSTEAD OF JUST TWO.

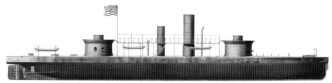

USS *MIANTANOMOH*

She had an integrated crew, with her December 1864 muster role listing at least 18 blacks. The *Onondaga* spent her entire active career with the James River Flotilla, covering the water approaches to Richmond, Virginia. When most of the other vessels of the flotilla were dispatched to North Carolina to participate in the attack on Fort Fisher, the *Onondaga* was left as the only monitor to defend, with a handful of wooden vessels, the important Federal supply depot at City Point. On January 23, 1865, the Confederate ironclads *Virginia II*, *Richmond,* and *Fredericksburg* and five smaller vessels descended the James River in an effort to attack the vulnerable Federal position. The Confederates had successfully slipped past Fort Brady, but then ran into river obstructions at Trent's Reach. The obstructions disrupted the Confederate attack, grounding several of the vessels. The *Onondaga* arrived on the scene in time to deliver a heavy pounding on both the *Virginia II* and the *Richmond* as they struggled in the obstructions. Before the *Virginia II* could escape, the *Onondaga* had blasted a hole in the Confederate ship's armor. The Confederate ships sought shelter in a bend of the river just opposite Battery Dantzler before retiring upriver to Chaffin's Bluff. The *Onondaga* had successfully repulsed this brief threat to the Federal supply depot.

The *Onondaga* was decommissioned in Philadelphia, Pennsylvania in June 1865. In March 1867, she was then sold back to her builder, who immediately resold her to France, where she served in the French Navy.

USS *Miantonomoh* (1865)

The twin-screw, wooden-hulled monitor *Miantonomoh* was designed by John Lenthall, who replaced John Ericsson's raft hull with a more streamlined design. He also raised the freeboard, which increased the vessel's seaworthy characteristics but decreased her protection. This tradeoff was deemed acceptable because the *Miantonomoh* was armored by 4½ inches (114 mm) of iron backed by oak. Her powerful engines were designed by Benjamin Isherwood and could reach speeds of 9 knots. One design flaw was that Lenthall relied on wooden frames to support the twin turrets. The weight of the turrets weakened the structural integrity of the vessel, leaving the hull prone to rotting and cracking.

The *Miantonomoh* was constructed at the New York Navy Yard in Brooklyn in 1862. She was launched August 15, 1863 and commissioned September 18, 1865. She was commanded by Commander Daniel Ammen, but saw no wartime service.

SPECIFICATIONS

DISPLACEMENT: 2,592 tons (2,351 tonnes)

DIMENSIONS: 226 ft x 49 ft 3 in x 12 ft 10 in (69 m x 15.01 m x 3.91 m)

ARMAMENT: Two 15 in (381 mm) Dahlgren smoothbores; two 150 pounder Parrott rifles

ARMOR: Turret: 11 in (279 mm); hull sides: 5.5 in (140 mm); deck: 1 in (25.4 mm)

MACHINERY: Four horizontal back-acting engines driving twin screws, developing 642 hp (479 kW)

SPEED: 6–7 knots

CREW: 150

USS *Onondaga*

SHIELDS
DURING HER CAREER, BULLET-PROOF SHIELDS WERE FITTED TO THE TOPS OF THE TURRETS.

TURRETS
ONONDAGA WAS THE FIRST DOUBLE-TURRETED MONITOR COMPLETED FOR THE US NAVY.

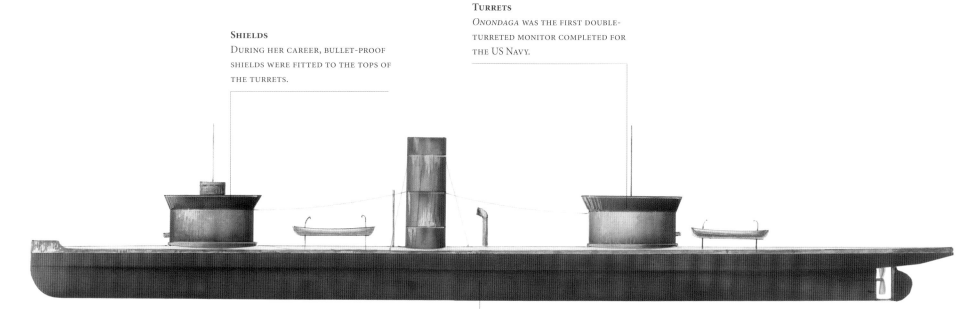

COAL CAPACITY
WHILE SHE HAD CAPACITY FOR 268 TONS (243 TONNES) OF COAL, SHE ONLY HAD BUOYANCY FOR 160 TONS (145 TONNES).

USS *Ozark* (1864)

THE USS *OZARK* WAS PART OF THE NEOSHO CLASS OF MONITORS DESIGNED BY JAMES EADS FOR SERVICE ON THE WESTERN RIVERS. SHE WAS BUILT BY CONTRACT WITH GEORGE BESTER IN PEORIA, ILLINOIS, LAUNCHED FEBRUARY 18, 1863 AND COMMISSIONED FEBRUARY 18, 1864 WITH ACTING VOLUNTEER LIEUTENANT GEORGE BROWN IN COMMAND.

It was common for builders to subcontract the armor and machinery, but the *Ozark* was unusual in that Bester contracted out the entire vessel.

The *Ozark* combined a single turret mounting two 11-inch (279 mm) Dahlgrens and a casemate with one 10 inch (254 mm) and three 9 inch (228 mm) Dahlgrens. The Neosho class was unique in being propelled by stern wheels. A drawback to this design was that it did not allow full 360-degree fire for the two turret-mounted Dahlgrens.

From March to May 1864, the *Ozark* took part in the Red River Campaign. The expedition failed in large part due to Major General Nathaniel Banks' leadership. As Banks retreated to Gran Ecore, the river continued to drop, reaching a depth of less than 3½ feet (1 m) over the falls in Alexandria, Louisiana. When Admiral David Porter

arrived there on April 28, he found that nine ironclads, including the *Ozark*, which required 7 feet (2 m), were trapped above the falls. The vessels were saved by the quick thinking of Colonel Joseph Bailey who proposed building a dam below the lower falls at a point where the river was 238 feet (225 m) wide. Porter thought the plan "looked like madness, and the best engineers ridiculed it," but in the desperation of the situation, Banks detailed Bailey's 3,000 men and 400 wagons and teams.

Difficult Passage

Bailey's crews worked heroically to gather the required construction materials, and soldiers struggled waist-deep in a 9-knot current to put everything in place. By May 9, after eight days of difficult labor, the water over the upper falls had risen enough for four of the trapped vessels to enter the deep channel. Part of the dam

gave way, but somehow the vessels made it through. Bailey then built a series of light "wing dams" across the upper falls and on May 11 three more vessels made the passage. The next day, it was the *Ozark*'s turn, making the journey with the *Chillicothe*. The last vessel, the *Baron De Kalb*, still had 6 inches (152 mm) too much draft, but was ultimately hauled over the falls by 2,000 men manning a series of 4 inch (101 mm) hawsers under the direction of the irrepressible Bailey.

The *Ozark* was quiet during the rest of the war and was decommissioned in Mound City, Illinois on July 25, 1865. She was sold on November 29.

SPECIFICATIONS

DISPLACEMENT: 578 tons (524 tonnes)

DIMENSIONS: 180 ft x 50 ft x 5 ft (55 m x 15.3 m x 1.5 m)

ARMAMENT: One 10 in (250 mm) gun; three 9 in (230 mm) guns

ARMOR: Turret: 6 in (152.4 mm); sides: 2.5 in (63.5 mm); deck: 1.25 in (31.75 mm)

MACHINERY: Four engines driving two screws

SPEED: 2.5 knots

CREW: 120

USS *Ozark*

TURRET
Ozark HAD A LARGE TURRET WITH AN INSIDE DIAMETER OF 20 FT (6 M).

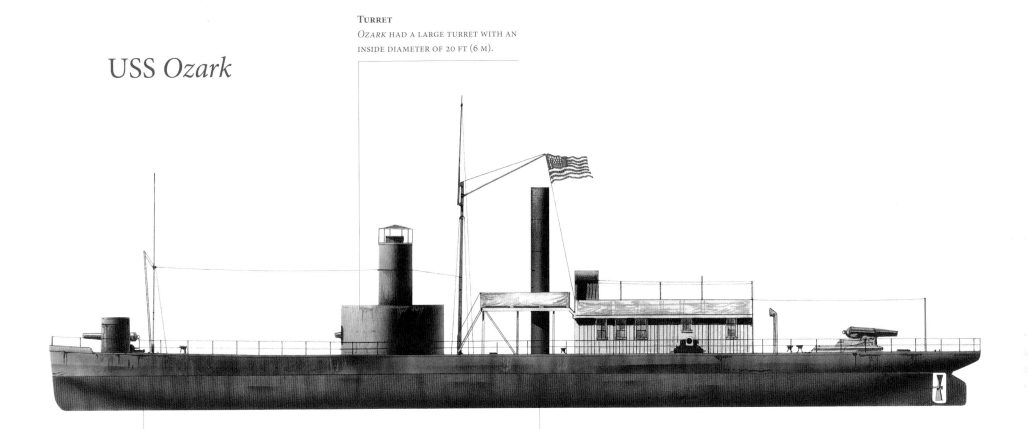

DRAFT
Ozark HAD AN EXTREMELY SHALLOW DRAFT OF 5 FT (1.5 M), ENABLING HER TO NAVIGATE SHALLOW WATERS.

ENGINES
Ozark COULD ONLY REACH A SPEED OF 2.5 KNOTS.

CSS *Tennessee* (1864)

THE CSS *TENNESSEE* WAS A 1,273 TON (1,155 TONNE) IRONCLAD RAM BUILT IN SELMA, ALABAMA AND LAUNCHED IN FEBRUARY 1863. SHE SAILED TO MOBILE TO COMPLETE HER OUTFITTING AND WAS COMMISSIONED IN FEBRUARY 1864, THE MOST COSTLY SHIP BUILT BY THE CONFEDERACY AND THE ONE THAT TOOK THE LONGEST TO COMPLETE.

She had 6 inches (152 mm) of armor on her casemate, 5 inches (127 mm) on her sides and 2 inches (50 mm) on her deck, along with firepower provided by six Brooke rifles. Under the experienced command of Admiral Franklin Buchanan, the *Tennessee* posed a serious threat to the wooden ships planning to attack Mobile. To counter the *Tennessee*, Admiral David Farragut's Federal fleet was reinforced by four monitors. Still Farragut respected the *Tennessee*, which by all accounts was one of the Confederacy's most powerful ironclads. He wrote to his son, "Buchanan has a vessel which he says is superior to the *Merrimack* with which he intends to attack us…. So we are to have no child's play."

Farragut attacked Mobile Bay on August 5, 1864. Famously ordering, "Damn the torpedoes. Full speed ahead!" he steamed past Forts Morgan and Gaines into Mobile Bay, where the *Tennessee* awaited him. The *Tennessee*'s engines had been taken from a riverboat steamer, and she was inadequately powered for her weight and therefore hard to maneuver. Though she was able to inflict some damage on the Federal ships, she was quickly surrounded. The *Tennessee*'s main weakness was the fact that her rubber chains ran across the after deck. These were soon shot away, largely by the *Chickasaw*, which fired more than 50 solid shots into her. Unable to steer, the *Tennessee* was repeatedly rammed and shelled.

Dead in the Water

One shot struck the after port shutter, killing the two men behind it and badly wounding Buchanan who was taken below. Commander James Johnston assumed command. With his vessel virtually dead in the water, ammunition nearly gone, and the bow, stern and one of the port gunport shutters jammed shut, Johnston knew there was little hope. He reported the situation to Buchanan who replied, "Do the best you can, sir, and when all is done, surrender." With the *Ossippee* bearing down on the *Tennessee* with the intent of ramming her hard, Johnston "decided, although with an almost bursting heart, to hoist the white flag." Farragut took Buchanan's sword as a prize.

The Federals repaired the Confederate ship, rechristened it the USS *Tennessee*, and used it to help capture Fort Morgan later in August. She was then sent to New Orleans, Louisiana for further repairs and served with the Mississippi Squadron until after the end of the Civil War. She was decommissioned August 19, sold on November 27, 1865 and scrapped.

SPECIFICATIONS

DISPLACEMENT: 1,273 tons (1,155 tonnes)

DIMENSIONS: 209 ft x 48 ft x 14 ft (64 m x 15 m x 4.3 m)

ARMAMENT: Two 8 in (203 mm) Brooke rifles; four 6.4 in (160 mm) Brooke rifles

ARMOR: Sides: 5 in (127 mm); forward end: 6 in (152 mm); deck: 2 in (51 mm)

MACHINERY: Two geared non-condensing engines with 24 in (610 mm) cylinders and a 7 ft (2.1 m) stroke.

SPEED: 5 knots

CREW: 133

CSS *Tennessee*

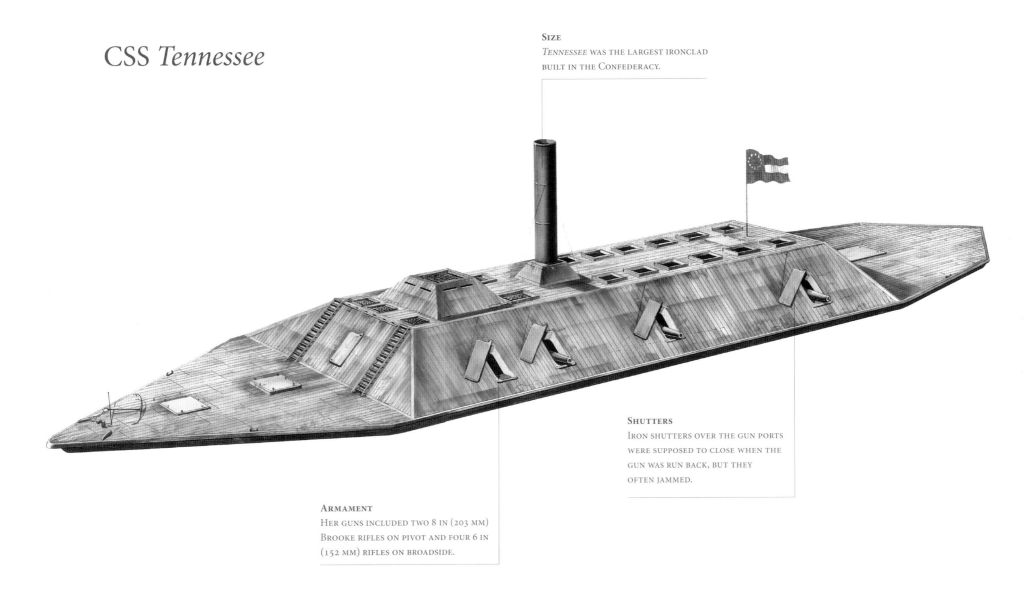

SIZE
TENNESSEE WAS THE LARGEST IRONCLAD
BUILT IN THE CONFEDERACY.

SHUTTERS
IRON SHUTTERS OVER THE GUN PORTS
WERE SUPPOSED TO CLOSE WHEN THE
GUN WAS RUN BACK, BUT THEY
OFTEN JAMMED.

ARMAMENT
HER GUNS INCLUDED TWO 8 IN (203 MM)
BROOKE RIFLES ON PIVOT AND FOUR 6 IN
(152 MM) RIFLES ON BROADSIDE.

USS *Winnebago* (1864)

THE CONFEDERATE DEFENDERS AT MOBILE BAY HAD SEVERAL ADVANTAGES. ALTHOUGH THE BAY STRETCHED SOME 30 MILES (48 KM) INLAND, ITS ENTRANCE WAS ONLY 3 MILES (5 KM) WIDE. THE CHANNEL WAS FURTHER REDUCED BY A SERIES OF SUNKEN PILINGS, SHALLOW WATER AND THREE LINES OF TORPEDOES.

On the eastern edge of the minefield was a thin opening stretching some 200 yards (183 m) to Mobile Point that provided a passageway for blockade runners. However, this route was covered by the powerful Fort Morgan, a massive pentagon-shaped, three-tiered structure with 47 guns. Fort Gaines covered the western side from Dauphin Island and a much smaller Fort Powell blocked Grant's Pass, a narrow inter-coastal passage north of Dauphin Island via the Mississippi Sound. Behind these forts were the formidable ironclad *Tennessee* and three wooden gunboats under the able command of Admiral Franklin Buchanan.

The Federals knew such defenses posed a serious threat to wooden vessels, so in January 1864, Assistant Secretary of the Navy Gustavus Fox had asked Admiral David Farragut how many ironclads he thought he would need to blast his way into Mobile Bay. Farragut replied, "Just as many as you can spare; two would answer me well, more would do better." By July, the Navy had four monitors on the way to Farragut. The *Manhattan* and the *Tecumseh* were large, improved vessels, mounting a pair of 15 inch (381 mm) Dahlgren guns behind 11 inches (279 mm) of turret armor. They were the most powerful warships then in existence. Complementing them were the *Chickasaw* and the *Winnebago*, twin-turret, quadruple-screwed river monitors with batteries of four 11 inch (279 mm) guns.

Mobile Bay Attack

The *Winnebago* had been built in Carondelet, Missouri. She was commissioned in April 1864 and assigned to the Mississippi Squadron. On June 15, she participated in an engagement with Confederate artillery at Ratliff's Landing, Louisiana, before being reassigned to the West Gulf Blockading Squadron in July. When Farragut attacked Mobile Bay on August 5, the *Winnebago* engaged both Fort Morgan and the *Tennessee*. After the battle, she remained in Mobile Bay, supporting operations to blockade and ultimately capture the city of Mobile. She took part in a March 1865 attack on nearby Spanish Fort, and in April, she convoyed troops to Selma and Montgomery, Alabama, and blockaded the Tombigbee River.

SPECIFICATIONS

DISPLACEMENT: 1,300 tons (1179 tonnes)

DIMENSIONS: 228 ft x 56 ft x 6 ft (70 m x 17 m x 1.8 m)

ARMAMENT: Four 11 in (279 mm) Dahlgren smoothbore guns

ARMOR: 8 in (203 mm) on turrets; 3 in (76 mm) on sides

MACHINERY: Four non-condensing horizontal engines; four screws and three rudders

SPEED: 9 knots

CREW: About 120

USS *Winnebago*

STEAM
EXTENSIVE USE OF STEAM POWER WAS
USED TO ELEVATE THE GUNS AND TO
LOWER THEM INTO THE HOLD.

GUNS
EACH TURRET HAD TWO 11 IN (279 MM)
DAHLGREN SMOOTHBORE GUNS.

ARMOR
THE ARMOR WAS 8 IN (203 MM) THICK
ON THE TURRETS AND 3 IN (76 MM)
THICK ON THE SIDES.

CSS *Stonewall* (1865)

HOPING TO ACCELERATE THE BUILDING OF ITS FLEDGLING NAVY, THE CONFEDERATE GOVERNMENT DISPATCHED JAMES BULLOCH TO ENGLAND AS A NAVAL AGENT TO ARRANGE FOR SHIPS TO BE BUILT FOR THE CONFEDERACY. BULLOCH OPERATED OUT OF LIVERPOOL, A SITE OF CONSIDERABLE CONFEDERATE SYMPATHY.

Under scrutiny from U.S. political consul Thomas Haines Dudley, Bulloch slipped out of Liverpool and in March 1863 went to Bordeaux, France, where he found Lucien Arman. On July 16 they signed a contract for Arman to build two armored ships, tentatively named the *Cheops* and the *Sphinx*.

The indefatigable Dudley redoubled his counter-intelligence efforts and kept pressure on Bulloch, and European authorities began to take a harder look at Bulloch in light of existing neutrality laws. When Arman met with Louis-Napoleon, he expected the emperor to quietly approve his business with Bulloch. Instead, Louis-Napoleon threatened to throw Arman in jail if he did not sell all his ships immediately to bona fide buyers. Arman quickly unloaded the vessels according to the emperor's instructions.

The vessel that ultimately became the *Stonewall* was sold to Denmark for use in the Schleswig-Holstein War. However, the war abruptly ended before the ship reached its destination. No longer needing her, the Danes refused acceptance. This development provided Bulloch the opportunity he needed, and arrangements were made to purchase the vessel for the Confederacy.

Captain Thomas Jefferson Page took control of the vessel and brought her to a rendezvous point off Quiberon, France, where he met Lieutenant H. Davidson and the steamer *City of Richmond*. Davidson had with him the crew and supplies Page needed for the new vessel. The Confederate flag was hoisted and the *Sphinx* was rechristened the *Stonewall*.

Truncated Service

It was soon discovered that the *Stonewall* had a leak, and Page took her to Spain for repairs. His initial welcome there was short-lived when American protests caused the Spanish authorities to order Page away. By this time, the Federal frigate *Niagara* and the sloop-of-war *Sacramento* had anchored at Corunna to watch the *Stonewall*. Surprisingly to Page, when he steamed the *Stonewall* out of the harbor at Ferrol on March 24, 1865, the Federal ships remained at anchor and allowed him to pass unmolested.

Proceeding on, Page reached Nassau on May 6 and then moved to Havana. He had intended to attack at Port Royal, South Carolina, but learning in Cuba that the war was over, he relinquished control of the *Stonewall* to Spanish authorities who voluntarily turned her over to the United States in July.

SPECIFICATIONS

DISPLACEMENT: 1,560 tons (1,415 tonnes)

DIMENSIONS: 194 ft x 31 ft 6 in x 15 ft 8 in (59 m x 9.6 m x 4.77 m)

ARMAMENT: One 9 in (228 mm) 300 pounder gun; two 70 pounder guns

ARMOR: 4.5 in (114 mm) on sides and 3.5 in (89 mm) at ends; 4 in (102 mm) on aft turret; 5.5 in (140 mm) over bow gun; 24 in (610 mm) of wood backing behind side armor

MACHINERY: Horizontal direct-acting Mazeline engines driving twin screws.

SPEED: 10.8 knots

CREW: 135

CSS *Stonewall*

SPEED
STONEWALL COULD REACH
A SPEED OF 10.8 KNOTS.

TURRET
TWO 70 POUNDER GUNS WERE
CARRIED AFT IN A FIXED TURRET.

FORWARD GUN
THE 9 IN (228 MM) GUN WAS HOUSED
FORWARD, FIRING DIRECTLY AHEAD.

USS *America* (1851)

THE USS *AMERICA* WAS ORIGINALLY BUILT AS A SCHOONER-RIGGED YACHT IN NEW YORK CITY AND LAUNCHED ON MAY 3, 1851. THE YACHT WAS CONSTRUCTED FOR A SYNDICATE HEADED BY JOHN COX STEVENS, THE COMMODORE OF THE NEW YORK YACHT CLUB. STEVENS AND HIS COLLEAGUES HOPED TO USE THE VESSEL TO PROMOTE AMERICAN SHIPBUILDING AND SAILING SKILL.

Indeed, the *America* won the Queen's Cup at Cowes, England on August 22, 1851 and became the namesake for the America's Cup yacht race.

The vessel had a sharp entry and was wider around the middle section, a feature common in Virginia pilot boats. The claims that she was the fastest American yacht of her period cannot be borne since she was not comprehensively raced against other American vessels. However, this in no way detracts from her performance.

Confederate Service

Cox and his syndicate sold the *America* after the race, and she was not well maintained as a racing vessel. A new owner renamed her the *Camilla*. She was brought back to America and acquired by the Confederate government for $60,000 to serve as a blockade runner and dispatch boat. She arrived at Savannah, Georgia in April 1861, just after the surrender of Fort Sumter. Renamed the *Memphis,* she apparently was never employed in her intended role. Although she was certainly a fast vessel, her lack of cargo space ill-suited her as a blockade runner. Instead, she was scuttled in Haw Creek off the Saint John's River at the head of Dunn's Lake in Florida to prevent Federal capture.

America Rises

In spite of Confederate attempts to prevent the operation, the vessel was raised by the Federal Navy in March 1862, reconditioned, and recommissioned under her former name, *America*. She served with the South Atlantic Blockading Squadron, taking part in two captures.

She was withdrawn from blockading service in 1863 and served as a training ship for Naval Academy midshipmen, first at Newport, Rhode Island and then at Annapolis, Maryland, until sold in 1873. In 1921, the yacht was presented to the Navy Department by the Eastern Yacht Club of Marblehead, Maine, to be preserved as a relic. The hulk was eventually broken up in 1945.

SPECIFICATIONS

DISPLACEMENT: 100 tons (91 tonnes)

DIMENSIONS: 111 ft x 25 ft x 12 ft (245 m x 7.62 m x 3.7 m)

ARMAMENT: One 12 pounder rifle gun; two 24 pounder smoothbore

MACHINERY: Sail

SPEED: Not known

CREW: 9 (when racing)

USS *America*

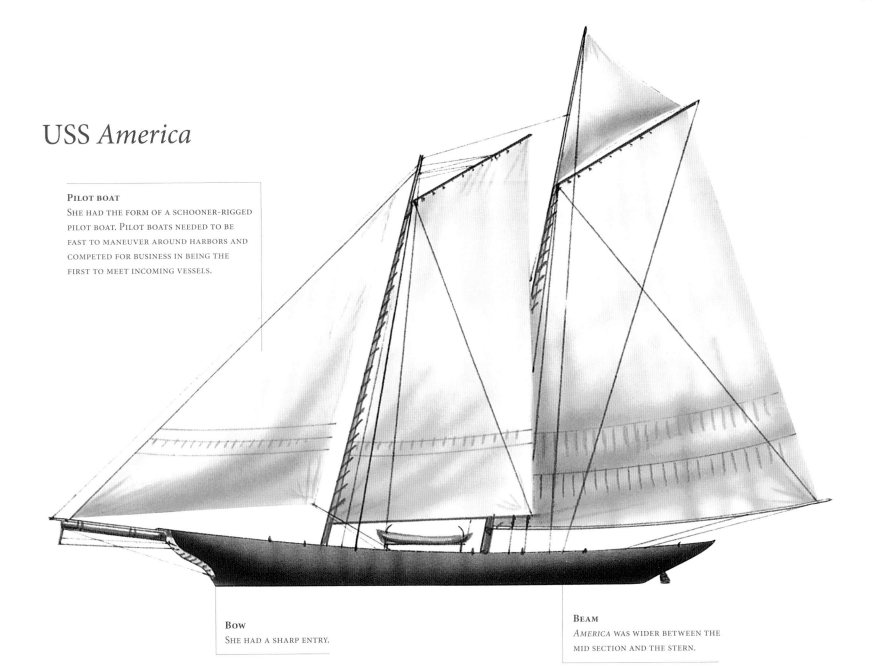

PILOT BOAT
SHE HAD THE FORM OF A SCHOONER-RIGGED
PILOT BOAT. PILOT BOATS NEEDED TO BE
FAST TO MANEUVER AROUND HARBORS AND
COMPETED FOR BUSINESS IN BEING THE
FIRST TO MEET INCOMING VESSELS.

BOW
SHE HAD A SHARP ENTRY.

BEAM
AMERICA WAS WIDER BETWEEN THE
MID SECTION AND THE STERN.

USS *Water Witch* (1853)

THE *WATER WITCH* WAS A WOODEN-HULLED, SIDE-WHEEL GUNBOAT COMMISSIONED DURING THE WINTER OF 1852 AND 1853 WITH LIEUTENANT THOMAS JEFFERSON PAGE IN COMMAND. SHE ACHIEVED SOME PRE-CIVIL WAR NOTORIETY IN FEBRUARY 1855 WHEN, WHILE SURVEYING THE LA PLATA RIVER, SHE WAS FIRED UPON BY A PARAGUAYAN FORT.

One member of her crew was killed, and in 1859 an armed commission to Paraguay exacted an apology, indemnity for the family of the deceased sailor, and an advantageous commercial treaty for the United States.

The *Water Witch* was in and out of commission until April 10, 1861. She joined the Gulf Blockading Squadron off Pensacola, Florida on May 2, with her initial duty involving dispatch service and shuttling mail between the blockaders and their base at Key West. She also carried mail to Havana, Cuba. Late that summer she was moved to the mouth of the Mississippi River, where she served until the beginning of 1862. Her shallow draft made her ideal for operating in such waters, and she made several reconnaissance trips into the mouth of the Mississippi.

When the Gulf Blockading Squadron was divided in two on January 20, the *Water Witch* was assigned to the East Gulf Blockading Squadron and began operating off the gulf coasts of Alabama and Florida. On March 5, she pursued the schooner *William Mallory* for five hours before finally capturing the blockade runner late in the day. During this period of service she also performed duties as a dispatch vessel and mail packet.

St. John's River Blockade

After undergoing repairs between April and September, she was recommissioned and ordered to the South Atlantic Blockading Squadron, where she took up a blockade station in the St. John's River in northeastern Florida. In October she participated in a mission up the river that forced the Confederates to abandon their position at St. John's Bluff. She continued to serve with the South Atlantic Blockading Squadron until she broke down and had to be towed north

for repairs in February 1863. She returned to Port Royal on June 14 and performed blockade duty until June 3, 1864 when a Confederate boat force commanded by Lieutenant Thomas Pelot boarded and captured her in Ossabaw.

The *Water Witch* was taken into the Confederate Navy where she served under the same name. On December 19 she was burned at White Bluff, Georgia to prevent her capture. In 2007, a team led by the Georgia Department of Natural Resources found what is believed to be her wreck off the coast of Savannah beneath approximately 15 feet (4.5 m) of sediment. A full-scale replica of the *Water Witch* is on display at the National Civil War Naval Museum in Columbus, Georgia.

SPECIFICATIONS

DISPLACEMENT: 464 tons (421 tonnes)

DIMENSIONS: 163 ft x 24 ft 4 in x 11 ft 9 in (50 m x 7.42 m x 3.58 m)

ARMAMENT: Four 32 pounders; one 12 pounder smoothbore; one 20 pounder Parrott rifle; four 32 pounders

MACHINERY: Side-wheel steamer

SPEED: 9 knots

CREW: 64

USS *Water Witch*

CREW
USS *WATER WITCH* CARRIED A CREW OF 64.

DRAFT
HER SHALLOW DRAFT OF 11 FT 9 IN (3.58 M) MADE HER IDEAL FOR OPERATING ON THE MISSISSIPPI RIVER.

DISPLACEMENT
HER DISPLACEMENT WAS 464 TONS (421 TONNES).

USS *Harriet Lane* (1857)

WILLIAM WEBB BUILT THE *HARRIET LANE* FOR THE TREASURY DEPARTMENT IN 1857 FOR USE AS A REVENUE CUTTER. SHE WAS TRANSFERRED TO THE NAVY ON MARCH 30, 1861 TO PARTICIPATE IN AN EXPEDITION TO SUPPLY THE BELEAGUERED FORT SUMTER GARRISON. SHE ARRIVED OFF CHARLESTON HARBOR ON APRIL 11, AND THE NEXT DAY SHE FIRED A SHOT ACROSS THE BOW OF THE MERCHANT SHIP *NASHVILLE*, WHICH WAS FLYING NO COLORS.

The *Nashville* promptly hoisted the United States ensign, but two days later raised the Palmetto flag and began her career as a Confederate privateer. Many consider this the first naval shot fired of the Civil War. The small Federal fleet of which the *Harriet Lane* was a part did little else to assist the garrison at Fort Sumter and when Major Robert Anderson surrendered on April 13, the, *Harriet Lane* withdrew to New York with her sister ships and Anderson's men.

The *Harriet Lane* next participated in the decisive Federal victory at Hatteras Inlet, but ran aground while attempting to enter Pamlico Sound on August 29. She was refloated but in the process much of her armament and equipment was jettisoned. After temporary repairs, she reached Hampton Roads, Virginia on September 8.

The *Harriet Lane* sailed on February 10, 1862 to join Commander David Porter's Mortar Flotilla in Key West in preparation for the attack on New Orleans, where she served as Porter's flagship and engaged Forts Jackson and St. Philip. After Admiral David Farragut's victorious attack there on April 24, the *Harriet Lane* served in operations at Pensacola, Florida; Vicksburg, Mississippi; and Mobile Bay, Alabama.

Galveston Fight

On October 4, the *Harriet Lane* was part of a squadron that captured Galveston, Texas. However, on January 1, 1863, Major General John Magruder led a surprise attack against the poorly defended position that recaptured the port for the Confederacy. Leon Smith led a three ship Confederate flotilla that descended on the *Harriet Lane*. Her large paddlewheels on each side made her vulnerable to ramming, and she was attacked by both the *Bayou City* and the *Neptune*. She ultimately became entangled with the *Bayou City*, whose troops boarded the *Harriet Lane* and took her by storm.

Although the Confederates succeeded in recapturing Galveston, the Federals soon reestablished the blockade. Early in 1864 the *Harriet Lane* was converted to a blockade runner, the *Lavinia*. She ran the blockade on April 30 and reached Cuba with a cargo of cotton. There, however, Spanish authorities detained her until the war's end. She was returned by Spain to the United States in 1867.

USS *Harriet Lane*

COPPER
THE ENTIRE SHIP WAS
SHEATHED AND FASTENED
WITH COPPER.

PADDLES
HARRIET LANE WAS PROPELLED BY
TWO SIDE PADDLES SUPPORTED BY
TWO MASTS.

ARMAMENT
RUNNING AGROUND IN 1861, CREW
THREW HER FOUR 32 POUNDER RIFLES
OVERBOARD TO LIGHTEN HER LOAD.

USS *Pawnee* (1860)

THE *PAWNEE* WAS COMMISSIONED ON JUNE 11, 1860 WITH COMMANDER H.J. HARTSTENE IN COMMAND. SHE WAS THE FIRST VESSEL IN THE U.S. NAVY TO BE EQUIPPED WITH TWIN PROPELLERS. SHE MADE A SHORT CRUISE TO MEXICO BEFORE THE CIVIL WAR AND WAS LOCATED IN WASHINGTON, D.C. FOR THE FIRST THREE MONTHS OF 1861.

With the mounting crisis at Fort Sumter, she was sent to Charleston, South Carolina on April 6 under the command of Commander Stephen Rowan as part of an ill-fated mission to relieve Major Robert Anderson's besieged command. The anticipated rendezvous of several ships did not come to fruition. The *Pawnee* was delayed by bad weather and did not arrive until April 12 with the *Pocahontas*. The ships also lost valuable time waiting for the *Powhatan*, which had been detached from the mission without their knowledge. By the time the ships arrived, Anderson had been compelled to surrender.

The *Pawnee* returned to Washington and was immediately dispatched to Norfolk, Virginia to secure the ships and stores at the Gosport Navy Yard from falling into Confederate hands. She had brought with her several key officers to command the ships, but upon her arrival on August 20 she found that, except for the *Cumberland*, all had been scuttled. She towed the *Cumberland*, whose crew greeted her "with a hurricane of heartiness," to safety.

Potomac River Patrol

From May to August 1861 the *Pawnee* was based in Washington and operated on the Potomac River. She then joined the Atlantic Blockade Squadron and participated in the capture of Hatteras Inlet on August 28–29. On October 29, she sailed with Admiral Samuel Du Pont's force that captured Port Royal, South Carolina.

Throughout 1862, the *Pawnee* operated along the coast of South Carolina, Georgia, and Florida as Du Pont pushed the limits of his Port Royal base. She took part in the occupation of Fernandina, Florida on March 3, 1862 and supported operations on the Stono River, South Carolina on May 28–30. In November she sailed to Philadelphia for repairs.

The *Pawnee* returned to Port Royal on February 10, 1863 with the ironclad *Pataspsco* in tow. For the duration of the war she served with the South Atlantic Squadron. Of significance was the role she played in helping capture the Confederate steamers *General Sumter* and *Hattie Brock* with their cargoes of cotton, turpentine, rosin, and railroad iron. She also participated in offensive operations up the Togoda Creek at North Edisto, South Carolina and assisted in the occupation of Georgetown, South Carolina, both in February 1865.

She was decommissioned on July 26, 1865 but was later recommissioned for further service to her nation.

SPECIFICATIONS

DISPLACEMENT: 1,533 tons (1,391 tonnes)

DIMENSIONS: 221 ft 6 in x 47 ft x 10ft (67.51 m x 14 m x 3.0 m)

ARMAMENT: Eight 9 in (230 mm) guns; two 12 pounder guns

MACHINERY: Two horizontal direct-acting engines

SPEED: 10 knots maximum; 5 knots average

CREW: 181

USS *Pawnee*

ENGINES
SHE HAD THE UNUSUAL CONFIGURATION
OF TWIN 9 FT (2.74 M) DIAMETER SCREW
ENGINES.

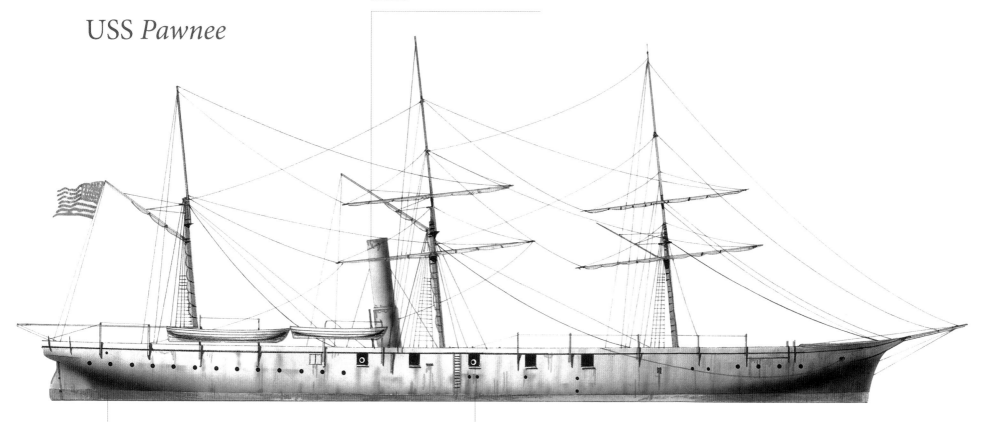

HULL
HER HULL HAD AN UNUSUAL CONCAVE
BASE DESIGNED TO SUPPORT THE HEAVY
ARMAMENT AND ENGINES.

DRAFT
SHE WAS ABLE TO CARRY A HEAVY
ARMAMENT ON A SHALLOW DRAFT OF
10 FT (3 M).

CSS *Planter* (1860)

THE *PLANTER* WAS BUILT IN 1860 IN CHARLESTON, SOUTH CAROLINA. WHILE THE FEDERAL FLEET BLOCKADED THE HARBOR, SHE SERVED AS AN ARMED DISPATCH BOAT AND TRANSPORT ATTACHED TO THE ENGINEER DEPARTMENT AT CHARLESTON. C.J. RELYEA WAS HER CAPTAIN, AND ROBERT SMALLS, A 23-YEAR-OLD SLAVE, WAS IMPRESSED INTO DUTIES AS HER PILOT. ON MAY 13, WHILE RELYEA WAS ON SHORE AWAY FROM THE SHIP, THE ENTERPRISING SMALLS ESCAPED WITH THE *PLANTER*.

Flying the Confederate flag, he steamed past the series of Confederate forts, nonchalantly blowing the *Planter*'s steam whistle in the usual manner of salute. Once he was out of range of the Confederate guns, Smalls replaced the Confederate flag with a white one, and turned the *Planter* over to the Federal blockade ship *Onward*.

In addition to the *Planter*, Smalls brought with him valuable news that the Confederates had abandoned their positions guarding the seaward approaches to James Island. This development left Charleston vulnerable to an attack from the rear across the island. Admiral Samuel Du Pont immediately saw the opportunity for a coup de main joint operation to seize Charleston, and on June 2 he landed two divisions, backed by considerable naval support, on James Island. The operation was grossly mismanaged and resulted in the Federal defeat near the town of Secessionville on June 16 and a subsequent withdrawal from James Island. Du Pont was disgusted by what he considered a missed opportunity, complaining, "Oh those soldiers. I put them nearly on *top* of the house in Charleston, but I did not push them into the windows and they came back."

Prize Winner

In spite of this failure, Smalls' bold action attracted national attention, and he was accorded status as a hero. He received $1,500 in prize money for delivering the *Planter* to Federal authorities. The ship, along with Smalls, entered into Federal service. After participating in a minor expedition to test Confederate defenses up the North Edisto River in June, Smalls was transferred to Du Pont's flagship *Wabash* to serve as pilot. He was often called away from military service, however, to serve as a spokesman on behalf of the cause of black advancement. After the war, he enjoyed an active and lengthy political career from his base of power in Beaufort.

The *Planter* was commanded in sequence by Acting Master Philemon Dickenson and Acting Master Lloyd Phoenix. Designed to burn wood— a scarce fuel source in the blockading fleet—the *Planter* was of limited utility to Du Pont, and he transferred her to the Army for service near Fort Pulaski, Georgia.

SPECIFICATIONS

DISPLACEMENT: 313 tons (284 tonnes)

DIMENSIONS: 147 ft x 30 ft x 3 ft 9 in (45 m x 9.1 m x 1.14 m)

ARMAMENT: One long 32 pounder gun; one short 24 pounder howitzer

MACHINERY: Two non-condensing engines with a 6 ft (1.8 m) stroke

SPEED: Unknown

CREW: Unknown

CSS *Planter*

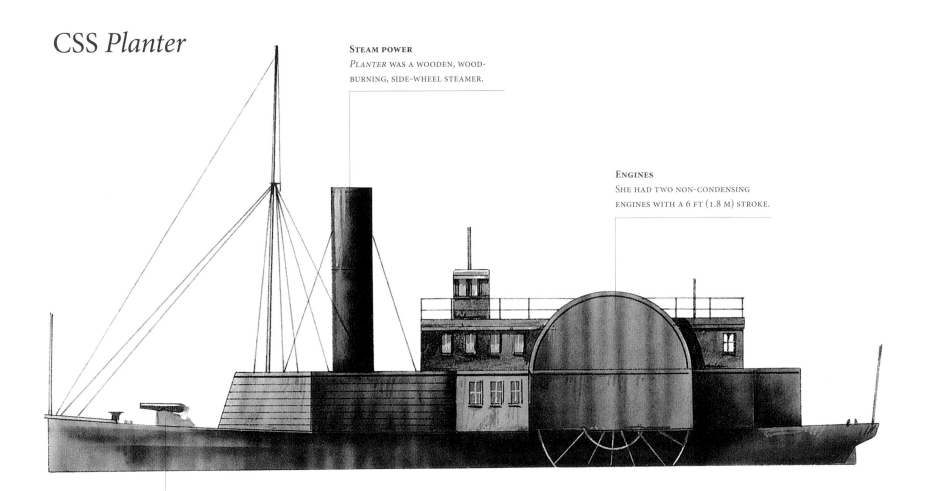

STEAM POWER
PLANTER WAS A WOODEN, WOOD-
BURNING, SIDE-WHEEL STEAMER.

ENGINES
SHE HAD TWO NON-CONDENSING
ENGINES WITH A 6 FT (1.8 M) STROKE.

ARMAMENT
SHE HAD ONE LONG 32 POUNDER AND
ONE 24 POUNDER HOWITZER.

USS *Commodore Perry* (1861)

THE *COMMODORE PERRY* WAS BUILT IN 1859 IN WILLIAMSBURG, NEW YORK AND PURCHASED BY THE NAVY ON OCTOBER 2, 1861. SHE WAS COMMISSIONED LATER IN THE MONTH WITH ACTING MASTER F.J. THOMAS IN COMMAND.

She joined the North Atlantic Blockading Squadron in time to take part in the February 7–8 attack on Roanoke Island, North Carolina. She then helped capture Elizabeth City on February 10, ramming and sinking the *Sea Bird*. The next day she captured the schooner *Lynnhaven*. In March, the *Commodore Perry* helped seize *New Bern* and *Washington*.

A converted ferry boat, the *Commodore Perry* was ideal for steaming through shallow waterways. One such mission occurred on October 3, 1862 when she took part in an Army–Navy expedition against Franklin, Virginia. The *Commodore Perry* led two other gunboats up the Blackwater River, whose narrow, high banks provided excellent positions for Confederate sharpshooters. Near Franklin, where the naval contingent was supposed to rendezvous with the Army troops, the *Commodore Perry* lost control at a narrow, sharp bend and ran aground. Quick action by Lieutenant William Cushing, later famous for destroying the *Albemarle*, saved the day.

Medal of Honor Award

There were other heroes besides Cushing that day. Among those onboard the *Commodore Perry*, Seaman John Williams was awarded the Medal of Honor. His citation read in part, "With enemy fire raking the deck of his ship and blockades thwarting her progress, Seaman Williams remained at his post and performed his duties with skill and courage as the *Commodore Perry* fought a gallant battle to silence many rebel batteries as she steamed down the Blackwater River."

On December 10, the *Commodore Perry* participated in the attack on Plymouth, North Carolina and on January 30, 1863 was part of a joint expedition against Hertford. She continued to patrol the area of the Pamlico and Albemarle Sounds until she went to Norfolk and Baltimore for repairs late in 1863. She was back on duty in March 1864, patrolling the inland and coastal waters of Virginia for the rest of the war. She was decommissioned in New York on June 26, 1865 and sold on July 12.

SPECIFICATIONS

DISPLACEMENT: 512 tons (464 tonnes)

DIMENSIONS: 143 ft x 33 ft x 10 ft (44 m x 10 m x 3 m)

ARMAMENT: Two 9 in (230 mm) guns; two 32 pounder smoothbore guns; one 12 pounder howitzer

MACHINERY: Side-wheel-propelled steam engine

SPEED: 7 knots

CREW: 125

USS *Commodore Perry*

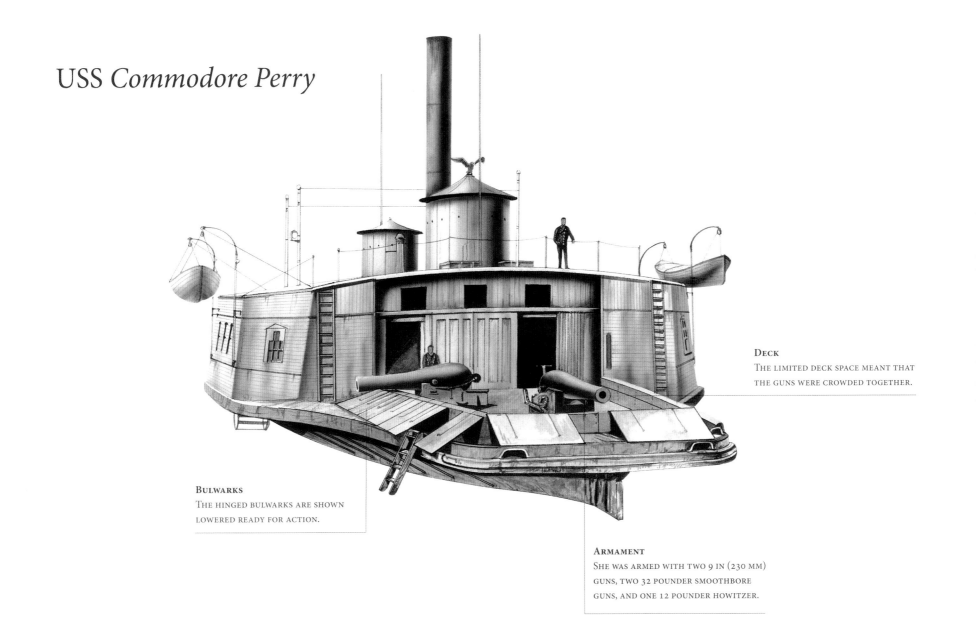

DECK
THE LIMITED DECK SPACE MEANT THAT
THE GUNS WERE CROWDED TOGETHER.

BULWARKS
THE HINGED BULWARKS ARE SHOWN
LOWERED READY FOR ACTION.

ARMAMENT
SHE WAS ARMED WITH TWO 9 IN (230 MM)
GUNS, TWO 32 POUNDER SMOOTHBORE
GUNS, AND ONE 12 POUNDER HOWITZER.

USS *Hetzel* (1861)

THE *HETZEL* WAS A SIDE-WHEEL STEAMER BUILT IN 1861 IN BALTIMORE, MARYLAND FOR THE UNITED STATES COAST SURVEY. SHE WAS TRANSFERRED TO THE NAVY DEPARTMENT ON AUGUST 21. SHE WAS ASSIGNED TO THE NORTH ATLANTIC BLOCKADING SQUADRON, AND ARRIVED AT NEWPORT NEWS, VIRGINIA ON NOVEMBER 18 WITH LIEUTENANT H.K. DAVENPORT AS HER COMMANDING OFFICER.

She soon saw action when on December 2 she and other Federal gunboats damaged the *Patrick Henry* in a two-hour engagement. In February 1862 she participated in Brigadier General Ambrose Burnside's capture of Roanoke Island, North Carolina and then moved up the Pasquotank River, where she and other ships engaged Confederate batteries and destroyed or captured five Confederate gunboats at Elizabeth City.

With Roanoke Island securely in Federal hands, the Burnside Expedition had the opportunity to greatly expand the logistical impact of the coastal war. Heretofore, the Federal attacks had primarily affected Confederate seagoing operations. By moving up the Neuse River from Pamlico Sound, Burnside could now seize New Bern, which was not only North Carolina's second largest port, but also the site of an important railroad.

The *Hetzel* first helped raise the steamer *Isaac N. Seymour*, which had struck an abandoned anchor and sank in the Neuse River, and then supported the successful attack at New Bern on March 13 and 14. Following this victory, the *Hetzel* spent much of the rest of the war on blockading duty in the North Carolina sounds. Throughout the course of the war, she shared in the capture of five steamers, six schooners and one sloop, and she served as the command ship for the area.

North Carolina Expedition

In addition to enforcing the blockade, the *Hetzel* went on an expedition to Hamilton and Williamston, North Carolina from November 2–9, 1862 in an unsuccessful hunt for ironclads rumored to be under construction in the area. On March 13–14, 1863, she helped defend Fort Anderson, opposite New Bern, from a Confederate attack.

The *Hetzel* sailed to Hampton Roads in November 1864 for much-needed repairs, returning to her North Carolina blockading station on May 29, 1865. She was relieved of her post in October and was returned to the Coast Survey.

SPECIFICATIONS

DISPLACEMENT: 200 tons (181 tonnes)

DIMENSIONS: 150 ft x 22 ft x 7.5 m (46 m x 6.7 m x 2.3 m)

ARMAMENT: One 9 in (228 mm) gun; one 80 pounder gun

MACHINERY: Side-wheel propelled steam engine

SPEED: Unknown

CREW: Unknown

USS *Hetzel*

ARMAMENT
HETZEL HAD ONE 9 IN (228 MM) GUN
AND ONE 80 POUNDER GUN.

LENGTH
HETZEL WAS 150 FT (46 M) LONG.

DISPLACEMENT
HETZEL WAS A SIDE-WHEEL STEAMER WITH
A DISPLACEMENT OF 200 TONS (181 TONNES).

USS *Jacob Bell* (1861)

THE *JACOB BELL* WAS ORIGINALLY A SIDE-WHEEL STEAMER BUILT IN NEW YORK CITY IN 1842. THE U.S. GOVERNMENT PURCHASED HER ON AUGUST 22, 1861, AND SHE WAS COMMISSIONED THE SAME DAY WITH LIEUTENANT EDWARD MCCREA IN COMMAND. SHE IMMEDIATELY SAILED FOR THE POTOMAC, WHERE SHE JOINED THE STEAMER *ICE BOAT* IN SHELLING A CONFEDERATE BATTERY AT THE MOUTH OF POTOMAC CREEK.

This proved to be routine duty for the *Jacob Bell*: reconnoitering along the shore of the Potomac and in its tributaries for Confederate fortifications and shelling any batteries found. She also helped enforce the blockade of the Virginia coast.

When Major General George McClellan launched his Peninsula Campaign in March 1862, he encountered more resistance than anticipated and sought to gather updated information about the enemy and terrain. McCrea took his *Jacob Bell* along with the *Satellite, Island Belle, Resolute, Reliance,* and *Piedmontese* on a reconnaissance up the Rappahannock River. He landed at Tappahannock, about 50 miles (80 km) from Richmond and took temporary possession of the town. There he gathered information about the Confederate troop presence at Fredericksburg and the defenses at Fort Lowry. Because

of unfamiliarity with the river, McCrea did not travel further. On his return trip, however, he reported capturing two schooners.

On May 19, the *Jacob Bell* was ordered to report to the North Atlantic Blockading Squadron at Hampton Roads in support of the Peninsula Campaign. On May 31, she joined the *Mahaska* and the *Aroostook* in ascending the James to a point 3 miles (5 km) below Drewry's Bluff on a reconnaissance. The three ships then returned to their anchorage off Turkey Island.

Shore Action

The *Jacob Bell*'s most serious action came while delivering dispatches to the *Monitor* on June 20 when she came under fire by two field batteries and, by McCrea's estimate, about 500 sharpshooters at Watkin's Bluff. The narrow channel left the *Jacob Bell* dangerously exposed and

she suffered 10 hits from the batteries and numerous hits from bullets. On September 2, she left the Peninsula to return to the Potomac Flotilla.

For the remainder of the war, the *Jacob Bell* operated on the Potomac and the Rappahannock. She captured the *C.F. Ward* with a contraband cargo on October 17 and destroyed two schooners on November 4 while on a reconnaissance mission up Nomini Creek. On August 23, 1863, she intercepted the schooner *Golden Leaf* trying to slip into Hosier's Creek with a cargo of sugar. She took two more ships in 1864.

The *Jacob Bell* was decommissioned at Washington Navy Yard on May 13, 1865, and was lost at sea on November 6 while being towed by the Banshee towards New York.

SPECIFICATIONS

DISPLACEMENT: 229 tons (208 tonnes)

DIMENSIONS: 141 ft 3 in x 21 ft x 8 ft 1in (43.05 m x 6.4 m x 2.46 m)

ARMAMENT: One 8 in (203 mm) Dahlgren smoothbore gun; one 32 pounder gun

MACHINERY: Side-wheel propelled steam engine

SPEED: Unknown

CREW: 49

USS *Jacob Bell*

ARMAMENT
SHE HAD ONE 8 IN (203 MM)
DAHLGREN SMOOTHBORE
AND ONE 32 POUNDER GUN.

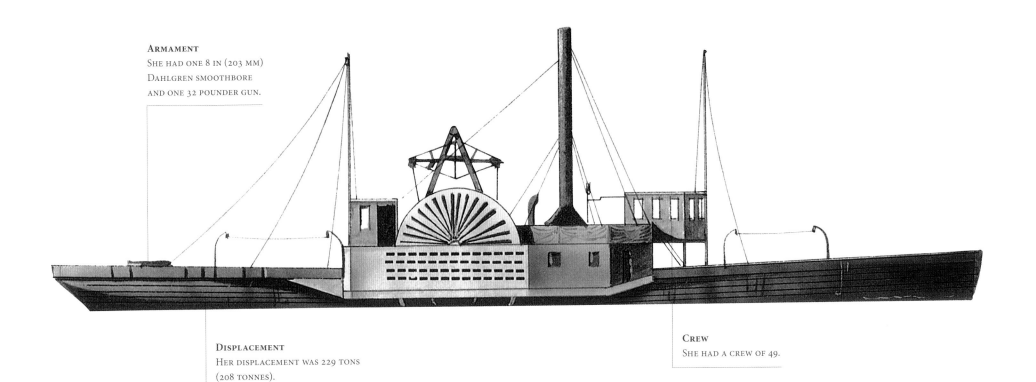

DISPLACEMENT
HER DISPLACEMENT WAS 229 TONS
(208 TONNES).

CREW
SHE HAD A CREW OF 49.

USS *Lexington* (1861)

THE *LEXINGTON* WAS A SIDE-WHEEL STEAMER BUILT IN PITTSBURGH, PENNSYLVANIA IN 1861. WITH THE *CONESTOGA* AND *TYLER*, SHE WAS THE FIRST OF THE UNION'S WESTERN GUNBOATS. SHE WAS PURCHASED IN JUNE 1861 AND RAPIDLY CONVERTED INTO A GUNBOAT IN CINCINNATI, OHIO UNDER THE DIRECTION OF COMMANDER JOHN RODGERS AND NAVAL CONSTRUCTOR SAMUEL POOK.

The three vessels were known as "timberclads," with their only protection being the addition of 5 inch (127 mm) thick oak planks. The *Lexington* displaced 362 tons (328 tonnes) and mounted two 32 pounder and four 8 inch (203 mm) shell guns. She joined the Western Gunboat Flotilla at Cairo, Illinois on August 12, 1861.

The *Lexington* quickly saw action, helping thwart the Confederate effort to coax Kentucky and Missouri out of the Union. She saw action in Columbus, Kentucky in August and September and in Belmont, Missouri in November, among other places. In February 1862, she helped capture Fort Henry but did not participate in the next attack on Fort Donelson, because an accident forced her to return to Cairo for repairs.

Back in action, the *Lexington* joined the *Tyler* in protecting Army transports and supporting troop movements along the Tennessee River. On April 7, they were critical in helping Grant survive the disastrous first day of the Battle of Shiloh. When the Confederate surprise attack sent Grant's men in an inglorious retreat to the banks of the Tennessee, fire from the gunboats quickened their nerve and helped persuade Confederate General Pierre Gustav Toutant Beauregard to call a halt to the attack.

Shore Action

Transferred to the Navy with the rest of the Western Gunboat Flotilla on October 1, the *Lexington* supported Major General William Sherman's unsuccessful assault on Chickasaw Bluffs outside Vicksburg, Mississippi on December 27 and Major General John McClernand's inconsequential attack on Fort Hindman, Arkansas on January 10, 1863. Ordered down the Mississippi on June 2 to support final operations against Vicksburg, the *Lexington* joined the *Choctaw* to hold off a Confederate attack at Milliken's Bend, Louisiana on June 7.

The *Lexington* participated in the Red River Campaign from March to May. On March 15, she helped chase Confederate steamers fleeing towards safety above the Alexandria rapids. Six of the steamers narrowly escaped, but the Confederates were forced to burn to prevent capture the *Countess*, which grounded in flight and a barge that was left behind. The campaign ended rather ingloriously with the *Lexington* joining several other vessels in narrowly escaping the falling river above the Alexandria rapids thanks to Colonel Joseph Bailey's ingenious dam. She spent the rest of the war on patrol and convoy duty and was decommissioned in Mound City, Illinois on July 2, 1865 and sold on August 17.

SPECIFICATIONS

DISPLACEMENT: 362 tons (328 tonnes)

DIMENSIONS: 177 ft 7 in x 36 ft 10 in x 6 ft (54.13 m x 11.23 m x 1.8 m)

ARMAMENT: Four 8 in (203 mm) Dahlgren smoothbore guns; two 32 pounder guns

MACHINERY: Steam engine

SPEED: 7 knots

CREW: Unknown

USS *Lexington*

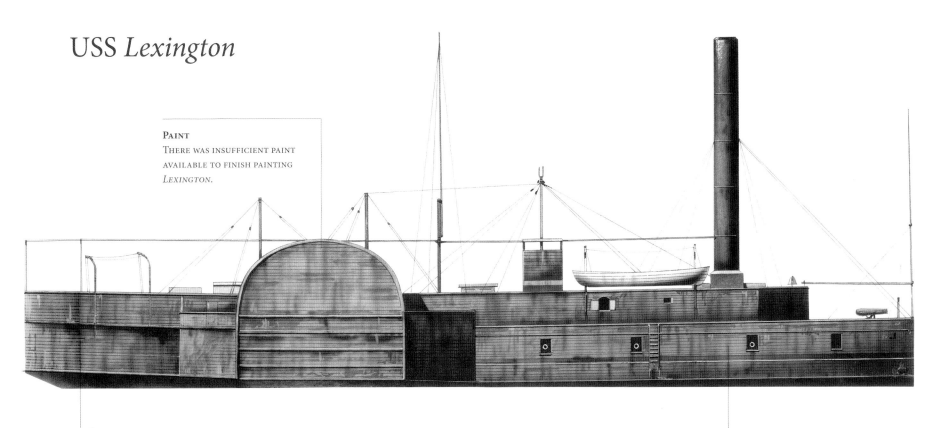

PAINT
THERE WAS INSUFFICIENT PAINT
AVAILABLE TO FINISH PAINTING
LEXINGTON.

BULWARK
A HIGH, 5 IN (127 MM) OAK BULWARK
PROTECTED THE CREW FROM RIFLE FIRE.

BOILERS
IN BEING CONVERTED FROM A FREIGHT
AND PASSENGER STEAMER, THE BOILERS
AND STEAMPIPES WERE LOWERED INTO
THE HOLD.

CSS *McRae* (1861)

THE *McRae* WAS THE FORMER BARK-RIGGED MEXICAN PIRATE SHIP *MARQUES DE LA HABANA*, WHICH HAD BEEN CAPTURED BY USS *SARATOGA* IN MARCH 1860. SHE WAS PURCHASED BY THE CONFEDERATE STATES IN NEW ORLEANS ON MARCH 17, 1861 AND CONVERTED TO A COMMERCE RAIDER WITH ONE 9 INCH (228 MM) PIVOT GUN AND SIX 32 POUNDERS IN BROADSIDE.

Renamed the *McRae*, she was placed under command of Lieutenant Thomas Huger. The *McRae*'s chronic engine problems prevented Huger from ever taking her to sea, and instead she became part of Captain George Rollins' defenses of the lower Mississippi River. Desperate for resources, on October 11, Rollins dispatched the *McRae* with Lieutenant Alexander Warley and a boarding party to seize the privately owned ironclad *Manassas* and impress her into service with the Confederate Navy. The next day, the *McRae* joined other ships in attacking the unsuspecting Federal fleet at the Head of the Passes and gaining a tactical victory.

New Orleans Attack

When Admiral David Farragut launched his attack on New Orleans on April 24, 1862, the *McRae* was initially positioned on the east bank, but Huger quickly moved her midstream and began engaging the Federal ships that had streamed past the Confederate forts. She became one of only three Confederate vessels actively participating in the fight. The smoke was so thick that the *McRae* narrowly escaped being run down twice by Federal ships as they emerged from the haze. In the confusion, many Federal ships passed the *McRae* without firing a shot, thinking she was one of their own.

Her exchange with the *Iroquois* was especially fierce, and it was probably a shell from the *Iroquois* that exploded in the *McRae*'s sail room that set the ship on fire. Huger desperately nosed the *McRae* to the bank to extinguish the flames. As he backed off the bank, Huger was struck by a fragment and mortally wounded. Lieutenant Charles Read assumed command and began pursuing the Federal fleet upriver, only to find himself alone among 11 enemy ships.

He reversed course and headed downriver, where he saw the *Defiance* flying a white flag. He dispatched Lieutenant Thomas Arnold to order the vessel, which did not appear damaged, to return to the fight. The *McRae* then continued on to Fort St. Philip.

Severely damaged, the *McRae* came upriver to New Orleans under a flag of truce on the evening of April 27 and landed Confederate wounded from the forts below. This last mission completed, she was abandoned, and Federal forces found her the next morning sunk alongside the city wharf.

SPECIFICATIONS

DISPLACEMENT: 830 tons (753 tonnes)

DIMENSIONS: Unknown

ARMAMENT: One 9 in smoothbore gun; six 32 pounder smoothbores; one 6 pounder rifle

MACHINERY: Single-screw, single-expansion steam engine; three-masted sail

SPEED: Unknown

CREW: Unknown

CSS *McRae*

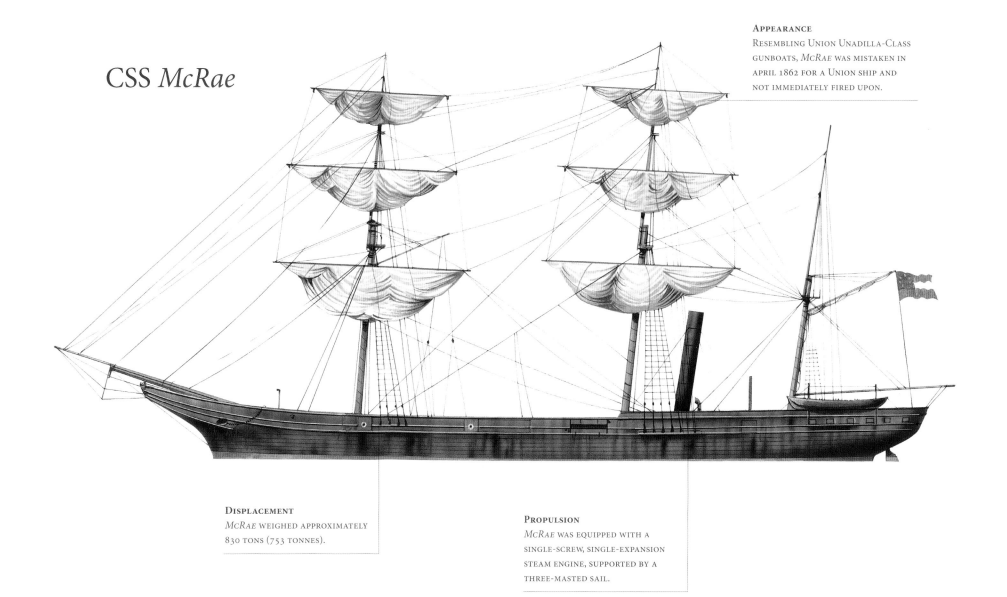

APPEARANCE
RESEMBLING UNION UNADILLA-CLASS
GUNBOATS, *McRae* WAS MISTAKEN IN
APRIL 1862 FOR A UNION SHIP AND
NOT IMMEDIATELY FIRED UPON.

DISPLACEMENT
McRae WEIGHED APPROXIMATELY
830 TONS (753 TONNES).

PROPULSION
McRae WAS EQUIPPED WITH A
SINGLE-SCREW, SINGLE-EXPANSION
STEAM ENGINE, SUPPORTED BY A
THREE-MASTED SAIL.

USS *Norwich* (1861)

THE *NORWICH* WAS A WOODEN SCREW STEAMER BUILT IN NORWICH, CONNECTICUT IN 1861 AND PURCHASED BY THE NAVY IN NEW YORK CITY ON SEPTEMBER 26. SHE WAS COMMISSIONED ON DECEMBER 28 WITH LIEUTENANT JAMES DUNCAN IN COMMAND. ON JANUARY 2, 1862, SHE DEPARTED FOR PORT ROYAL, SOUTH CAROLINA FOR DUTY WITH THE SOUTH ATLANTIC BLOCKADING SQUADRON.

The *Norwich* helped blockade Savannah, Georgia for two months, while Admiral Samuel Du Pont decided how to exploit his capture of Port Royal. Du Pont first captured Fernandina, Florida and this easy victory convinced him to advance on Jacksonville, about 30 miles (50 km) from the bar up the narrow and twisting St. John's River. As part of this operation, on March 10, 1863, the *Norwich* and the *Uncas* escorted troop transports up the St. John's and shelled Confederate positions defending Jacksonville, clearing the way for Army landings.

Shortly thereafter, cooperation between Du Pont and his Army counterpart Major General Thomas Sherman began to unravel, and the Federals withdrew from Jacksonville on April 9, and Du Pont's vessels moved back to the mouth of the St. John's. Jacksonville then became the site of much guerrilla fighting and brown water naval operations, such as on August 19 when a raid from the *Norwich* and the *Hale* destroyed a Confederate signal station near the town.

Convoy Duties

Jacksonville changed hands numerous times until February 7, 1864 when Federal forces occupied it for a fourth and final time. Major General Quincy Gillmore requested Rear Admiral John Dahlgren, who had replaced Du Pont, provide naval support for an attack into Florida on the west bank of St. John's, and Dahlgren dispatched, among other vessels, the *Ottawa* and the *Norwich* to convoy the Army troops to Jacksonville. On February 7, the *Norwich* trapped the blockade runner *St. Mary's* in Me Girt's Creek above Jacksonville where the *St. Mary's* was scuttled and her cargo of cotton destroyed to prevent capture.

Once Jacksonville was secured, the *Norwich* returned to her blockade duty along the coast and in the rivers of Florida and Georgia for the duration of the war. She was decommissioned in Philadelphia on June 30, 1865 and sold at public auction on August 10.

SPECIFICATIONS

DISPLACEMENT: 450 tons (408 tonnes)

DIMENSIONS: 132 ft 5 in x 24 ft 6 in x 10 ft (40.36 m x 7.47 m x 3.0 m)

ARMAMENT: One 30 pounder Parrott rifle; four 8 in (203 mm) guns

MACHINERY: Steam engine

SPEED: 9.5 knots

CREW: Not known

USS *Norwich*

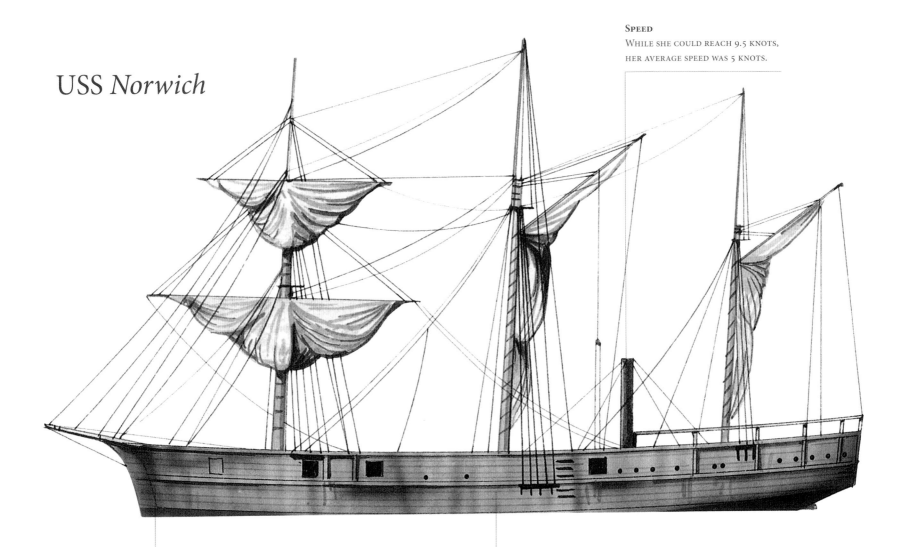

CSS *Patrick Henry* (1861)

THE CSS *PATRICK HENRY* WAS THE FORMER SIDE-WHEEL PASSENGER AND FREIGHT STEAMER *YORKTOWN*, WHICH RAN BETWEEN RICHMOND, VIRGINIA AND NEW YORK BEFORE THE CIVIL WAR. SHE WAS BUILT BY WILLIAM WEBB IN NEW YORK IN 1859. THE *YORKTOWN* WAS IN THE JAMES RIVER WHEN VIRGINIA SECEDED FROM THE UNION ON APRIL 17, 1861.

She was seized by the state and subsequently turned over to the Confederate Navy where Commander John Tucker, commander of the newly organized James River Squadron, directed she be converted into a lightly protected ship-of-war. She was assigned to a position near Mulberry Island in the James to protect the right flank of the Confederate Peninsula Army.

During the March 8, 1862 Battle of Hampton Roads, the *Patrick Henry* joined the *Virginia, Beaufort,* and *Raleigh* in shelling the beleaguered *Congress*. After an hour of pounding, the *Congress* surrendered but not before the *Patrick Henry* herself had come under fire from other Federal ships and shore batteries. One shot through her steam chest killed four of her crew. She was towed out of action long enough to make repairs, and then she resumed her former position. When the *Monitor* arrived to challenge

the *Virginia* the next day, the *Patrick Henry* kept her distance, engaging the *Monitor* only at long range. When the Confederates evacuated Norfolk on May 10, the *Patrick Henry* retired up the James River with the entire James River Squadron to Drewry's Bluff, where a Federal attack was repulsed on May 15.

Academy Role

The *Patrick Henry*'s most notable service to the Confederacy was with the fledgling Confederate States Naval Academy, established in 1863 on the James River at Drewry's Bluff. To support this activity, the *Patrick Henry* was made into a school ship manned by 13 faculty and staff. Lieutenant William Parker was appointed superintendent. The first class had about 50 midshipmen, but was later increased to 60. Confederate law limited the number of acting midshipmen to 106, but a more practical size restriction

was the fact that the *Patrick Henry* could only accommodate about 30 of the midshipmen. The remainder was housed on other ships in active service, which gave the midshipmen valuable experience, but also disrupted the course of instruction.

As the enemy closed in on Richmond, Rear Admiral Raphael Semmes ordered the *Patrick Henry* and other vessels of the James River Squadron destroyed on April 3, 1865. Sixty midshipmen from the *Patrick Henry* performed one last service to the cause in helping guard a train carrying $528,000 in gold the Confederate Treasury Department desperately tried to evacuate from Richmond.

SPECIFICATIONS

DISPLACEMENT: 1,300 tons (1,179 tonnes)

DIMENSIONS: 250 ft x 34 ft x 13 ft (76 m x 10 m x 4.0 m)

ARMAMENT: One 10 in (254 mm) smoothbore; one 64 pounder gun; six 8 in (203 mm) guns; two 32 pounder rifles (1861)

MACHINERY: Side-wheel steamer

SPEED: Unknown

CREW: 150

CSS *Patrick Henry*

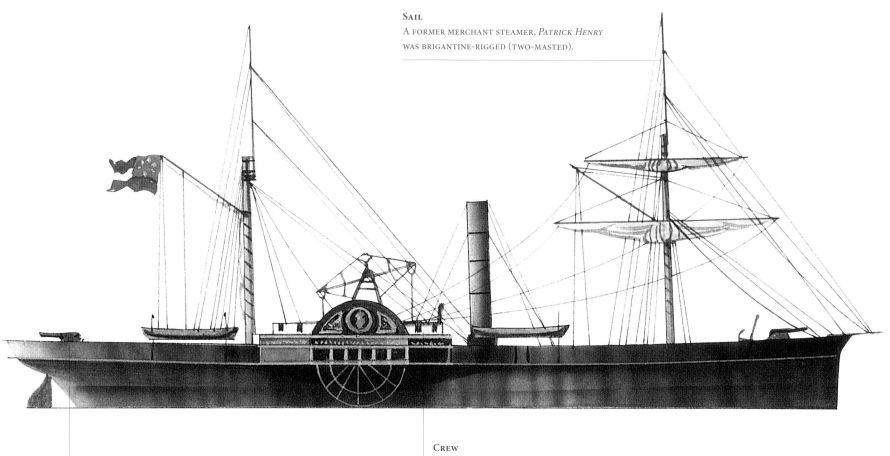

SAIL
A FORMER MERCHANT STEAMER, *PATRICK HENRY*
WAS BRIGANTINE-RIGGED (TWO-MASTED).

ARMAMENT
HER ARMAMENT CHANGED OVER TIME.
IN 1861, SHE HAD 10 GUNS; IN NOVEMBER
1863, SHE HAD FOUR.

CREW
PATRICK HENRY CARRIED A CREW
OF 150.

USS *Rhode Island* (1861)

THE SHIP THAT BECAME THE *RHODE ISLAND* WAS BUILT AS A WOODEN, SIDE-WHEEL STEAMER IN NEW YORK IN 1860 AS THE *JOHN P. KING*. THIS VESSEL WAS BURNED, REBUILT AND RENAMED THE *EAGLE* IN 1861. SHE WAS PURCHASED BY THE NAVY ON JUNE 27, RENAMED THE *RHODE ISLAND*, AND COMMISSIONED JULY 29 WITH COMMANDER STEPHEN TRENCHARD IN COMMAND.

Although mainly used as a supply ship, the *Rhode Island* also helped enforce the blockade. On her first cruise, she captured the schooner *Venus* attempting to run the blockade off Galveston, Texas with a cargo of lead, copper, tin and wood. More typically, between February 12 and March 18, 1862, she supplied 98 vessels. She supplied another 118 on a run between April 5 and May 20. While supporting the Gulf Blockading Squadron, she chased and forced ashore the British schooner *Richard O'Bryan* near San Luis Pass on July 4.

On December 29, the *Rhode Island* departed Hampton Roads with the *Monitor* in tow and the *Passaic* in company. Encountering a heavy storm off Cape Hatteras on December 30, the *Monitor's* pumps were unable to control flooding caused by leaks below the waterline. The crew was forced to abandon ship, but before they could completely transfer to the safety of the *Rhode Island*, the ironclad sank. Four officers and 12 sailors perished.

West Indies Patrol

On January 29, 1863, the *Rhode Island* was ordered to the West Indies to join in the search for the Confederate steamers *Oreto* and *Alabama*. While these ships evaded the Federals, the *Rhode Island* did succeed in forcing the blockade runner *Margaret and Jessie* ashore at Stirrup Cay on May 30. On August 16, she also captured the British blockade runner *Cronstadt* north of the Bahamas with a cargo of cotton, turpentine and tobacco.

The *Rhode Island* arrived at Boston Navy Yard on March 28, 1864 with defective boilers and in need of extensive overhaul. She was decommissioned on April 21 and transformed into an auxiliary cruiser mounting one 11 inch (280 mm) gun, eight 8 inch (203 mm) guns, one 30 pounder Parrott rifle and one 12 pounder rifle. She was recommissioned on October 3 and towed the monitor *Monadnock* from Boston to New York before joining the North Atlantic Blockading Squadron soon afterwards.

The *Rhode Island* captured the British blockade runner *Vixen* on December 1, and then participated in both attacks on Fort Fisher, North Carolina. She then towed the monitor *Saugus* to Norfolk, Virginia. She cruised to Mobile, Alabama before returning to Hampton Roads on May 22, 1865. She remained on duty after the war, helping to bring the Confederate armored ram *Stonewall* to the United States from Cuba on November 23. She was decommissioned in 1867.

SPECIFICATIONS

DISPLACEMENT: 1,517 tons (1376 tonnes)

DIMENSIONS: 236 ft 2 in x 36 ft 8 in x 15 ft (71.98 m x 11.18 m x 4.6 m)

ARMAMENT: One 11 in (280 mm) gun; eight 8 in (200 mm) guns; one 30 pounder Parrott rifle; one 12 pounder rifle (1864)

MACHINERY: Single beam engine with a 12 ft (3.6 m) stroke

SPEED: 16 knots max; 9 knots average

CREW: 257

USS *Rhode Island*

GUNS
FROM 1861 TO 1864, SHE WAS
EQUIPPED WITH FOUR 32
POUNDER GUNS.

DRAFT
HER DRAFT WAS 15 FT (4.6 M) WHEN
LOADED, AND 12 FT (3.7 M) WHEN LIGHT.

SPEED
SHE COULD REACH A MAXIMUM SPEED
OF 16 KNOTS.

USS *Santiago de Cuba* (1861)

THE *SANTIAGO DE CUBA* WAS A WOODEN, BRIGANTINE-RIGGED, SIDE-WHEEL STEAMER BUILT IN 1861 IN BROOKLYN, NEW YORK AND PURCHASED BY THE NAVY ON SEPTEMBER 6. SHE WAS COMMISSIONED ON NOVEMBER 5 WITH COMMANDER DANIEL RIDGELY IN COMMAND.

Ordered to Havana, Cuba ". . . to protect legitimate commerce and to suppress communications and traffic with or by the insurgents . . .", she arrived on November 17. She soon proved her worth, capturing the British blockade runner schooner *Victoria* some 90 miles (145 km) west of Point Isabel, Texas on December 3. After sending the prize to Galveston, the *Santiago de Cuba* next stopped the British schooner *Eugenia Smith* on December 7, but could not find evidence of contraband trade and released her.

The *Santiago de Cuba* was very active in the spring of 1862, taking the schooner *Mersey* off Charleston, South Carolina on April 26, the schooner *Maria* off Port Royal on April 30 and the schooner *Lucy C. Holmes* on May 27. Continuing into the summer, she seized the *Columbia* on August 3 and the *Lavinia* on August 27. Both these blockade runners were taken off Abaco in the Bahamas.

In September, the *Santiago de Cuba* was assigned to a newly organized "Flying Squadron," created to bring to bay the Confederate commerce raiders *Alabama* and *Florida*. Although these menaces eluded capture, the *Santiago de Cuba* had luck elsewhere. On June 21, 1863, she captured the British steamer *Victory* off Eleuthera Island after she had slipped through the blockade off Charleston with a cargo of cotton, tobacco and turpentine. Four days later, she took the steamer *Britannia* in the same area. On July 15, she seized the steamer *Lizzie* east of the Florida coast. That winter the *Santiago de Cuba* sailed north for repairs.

Recommissioned

She was recommissioned on June 6, 1864 and resumed her former duties chasing blockade runners. In September, she captured the *Advance* (often cited as the *A.D. Vance*) northeast of Wilmington,

North Carolina with a cargo of cotton headed for Europe. The *Advance* had been one of the Confederacy's most successful blockade runners with over 20 trips to her credit. On November, 2 the *Santiago de Cuba* captured the blockade runner *Lucy*. Future poet Sidney Lanier was among the sailors taken prisoner with the ship.

Setting aside her usual blockade duties, the *Santiago de Cuba* participated in both attacks on Fort Fisher, North Carolina. After the second successful attack, the *Santiago de Cuba* carried wounded men to Norfolk. She was decommissioned on June 17, 1865 at the Philadelphia Navy Yard and sold at public auction on September 21.

SPECIFICATIONS

DISPLACEMENT: 1,567 tons (1,422 tonnes)

DIMENSIONS: 229 ft x 38 ft x 6 ft 2 in (70 m x 11.6 m x 1.8 m)

ARMAMENT: Two 20 pounder Parrott rifles; eight 32 pounder guns

MACHINERY: Single beam engine with an 11 ft (3.3 m) stroke

CREW: 114

USS *Santiago de Cuba*

ARMAMENT

IN 1861, SHE HAD TWO 20 POUNDER PARROTT RIFLES AND EIGHT 32 POUNDER GUNS.

RIGGING

SHE WAS BRIGANTINE-RIGGED.

SIDE-WHEEL

SANTIAGO DE CUBA WAS A LARGE SIDE-WHEEL STEAMER WITH AN AVERAGE SPEED OF 8 KNOTS.

USS *Sciota* (1861)

ONE OF THE "90-DAY GUNBOATS" HURRIEDLY BUILT AT THE BEGINNING OF THE CIVIL WAR, THE *SCIOTA* WAS LAUNCHED ON OCTOBER 15, 1861 AND COMMISSIONED AT THE PHILADELPHIA NAVY YARD ON DECEMBER 15, 1861 WITH LIEUTENANT EDWARD DONALDSON IN COMMAND. SHE WAS ASSIGNED TO THE GULF BLOCKADING SQUADRON AND ARRIVED AT SHIP ISLAND, MISSISSIPPI ON JANUARY 8, 1862.

She quickly saw action, capturing the blockade runner *Margaret* with its load of cotton off Isle of Breton, Louisiana on February 6.

The *Sciota* joined Admiral David Farragut's West Gulf Blockading Squadron and contributed to the Federal victory at New Orleans on April 24. She then was part of the force Farragut led past the Vicksburg batteries up the Mississippi River on June 28. Unable to carry the defenses, Farragut returned his ships below Vicksburg and the *Sciota* operated on the lower Mississippi for most of the remainder of the year.

On January 3, 1863, Farragut ordered the *Sciota* and two other gunboats to Galveston, Texas in response to the Confederates' recapture of that port. The Federals found the Confederate defenses too strong during an attack on January 10, and the *Sciota* returned to blockade duty.

On July 14, the *Sciota* collided with the Union steamer *Anton* in the Mississippi

about 8 miles (13 km) above Quarantine and sank. She was raised late in August and taken to New Orleans to be refitted. In December, she was back on blockade duty off the Texas coast. On December 31, she and the *Granite City* landed soldiers on the gulf shore of Matagorda Peninsula. In the ensuing action, the *Sciota* shelled Confederate positions. The two ships supported a similar operation at Smith's Landing, Texas in January 1864.

Blockade Duties

Most of the *Sciota*'s remaining activity involved blockade duty. On April 4, she captured the schooner *Mary Sorly*, attempting to run the blockade at Galveston with a cargo of cotton. On September 13 she recovered 83 bales of cotton found floating at sea. On October 27 and 28, respectively, she captured the schooners *Pancha Larispa* and *Cora Smyser* attempting to run the blockade.

In November, the *Sciota* was ordered to Pensacola for repairs.

In January 1865, she steamed to Mobile Bay, where she struck a torpedo and sank on April 14. Her commanding officer, Acting Lieutenant James Magune, reported: "The explosion was terrible, breaking the beams of the spar deck, tearing open the waterways, ripping off starboard forechannels, and breaking fore-topmast." She was raised in early July, and her hulk was sold at public auction inNew York on October 25, 1865.

SPECIFICATIONS

DISPLACEMENT: 507 tons (460 tonnes)

DIMENSIONS: 158 ft x 28 ft x 9 ft 6 in (48 m x 8.5 m x 2.9 m)

ARMAMENT: One 11 in (279 mm) Dahlgren smoothbore; two 24 pounder smoothbores; two 20 pounder Parrott rifles

MACHINERY: Two horizontal back-acting engines driving a single screw

SPEED: 10–11 knots

CREW: 62–114

USS *Sciota*

ENGINE
SHE WAS EQUIPPED WITH TWO HORIZONTAL, BACK-ACTING ENGINES DRIVNG A SINGLE SCREW.

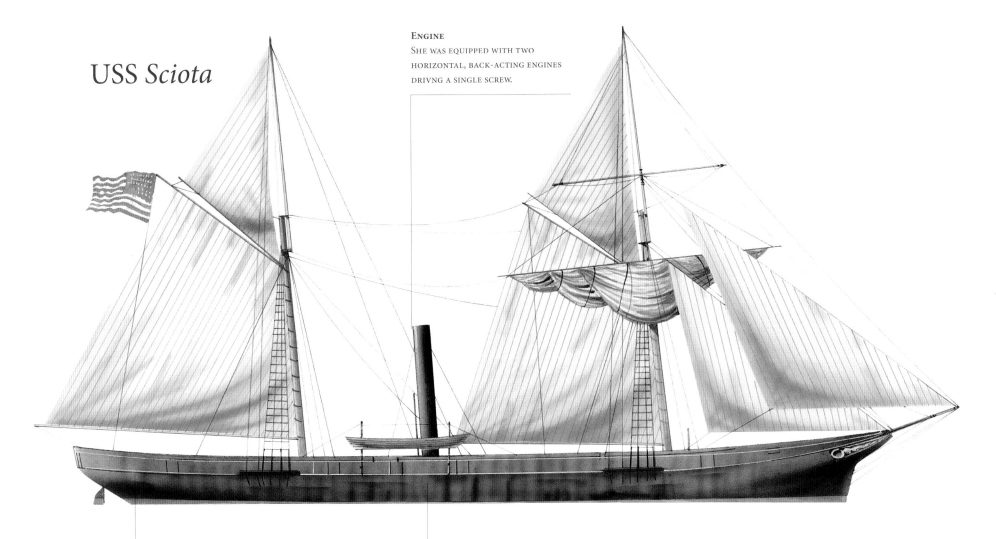

WOOD
HASTILY BUILT OF POORLY SEASONED WOOD, SHE WAS ALSO LIABLE TO ROLL BADLY.

SCHOONER
USS *SCIOTA* WAS A SCHOONER-RIGGED, WOODEN-HULLED GUNBOAT.

USS *Tyler* (1861)

THE CAREER OF THE USS *TYLER* PARALLELED THAT OF THE *LEXINGTON*. SHE WAS BUILT AS THE *A.O. TYLER* IN CINCINNATI, OHIO IN 1857 AS A SIDE-WHEEL STEAMER. SHE WAS PURCHASED IN JUNE 1861 AND, LIKE THE *LEXINGTON*, QUICKLY CONVERTED INTO A TIMBERCLAD GUNBOAT. THE *TYLER* DISPLACED 420 TONS (381 TONNES) AND MOUNTED ONE 32 POUNDER AND SIX 8 INCH (203 MM) SMOOTHBORES.

She joined the Western Gunboat Flotilla at Cairo, Illinois on August 12 and was commissioned in September.

Like the *Lexington*, the Tyler was active in the early operations that helped secure Kentucky and Missouri for the Union. With the *Lexington* she helped compel the surrender of Fort Henry in February 1862, but unlike the *Lexington*, the *Tyler* also was present for the twin victory at Fort Donelson. Between the two battles, she joined the *Conestoga* and the *Lexington* in a raiding expedition farther up the Tennessee River to Florence, Alabama between February 6 and 10. Along the way, the ships destroyed a railroad bridge and captured several vessels including the *Eastport*, which the Confederates were in the process of converting to an ironclad.

After Fort Donelson, the *Tyler* resumed operations on the Tennessee River in support of Major General Ulysses Grant's advance southwards along the river's banks through western Tennessee. With the *Lexington* she was instrumental in turning the tide of the Battle of Shiloh on April 7. Afterwards on April 19, the *Tyler* returned to Florence, Alabama, where she captured the Confederate transport *Albert Robb* and burned the *Dunbar*.

Yazoo River Patrol

On July 14, the *Tyler* joined the ram *Queen of the West* and the ironclad *Carondolet* in a reconnaissance up the Yazoo River above Vicksburg in search of the ironclad ram CSS *Arkansas*, which had eluded capture at Memphis and sought refuge far up the Yazoo. When the adversaries met on July 15, the *Carondolet* was disabled and the *Queen of the West* fled, leaving the *Tyler* to battle the powerful Confederate vessel alone. Outmatched, the *Tyler* wisely retreated with the *Arkansas* in pursuit. In a running fight all the way down the Yazoo, the *Tyler* finally reached the safety of the Federal fleet lying near the confluence of the Mississippi and Yazoo Rivers. The *Arkansas* blasted her way through the enemy and continued on to Vicksburg.

Like the *Lexington*, the *Tyler* saw action during the Vicksburg Campaign, the attack on Fort Hindman and on the White River, where her last major combat occurred near Camden, Arkansas on June 24, 1864. After the war she moved in June 1865 to Mound City, Illinois, where she remained until sold at auction in August.

SPECIFICATIONS

DISPLACEMENT: 420 tons (381 tonnes)

DIMENSIONS: 180 ft x 45 ft 4 in x 6 ft (55 m x 13.82 m x 1.8 m)

ARMAMENT: One 32 pounder gun; six 8 in (203 mm) guns

MACHINERY: Side-wheel steam engine

SPEED: 8 knots

CREW: 61

USS *Tyler*

GANGWAY
THE LACK OF A FORE AND AFT GANGWAY
MEANT THAT CREW HAD TO WALK OVER
THE EXPOSED BOILERS.

DISPLACEMENT
TYLER DISPLACED 420 TONS
(381 TONNES).

GUNS
TYLER MOUNTED ONE 32 POUNDER
AND SIX 8 IN (203 MM) SMOOTHBORES.

USS *General Bragg* (1862)

THE *GENERAL BRAGG* WAS BUILT IN NEW YORK CITY IN 1851 AS THE RIVER STEAMER *MEXICO*. SHE WAS OWNED BY THE SOUTHERN STEAMSHIP COMPANY, BUT WAS IMPRESSED INTO CONFEDERATE SERVICE IN NEW ORLEANS ON JANUARY 15, 1862. SHE WAS CONVERTED INTO A COTTON-CLAD RAM WITH A 4 INCH (102 MM) OAK SHEATH AND A 1 INCH (25 MM) IRON COVERING ON HER BOW, AND DOUBLE PINE BULKHEADS FILLED WITH COMPRESSED COTTON BALES.

On March 25, the *General Bragg's* conversion was completed, and she was sent to Fort Pillow, Tennessee to help defend the river approaches to Memphis. There on May 10 she participated in the Battle of Plum Point Bend under the command of Captain W.H.H. Leonard. Leading the attack, the *General Bragg* forced the *Cincinnati* into shallow water, pursuing her through intense fire from the Federal fleet. Although the *General Bragg* rammed the *Cincinnati*, she also was struck by the *Cincinnati's* broadside, and her tiller rope was cut. The *General Bragg* drifted downriver out of action, leaving *General Sterling Price* and *Sumter* to finish off the *Cincinnati*.

After Fort Pillow was evacuated on June 1, the *General Bragg* fell back with the other Confederate ships to Memphis to take coal on board. When the Federals attacked on June 6, the

General Bragg grounded on a sandbar and was captured.

The Federals assigned their new possession to the Western River Flotilla, with Lieutenant Joshua Bishop as her commander. She was fitted out of Cairo, Illinois and on August 16 began a period of patrolling the Mississippi River from Helena, Arkansas to the mouth of the Yazoo River. She remained in the vicinity of Vicksburg until December 13, 1863 when she reported for duty at the mouth of the Red River.

River Patrols

On June 15, 1864, the *General Bragg* joined other ships in driving the Confederates from their position near Tunica Bend, Louisiana, but she was disabled in the action. For the remainder of the war, the *General Bragg* patrolled the Mississippi from the mouth of the Red River to Natchez, Mississippi, occasionally

cruising as far south as Baton Rouge and New Orleans. She was decommissioned in Cairo on July 24, 1865 and sold on September 1.

SPECIFICATIONS

DISPLACEMENT: 1,043 tons (946 tonnes)

DIMENSIONS: 208 ft x 32 ft 8 in x 12 ft (63 m x 9.96 m x 3.7 m)

ARMAMENT: One 30 pounder gun; one 32 pounder gun; one 12 pounder gun

MACHINERY: Side-wheel propelled steam engine

SPEED: 10 knots

CREW: Unknown

USS *General Bragg*

BOWS
TO STRENGTHEN HER FOR BATTLE, A 4 IN (102 MM) OAK SHEATH WITH A 1 IN (25 MM) IRON COVERING WAS ADDED TO THE BOWS.

HOLD
HER HOLD WAS 15 FT (4.6 M) DEEP.

BULKHEADS
DURING CONVERSION, DOUBLE PINE BULKHEADS FILLED WITH COMPRESSED COTTON WERE ADDED.

USS *General Sterling Price* (1862)

THE *GENERAL STERLING PRICE*, WHICH SERVED BOTH THE CONFEDERACY AND THE UNION DURING THE CIVIL WAR, WAS BUILT AS THE *LAURENT MILLAUDON* IN CINCINNATI, OHIO IN 1856. THE CONFEDERACY ACQUIRED THE WOODEN, RIVER STEAMER FOR CAPTAIN JAMES MONTGOMERY'S RIVER DEFENSE FLEET.

On January 25, 1862, Montgomery began to convert her into a cotton-clad ram by placing a 4 inch (102 mm) oak sheath with a 1 inch (25 mm) iron covering on her bow and by installing double pine bulkheads filled with compressed cotton bales. On March 25, Captain J.H. Townsend sailed her from New Orleans to Memphis, Tennessee to have her ironwork completed. On April 10, she was sent to Fort Pillow, Tennessee to defend the river approaches to Memphis.

On May 10, 1862, the *General Sterling Price* and seven other vessels attacked the Federal Mississippi Flotilla at Plum Point Bend. After the Confederate ram *General Bragg* delivered a preliminary blow, the *General Sterling Price* struck the *Cincinnati* and decisively disabled her. The *General Sterling Price* also silenced the Federal *Mortar Boat No. 16*, which was being guarded by *Cincinnati*. However, the *General Sterling Price* was herself hit and heavily damaged in the action. She was soon repaired and helped hold off Federal vessels until Fort Pillow was successfully evacuated on June 1. She then retired to Memphis with the rest of the Confederate vessels to take coal.

Collision

After capturing Fort Pillow, the Federals pressed on to Memphis and attacked on June 6. Attempting to ram the *Monarch*, the *General Sterling Price* instead collided with the Confederate ram *General Beauregard*, which had also attacked the *Monarch*. While the two Confederate vessels were entangled, the Federals rammed the *General Sterling Price* until she sank.

The Federals raised the vessel, and she was sent to Cairo, Illinois on June 16 for repairs. Although she was renamed the *General Price*, she was still frequently referred to by her old name. Her repairs complete, on March 11, 1863 she departed Cairo for duty with the Mississippi Squadron in time to participate in the ill-fated Steele's Bayou Expedition. On April 17 she ran the gauntlet of the defenses at Vicksburg. The *General Price* took part in the capture of Alexandria, Louisiana and the bombardment of Fort De Russy in May before returning to support the siege of Vicksburg. After that city surrendered on July 4, the *General Price* went to Cairo for repairs.

She rejoined the squadron at Memphis on December 2, and took part in the Red River Campaign in May 1864. She spent the rest of the war patrolling the lower Mississippi River.

She was decommissioned in Mound City, Illinois on July 24, 1865 and sold on October 3.

SPECIFICATIONS

DISPLACEMENT: 633 tons (574 tonnes)

DIMENSIONS: 182 ft x 30 ft x 9.2 ft (55 m x 9 m x 3 m)

ARMAMENT: Not known

MACHINERY: Steam engine

SPEED: 12 knots

CREW: Not known

USS *General Sterling Price*

BULKHEADS
HER BULKHEADS WERE MADE OF DOUBLE
PINE AND FILLED WITH COMPRESSED
COTTON BALES.

RAM
HER BOW ARMOR INCLUDED A 4 IN
(102 MM) OAK SHEATH WITH A 1 IN
(25.4 MM) IRON COVERING.

CSS *Governor Moore* (1862)

THE CSS *GOVERNOR MOORE* WAS ORIGINALLY THE *CHARLES MORGAN*, BUILT FOR THE SOUTHERN S.S. COMPANY IN NEW YORK IN 1854. THIS SCHOONER-RIGGED, LOW-PRESSURE, WALKING BEAM-ENGINED, SEAGOING STEAMER WAS SEIZED AT NEW ORLEANS BY BRIGADIER GENERAL MANSFIELD LOVELL IN MID-JANUARY 1862 "FOR THE PUBLIC SERVICE."

She was renamed after Louisiana Governor Thomas Moore and made a gunboat whose armament included two rifled 32 pounders. Pine lumber and cotton bales protected her boilers. She was commanded by Captain Beverly Kennon.

Although Commander John Mitchell was placed in charge of the waterborne defenses of New Orleans on February 1, 1862, the River Defense Fleet remained outside his grasp and he showed little interest in assuming responsibility for state vessels like the *Governor Moore* and the *General Quitman*. Among the many problems complicating the Confederate defense of New Orleans was this failure to establish unity of effort.

In spite of the overall defeat, the *Governor Moore* fought valiantly when Admiral David Farragut attacked on April 24, 1862. This included a lively exchange of fire with the *Varuna*, which the *Governor Moore* rammed twice, enabling the *R.J. Breckinridge* of the River Defense Fleet to ultimately deliver a decisive third ramming that forced the *Varuna* to ground itself on the shore.

Scuttled

What happened next is explained differently in conflicting reports but, according to Kennon's account, as he headed in pursuit of the *Cayuga*, the *Governor Moore* ran into the bulk of the Federal fleet. Kennon tried to reverse course and engage the enemy, but his ship suffered damage to the engine and steerage that compelled him to lose control and, as a result, the *Governor Moore* grounded. Kennon then ordered the ship set on fire and blown up. He estimated that of his crew of 93, 64 were killed or wounded, 24 were captured and the rest either escaped or were unaccounted for.

Kennon was proud of his ship's performance, writing, "The pennant and remains of the ensign were never hauled down." He continued, "The flames that lit our decks stood faithful sentinels over their halyards until they, like the ship, were entirely consumed. I burned the bodies of the slain. Our colors were shot away three times. I hoisted them myself twice; finally every stripe was taken out of the [Louisiana state] flag, leaving a small constellation of four little stars only, which showed to our enemy how bravely we had defended them."

SPECIFICATIONS

DISPLACEMENT: 1,215 tons (1,102 tonnes)

DIMENSIONS: Unknown

ARMAMENT: Two 32 pounder rifled cannons

MACHINERY: Side-wheel, low pressure, walking-beam engine; schooner-rigged

SPEED: Unknown

CREW: 93

CSS *Governor Moore*

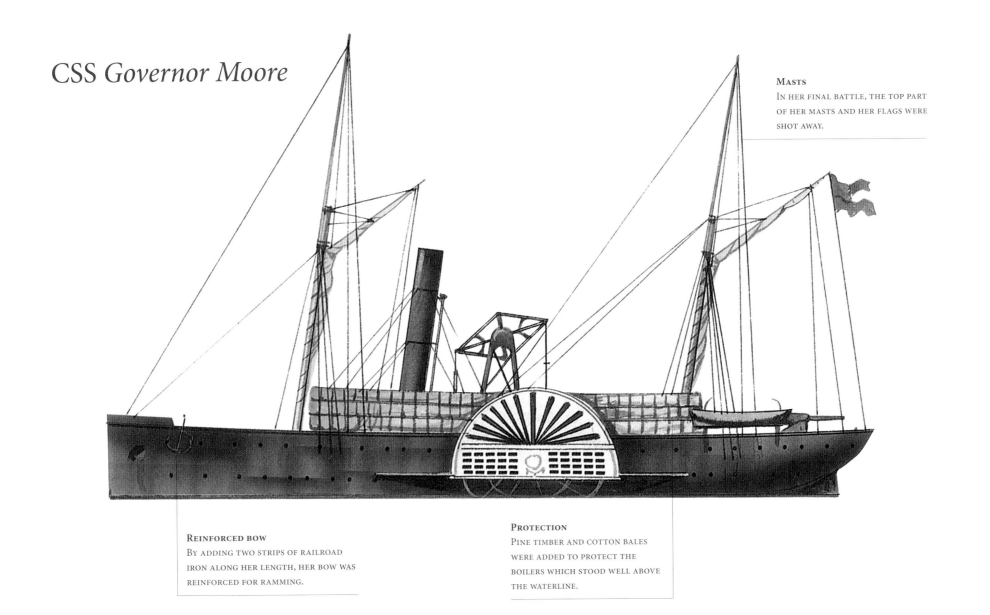

MASTS
IN HER FINAL BATTLE, THE TOP PART
OF HER MASTS AND HER FLAGS WERE
SHOT AWAY.

REINFORCED BOW
BY ADDING TWO STRIPS OF RAILROAD
IRON ALONG HER LENGTH, HER BOW WAS
REINFORCED FOR RAMMING.

PROTECTION
PINE TIMBER AND COTTON BALES
WERE ADDED TO PROTECT THE
BOILERS WHICH STOOD WELL ABOVE
THE WATERLINE.

USS *Housatonic* (1862)

THE *HOUSATONIC* WAS LAUNCHED ON NOVEMBER 20, 1861 FROM BOSTON AND COMMISSIONED THERE ON AUGUST 29, 1862 WITH COMMANDER WILLIAM ROGERS TAYLOR IN COMMAND. SHE DEPARTED BOSTON ON SEPTEMBER 11 AND ARRIVED AT CHARLESTON ON SEPTEMBER 19 TO JOIN THE SOUTH ATLANTIC BLOCKADING SQUADRON.

On January 29, 1863 her boats and crew helped refloat the Confederate blockade runner *Princess Royal*, which had been driven ashore as she attempted to enter Charleston with a valuable cargo that included two marine engines imported from England. Two days later the *Housatonic* helped repulse a sortie against the Federal fleet launched by the Confederate ironclad rams *Chicora* and *Palmetto State* in what may have been an effort to recover the *Princess Royal*.

More typical of the nature of the *Housatonic*'s duty was her capture of the *Neptune* as she attempted to run out of Charleston with a cargo of cotton and turpentine on April 19. The *Housatonic* likewise helped capture the steamer *Secesh* on May 15. This is not to say the *Housatonic* did not also conduct offensive operations such as her participation in the attack on Fort Wagner on July 10.

After that, she contributed to the nearly constant bombardment of Charleston as well as patrols, reconnaissance and transportation of raiding parties that kept up the relentless pressure on the Confederate stronghold.

Rammed and Sunk

In spite of this faithful service, however, what the *Housatonic* is most famous for is her demise. Just before 9 o'clock on the night of February 17, 1864, her officer of the deck, Acting Master J.N. Crosby, sighted an unidentified object approaching the ship from about 100 yards (90 m) away.

The *Housatonic* engaged the attacker with small arms and tried to escape, but within two minutes of being spotted, the Confederate submarine *H.L. Hunley* was able to ram her 130 pound (59 kg) spar torpedo into the *Housatonic*'s starboard side. As the ship sank, most of the crew escaped in two boats or, because the water was only 28 feet (8.5 m) deep, by climbing the rigging that remained above water as the ship settled to the bottom. Nonetheless, two officers and three men were lost. The blast, however, likely damaged the *Hunley* as well, and she sank while returning to shore, but not before she succeeded in making the *Housatonic* the first ship in naval history to be sunk by a submarine.

After the Civil War, several operations were conducted to lower the wreck of the *Housatonic* to reduce it as a navigational hazard. In 1999, a multi-agency archaeological fieldwork project recovered some hundred artifacts from the site.

SPECIFICATIONS

DISPLACEMENT: 1,934 tons (1,754 tonnes)

DIMENSIONS: 205 ft x 38 ft x 8 ft 7 in (62 m x 12 m x 2.62 m)

ARMAMENT: One 100 pounder Parrott rifle; three 30 pounder Parrott rifles; one 11 in (280 mm) Dahlgren smoothbore; two 32 pounders; two 24 pounder howitzers; one 12 pounder howitzer; one 12 pounder rifle

MACHINERY: Two horizontal direct-acting engines

SPEED: 10 knots

CREW: 214

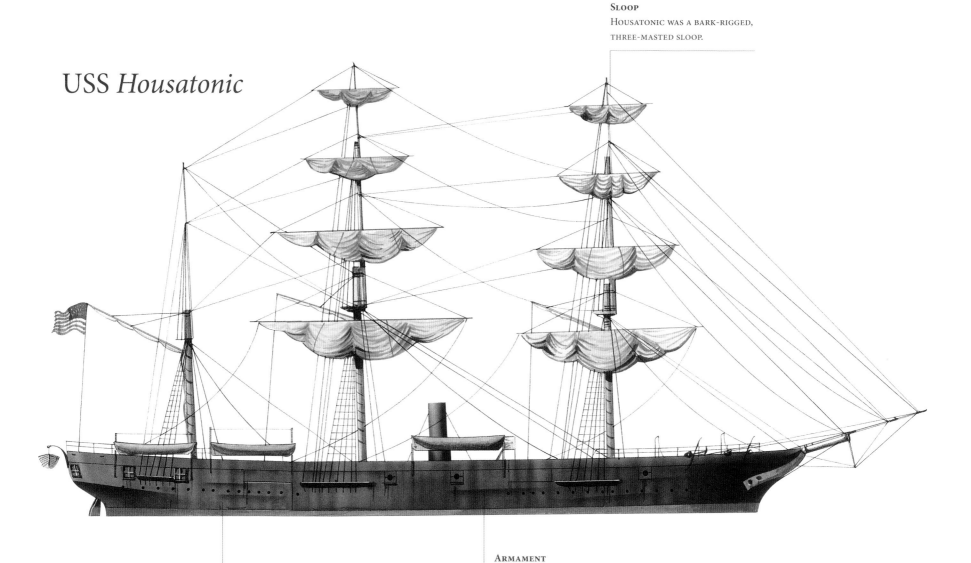

USS *Housatonic*

SLOOP
HOUSATONIC WAS A BARK-RIGGED, THREE-MASTED SLOOP.

TORPEDOED
HOUSATONIC WAS HIT BY A TORPEDO ON THE STARBOARD SIDE FORWARD OF THE MIZZENMAST.

ARMAMENT
IN 1862, SHE HAD ONE 100 PDR PARROTT RIFLE, THREE 30 PDR RIFLES, AND ONE 11 IN (279 MM) DAHLGREN SMOOTHBORE AND SMALLER GUNS.

USS *Marmora* (1862)

THE *MARMORA* WAS BUILT IN MONONGAHELA, PENNSYLVANIA AND PURCHASED BY THE NAVY ON SEPTEMBER 17, 1862. THE STERN WHEEL STEAMER WAS CONVERTED TO A TINCLAD AND COMMISSIONED IN CARONDELET, MISSOURI ON OCTOBER 21, 1862 WITH CAPTAIN ROBERT GETTY IN COMMAND. SHE IMMEDIATELY REPORTED FOR DUTY WITH THE MISSISSIPPI SQUADRON IN THE VICKSBURG CAMPAIGN.

Among the *Marmora*'s most important duties was keeping the Mississippi's tributaries open to Federal transports. While patrolling the Yazoo on December 11, 1862, she and the *Signal* saw numerous scows and floats that indicated torpedoes. One had exploded near the *Signal*, and the *Marmora* had successfully detonated another at a safe distance by rifle fire. The *Marmora* was part of a five-vessel flotilla dispatched the next day to investigate further.

Leading the patrol, the *Marmora* observed floating blocks of wood that served to hold Confederate torpedoes in place. Mistaking these buoys for the torpedoes themselves, the sailors began trying to safely detonate them with small arms fire.

Unaware of the true situation, Commander Thomas Selfridge thought the *Marmora* had come under Confederate attack from the shore, and he ordered his ironclad *Cairo* ahead to provide support. As the *Cairo* moved forward, she ran into a trigger line and two torpedoes exploded. She sank in less than 12 minutes, but the *Marmora* and the other Federal ships were able to rescue her entire crew.

Search and Destroy Expedition

The *Marmora* left her duties patrolling the Yazoo to take part in the attack on Fort Hindman, Arkansas from January 4–11, 1863. In March, she participated in an expedition that captured the *Fairplay* and destroyed newly constructed Confederate batteries 20 miles (32 km) up the Yazoo. The *Marmora* concentrated on patrol duty and supply runs until June, when she burned houses at Gaines' Landing in retaliation for Confederate guerrilla activity. In August, she conducted reconnaissance up the White and Little Red Rivers.

In November, the *Marmora* was on duty guarding the mouth of the Yazoo. When the Confederates attempted to retake Yazoo City on March 7–8, 1864, the *Marmora* and other ships steamed to the rescue. To dissuade further counterattacks, the *Marmora* was part of a force that remained in the area for several months, while other forces launched the Red River Campaign. With the pace of operations slowing, the *Marmora* was ordered to Mound City, Illinois and placed in reserve. She was decommissioned on July 7, 1865 and sold on August 17.

SPECIFICATIONS

DISPLACEMENT: 207 tons (188 tonnes)

DIMENSIONS: 155 ft x 33 ft 5 in x 4 ft 6 in (47 m x 10.19 m x 1.37 m)

ARMAMENT: Two 24 pounder guns; two 12 pounder guns (1862)

MACHINERY: Sternwheel river steamer

SPEED: 6–7 knots

CREW: Unknown

USS *Marmora*

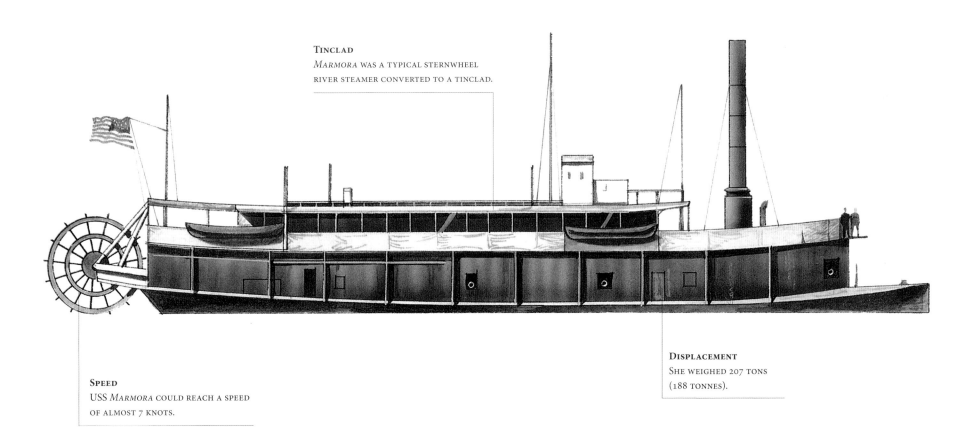

TINCLAD
MARMORA WAS A TYPICAL STERNWHEEL
RIVER STEAMER CONVERTED TO A TINCLAD.

DISPLACEMENT
SHE WEIGHED 207 TONS
(188 TONNES).

SPEED
USS *MARMORA* COULD REACH A SPEED
OF ALMOST 7 KNOTS.

USS *Memphis* (1862)

THE *MEMPHIS* HAD AN INTERESTING CAREER ON BOTH SIDES OF THE CIVIL WAR. BUILT BY WILLIAM DENNY & BROTHERS IN SCOTLAND IN 1861, SHE WAS CAPTURED BY THE GUNBOAT *MAGNOLIA* (HERSELF A FORMER BLOCKADE RUNNER PREVIOUSLY CAPTURED BY THE FEDERALS AND NOW ENFORCING THE BLOCKADE) WHILE RUNNING THE BLOCKADE FROM CHARLESTON, SOUTH CAROLINA WITH A CARGO OF COTTON AND ROSIN ON JULY 31, 1862.

The *Memphis* was towed to New York, where she was purchased by the Navy from a prize court on September 4, 1862. She was commissioned on October 4, 1862 with Acting Volunteer Lieutenant Pendleton Watmough in command.

The *Memphis* then began her own career enforcing the blockade with the South Atlantic Blockading Squadron off Charleston. On October 14, she captured the British steamer *Ouachita* bound for Havana. On January 4, 1863, she and the *Quaker City* took the Confederate sloop *Mercury* with a cargo of turpentine headed for Nassau.

Blockade Fight

Such duty was not without its dangers. On January 31, the Confederate ironclads *Palmetto State* and *Chicora* attacked the Federal blockade fleet in Charleston Harbor. The *Memphis* pulled the *Keystone State* to safety after that ship was struck 10 times by the *Chicora* in an attack that left a quarter of the *Keystone State*'s crew killed or wounded.

On March 6, 1864, the *Memphis* was operating in the North Edisto River when the Confederate torpedo boat *David* attacked her. The *David's* spar torpedo struck the *Memphis* in her port side but did not explode. The *Memphis* engaged the *David* with small arms fire as the *David* delivered another glancing blow to her starboard side. Again the torpedo misfired. By this time the *Memphis* was able to bring her heavy guns to bear, compelling the *David* to retreat upstream to safety. Having escaped this close brush uninjured, the *Memphis* continued her blockading duties to the end of the war.

The *Memphis* was decommissioned on May 6, 1867 and sold to V. Brown & Company in New York in 1869. Renamed the *Mississippi*, she operated as a freight ship until May 13, 1883 when she was gutted by a dock fire in Seattle, Washington.

SPECIFICATIONS

DISPLACEMENT: 791 tons (716 tonnes)

DIMENSIONS: 227 ft 6 in x 30 ft 1 in x 15 ft 6 in (69.4 m 9.17 m x 4.7 m)

ARMAMENT: Four 24 pounders; two 12 pounder guns; one 30 pounder rifle (1862)

MACHINERY: Two English-built vertical, direct-acting steam engines

SPEED: 14 knots

CREW: Not known

USS *Memphis*

SPEED
ALTHOUGH HER TOP SPEED WAS
14 KNOTS, HER AVERAGE SPEED
WAS 9 KNOTS.

ARMAMENT
BY 1865, SHE CARRIED ONE 30 POUNDER RIFLE,
FOUR 20 POUNDER DAHLGREN RIFLES, TWO 2
POUNDER RIFLES AND FOUR 24 POUNDER GUNS.

USS *Miami* (1862)

THE *MIAMI* WAS A SIDE-WHEEL, DOUBLE-ENDER GUNBOAT COMMISSIONED IN PHILADELPHIA, PENNSYLVANIA ON JANUARY 29, 1862 WITH LIEUTENANT ABRAM DAVIS HARRELL IN COMMAND. SHE WAS QUICKLY SENT TO SHIP ISLAND, MISSISSIPPI TO PREPARE FOR THE IMPENDING ATTACK ON NEW ORLEANS. CAPTAIN DAVID PORTER HAD PRESENTED A PLAN TO REDUCE FORTS ST. PHILIP AND JACKSON BY SUSTAINED MORTAR FIRE, ALLOWING THE SOLDIERS FROM SHIP ISLAND TO THEN MOVE FORWARD AND GARRISON THE CAPTURED FORTS.

The *Miami* towed three of Porter's 21 mortar schooners to pre-designated positions and on April 18, Porter began his bombardment. Admiral David Farragut allowed Porter to continue his attack for two days before determining mortar fire alone would be insufficient to defeat the forts. When Farragut attacked on April 24, the *Miami* remained below with the mortar schooners providing covering fire for the ships as they ran the gauntlet. She then transported Major General Benjamin Butler's troops to conduct their land attack.

With New Orleans secure, Farragut sent the *Miami* and the Mortar Flotilla to Ship Island to prepare to attack Mobile. However, when Farragut decided to ascend the Mississippi River to attack Vicksburg, he called for Porter's Mortar Flotilla. The *Miami* reached New Orleans on June 7 and began towing schooners upriver. On June 21, she reached Vicksburg, where she moved schooners in and out of firing positions and shelled Confederate positions. Nonetheless, Farragut found he could not carry the formidable defense without an accompanying Army force, and he returned to the lower river on July 15.

Fighting at Plymouth

The *Miami* was next sent to Fort Monroe, Virginia, where she arrived on September 9. After two months of reconnaissance duty up the James River, blockade duty in Hampton Roads, and refitting, the *Miami* moved to the North Carolina sounds. On April 17 and 18, she helped repulse a Confederate attack at Plymouth. The Federals then prepared for an attack by the Confederate ram *Albemarle*, and the *Miami* and *Southfield* were lashed together for mutual protection and concentration of firepower. When the *Albemarle* attacked on April 19, she rammed the *Southfield* and while the two ships were entangled, the *Miami* raked the *Albemarle* with fire but did little damage and was driven off. On April 20, the Confederates captured Plymouth.

After the *Albemarle* was destroyed on October 27, the *Miami* moved to the James River to support Major General Ulysses Grant's drive on Richmond. She served there until the end of the war and was decommissioned in Philadelphia on May 22, 1865. She was sold at auction on August 10.

SPECIFICATIONS

DISPLACEMENT: 730 tons (755 tonnes)

DIMENSIONS: 208 ft x 33 ft 2 in x 8 ft 6 in (63.5 m x 10.2 m x 2.6 m)

ARMAMENT: One 80 pounder Parrott rifle; one 9 in (228 mm) smoothbore Dahlgren gun; four 24 pounder guns

MACHINERY: One inclined direct acting engine

SPEED: 8 knots

CREW: 134

USS *Miami*

ENGINE
THE GUNBOAT WAS DRIVEN BY A SINGLE,
7-FT (2.1 M) STROKE STEAM ENGINE.

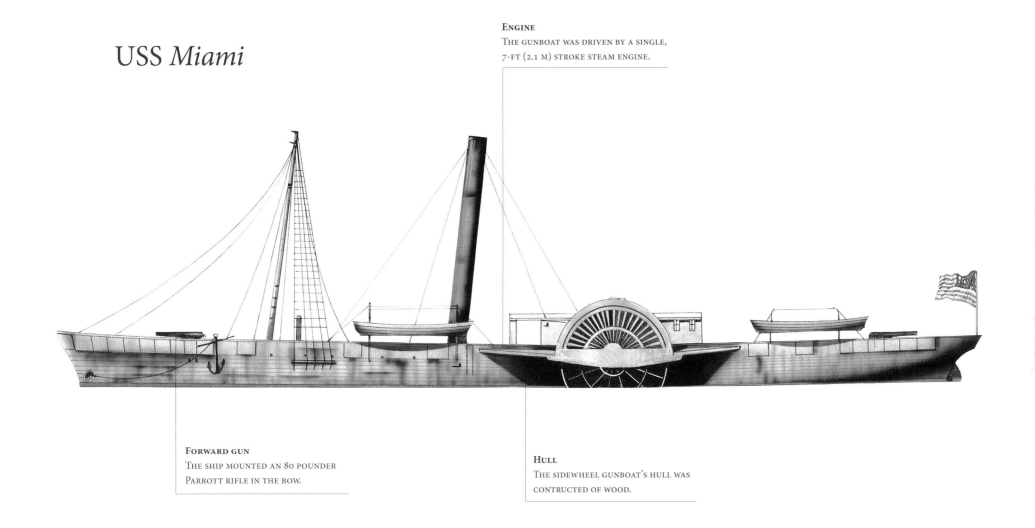

FORWARD GUN
THE SHIP MOUNTED AN 80 POUNDER
PARROTT RIFLE IN THE BOW.

HULL
THE SIDEWHEEL GUNBOAT'S HULL WAS
CONTRUCTED OF WOOD.

USS *Paul Jones* (1862)

THE *PAUL JONES* WAS A SIDE-WHEEL, DOUBLE-ENDED, STEAM GUNBOAT LAUNCHED ON JANUARY 30, 1862. SHE WAS COMMISSIONED ON JUNE 9, 1862 IN BALTIMORE, MARYLAND WITH COMMANDER CHARLES STEEDMAN IN COMMAND, AND JOINED THE SOUTH ATLANTIC BLOCKADING SQUADRON.

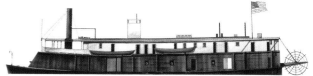

USS *SILVER LAKE*

On July 29, the blockade runner *Thomas L. Wragg* had been turned away from Charleston and Savannah by the Federal blockade and headed up the Ogeechee River in Georgia, seeking the protection of Fort McAllister's guns. Steedman led the *Paul Jones* and three other vessels in pursuit, and engaged the fort at long range with the *Paul Jones'* 100 pounder rifled cannon. The enemies exchanged shots for nearly an hour and a half before Steedman's fleet retreated to safety downriver. Admiral Samuel Du Pont decided to leave Fort McAllister alone until a cooperating army force could take it from the rear, and the *Paul Jones* then helped the *Patroon* and *Cimarron* silence the fort on St. John's Bluff on the St. John's River in Florida on September 17. Returning to blockade duty, the *Paul Jones* assisted in capturing the schooner *Major E. Willis* off Charleston on April 19, 1863 and

successfully took on the sloop *Mary* and her cargo of cotton off St. Simons Sound, Georgia.

The *Paul Jones* participated in the July 18–24 attacks on Fort Wagner in Charleston, before heading to New York for repairs. She rejoined her squadron on September 15 and continued to patrol the coast until late in August 1864. She then sailed to Boston and was decommissioned on September 19, only to be recommissioned on April 1, 1865 for service in the East Gulf Blockading Squadron. She was finally decommissioned and sold in July 1867.

USS *Silver Lake* (1862)

The *Silver Lake* was a wooden stern-wheel steamer purchased by the Navy on November 15, 1862 in Cincinnati, Ohio. She was commissioned on December 24, 1862 with Acting Volunteer Lieutenant Robert Riley in command.

In January and February 1863, the *Silver Lake* joined the *Lexington, Fair-play, St. Clair, Brilliant,* and *Robb* in helping repulse a Confederate attempt to retake Fort Donelson on the Cumberland River. The ships remained in the area, shelling Confederate forces and destroying the cotton works in Florence, Tennessee on March 31, 1863, and shelling Palmyra, Tennessee on April 3 in retaliation for Confederate guerrilla activity. In December 1863, the *Silver Lake* was part of an expedition that silenced Confederate batteries near Bell's Mills, Tennessee and recaptured three transports from the Confederates. She was then ordered out of harm's way to Nashville.

The *Silver Lake* was decommissioned on August 11, 1865 in Mound City, Illinois and sold at public auction six days later.

SPECIFICATIONS

DISPLACEMENT: 1,210 tons (1,098 tonnes)

DIMENSIONS: 216 ft 10 in x 35 ft 4 in x 8 ft (66.09 m x 10.77 m x 2.4 m)

ARMAMENT: One 100 pounder Parrott rifle; two 9 in (228 mm) Dahlgren smoothbores; one 11 in (279 mm) Dahlgren smoothbore; two 50 pounder guns; two 24 pounder howitzers

MACHINERY: Inclined direct-acting engine-driven side wheels

SPEED: 9.5 knots

CREW: 131

USS *Paul Jones*

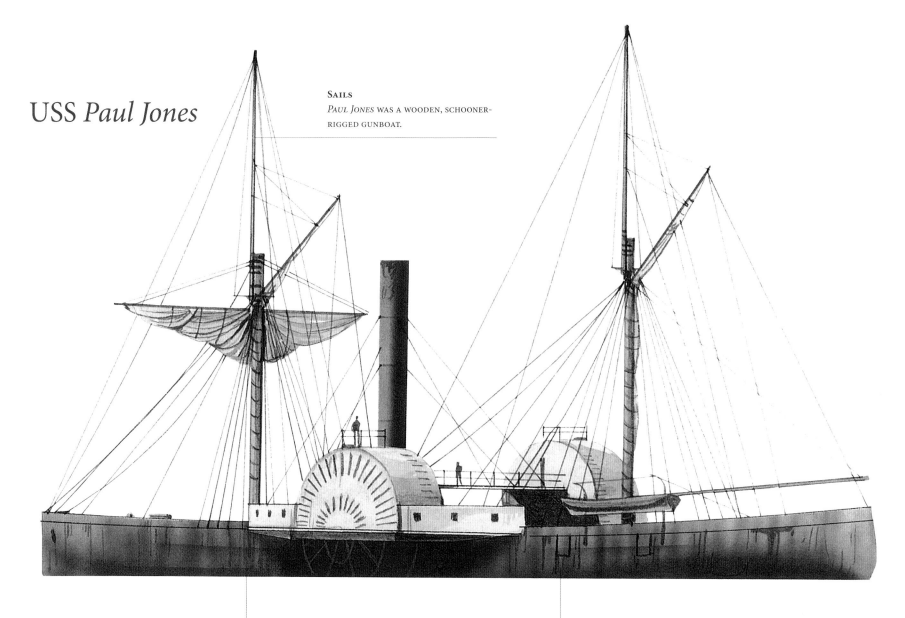

SAILS
PAUL JONES WAS A WOODEN, SCHOONER-
RIGGED GUNBOAT.

DESIGN
USS *PAUL JONES* WAS A DOUBLE-ENDER,
HAVING A RUDDER AT EACH END.

ARMAMENT
HEAVILY ARMED, IN 1862 *PAUL JONES* WAS
EQUIPPED WITH EIGHT GUNS OF VARIOUS KINDS.

USS *Port Royal* (1862)

THE *PORT ROYAL* WAS A WOODEN, DOUBLE-ENDED, SIDE-WHEEL GUNBOAT, LAUNCHED FROM NEW YORK ON JANUARY 17, 1862 BY THOMAS STOCK. SHE WAS COMMISSIONED ON APRIL 26 AND BEGAN A CAREER THAT SAW A VARIETY OF DUTIES IN THE ATLANTIC AND GULF OF MEXICO WATERS.

The *Port Royal* left New York on May 4 and steamed to Hampton Roads, where she joined the North Atlantic Blockading Squadron in supporting Major General George McClellan's Peninsula Campaign. As part of this effort, she engaged Confederate batteries at Sewell's Point, Virginia on May 8 and was part of the unsuccessful attack on Drewry's Bluff a week later. The heavy Confederate fire in this latter operation forced the unarmored *Port Royal* to keep her distance and she contributed little to the attack. Nonetheless, her captain was wounded by a Confederate sharpshooter.

With the failure of McClellan's drive on Richmond, the *Port Royal* relocated to the North Carolina Sounds, where she was part of the Federal naval force that reconnoitered the Neuse River and attacked Kingston on December 12–16. She then moved to the Florida coast and by the spring of 1863 was blockading the port of Apalachicola. On April 20, she dispatched a landing party that raided Apalachicola and captured cotton and ordnance.

Clandestine Mission

On May 24, Lieutenant Commander George Morris initiated a bigger operation sending Acting Master Edgar Van Slyck and 41 men to capture a sloop thought to have taken on board a load of cotton to run through the blockade. Van Slyck and his party slipped past Fort Gadsden under cover of darkness. At first they found no suspicious activity until they spotted a barge of the type used to transport cotton.

Reconnoitring the area, they found the sloop *Fashion* tied up on Brush Creek. The heavy rain disguising their advance, Van Slyck and his men cut the *Fashion* loose, towed her to the river, burned her, and returned safely to the *Port Royal*.

The raid caused much panic among the Confederates, and the *Chattahoochee* was sent in pursuit until her overheated boilers exploded.

In August 1864, the *Port Royal*, lashed alongside the *Richmond*, participated in the attack on Mobile Bay, Alabama. She spent the rest of the war on patrol duty. She was decommissioned on May 23, 1866 and sold in Boston on October 3.

SPECIFICATIONS

DISPLACEMENT: 974 tons (884 tonnes)

DIMENSIONS: 209 ft x 35 ft x 9 ft (63.7 m x 11 m x 2.74 m)

ARMAMENT: One 100 pounder rifle; one 10 in (254 mm) smoothbore; six 24 pounder howitzers

MACHINERY: Inclined direct-acting engines driving side wheels

SPEED: 9.5 knots

CREW: 131

USS *Port Royal*

SPEED
SHE COULD REACH A SPEED
OF 9.5 KNOTS.

MACHINERY
SHE HAD INCLINED, DIRECT-ACTING
ENGINES DRIVING SIDE WHEELS.

DOUBLE-ENDED
PORT ROYAL WAS A DOUBLE-ENDED
GUNBOAT ABLE TO TRAVEL EQUALLY
WELL IN BOTH DIRECTIONS.

USS *Rattler* (1862)

BUILT AS THE WOODEN SIDE-WHEEL STEAMER *FLORENCE MILLER* IN CINCINNATI, OHIO IN 1862, THIS VESSEL WAS PURCHASED BY THE NAVY ON NOVEMBER 11, 1862. SHE WAS CONVERTED TO A TINCLAD, RENAMED THE *RATTLER* OR *TINCLAD NO. 1*, AND COMMISSIONED ON DECEMBER 19 WITH ACTING MASTER AMOS LONGTHORNE IN COMMAND.

The *Rattler* was the lead vessel of Mississippi Squadron as it ascended the White and Arkansas Rivers to attack Fort Hindman, Arkansas on January 10, 1863. She closed within 50 yards (45 m) of the Confederate guns attempting to clear chevaux-de-frise before heavy fire forced her to withdraw. The next day she and the *Glide* turned the Confederate position, allowing the Federal troops to seize the fort.

The *Rattler* served as the flagship of the failed Yazoo Pass Expedition, an attempt to bypass and isolate Vicksburg. Once Vicksburg fell on July 4, 1863, the *Rattler* joined in raids from July 12 to 20 up the Red, Black, Tensas, and Ouachita Rivers. During these operations, she and the *Manitou* combined to capture the *Louisville* on the Little Red River.

The *Rattler* then patrolled the Mississippi River near Rodney, Mississippi. On September 13, her commanding officer, Acting Master Walter Fentress, and 16 others were captured by Confederate guerrillas while attending church in Rodney. Lieutenant Commander James Greer, commander of the Fourth District of the Mississippi Squadron, criticized Fentress for taking "no precaution whatever against capture."

A humiliated Fentress wrote to Admiral David Porter from Libby Prison in Richmond, Virginia on November 15: "I do not, sir, wish to excuse myself, for I am aware that excuses are of little value with you when an officer is at fault, but, sir, I do crave your forbearance in this most unfortunate mistake of mine." The *Rattler* continued to patrol near Rodney for over a year after Fentress's capture.

Wrecked

Her career came to an end on December 30, 1864 when her anchor cable parted during a heavy gale near Grand Gulf, Mississippi. She was driven ashore, struck a snag, and sank. Her crew was able to salvage her supplies and most of her guns before abandoning her. Confederate troops subsequently set her on fire, and she was destroyed.

SPECIFICATIONS

DISPLACEMENT: 165 tons (150 tonnes)

DIMENSIONS: Length: about 170 ft (52 m); beam and draft unknown

ARMAMENT: Varied over time; but included two 30 pounder Parrott rifles and four 24 pounder guns

MACHINERY: Side-wheel propelled steam engine

SPEED: Unknown

CREW: Unknown

USS *Rattler*

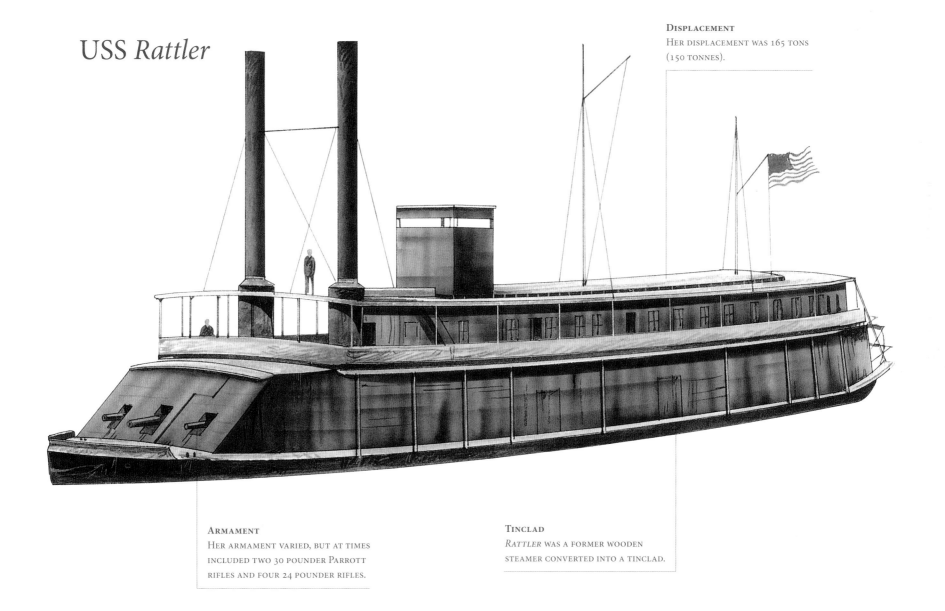

DISPLACEMENT
HER DISPLACEMENT WAS 165 TONS
(150 TONNES).

ARMAMENT
HER ARMAMENT VARIED, BUT AT TIMES
INCLUDED TWO 30 POUNDER PARROTT
RIFLES AND FOUR 24 POUNDER RIFLES.

TINCLAD
RATTLER WAS A FORMER WOODEN
STEAMER CONVERTED INTO A TINCLAD.

CSS *Selma* (1862)

THE *SELMA* WAS A COASTAL VESSEL BUILT IN MOBILE, ALABAMA FOR THE MOBILE MAIL LINE IN 1856. BECAUSE SHE WAS MOST LIKELY ORIGINALLY NAMED THE *FLORIDA*, SHE IS SOMETIMES CONFUSED WITH OTHER SHIPS BEARING THAT NAME, INCLUDING THE BLOCKADE RUNNER. SHE WAS ACQUIRED BY THE CONFEDERACY IN JUNE 1861 AND CONVERTED TO A GUNBOAT, PROBABLY IN THE LAKE PONTCHARTRAIN AREA OF NEW ORLEANS.

As part of this conversion, her upper deck was plated with ⅜ inch (9.5 mm) of iron. By November, she had been commissioned under the command of Lieutenant Charles Hays. She originally served in the New Orleans, Lake Pontchartrain and Mississippi Sound areas, before ending her career at Mobile Bay.

Largely blockaded, she made only occasional forays against the Federal fleet. She was able to engage the *Massachusetts* on October 19 and the *Montgomery* on December 4. In July 1862, she was renamed the *Selma* and placed under the command of Lieutenant Arthur Yates. By the time of Admiral David Farragut's attack on Mobile on August 5, 1864, she, the *Morgan* and the *Gaines* were the only lightly armed gunboats capable of defending lower Mobile Bay. All three ships suffered from desertions, and the *Selma* was reportedly down to a crew of 15 in mid-February. These three ships were of little concern to Farragut, who was able to focus his attention on the ironclad *Tennessee* as the only legitimate naval threat. Brazenly challenging the Confederate torpedoes, Farragut steamed past Fort Morgan's powerful guns, taking little notice of the *Selma* and her sister gunboats.

Pursuit

The best the *Selma* could muster was some raking fire to the *Hartford*, which had the gunboat *Metacomet* lashed to her. Once the pair passed the Confederate forts, Farragut ordered the *Metacomet* cut loose to deal with the annoying *Selma*, now commanded by Lieutenant Peter Murphey. The *Morgan* and the *Gaines* fled, leaving the *Selma* isolated with the *Metacomet*, and three other gunboats on the way, in hot pursuit. Murphey tried to escape to shallow water, but after an hour-long running battle was forced to surrender. The *Selma* lost seven killed and eight wounded, including her captain.

She was taken into the service of the U.S. Navy and helped bombard Fort Morgan later in August. She remained in Mobile Bay until January 1865 when she was transferred to New Orleans. She was decommissioned there on July 12 and was redocumented as a merchant ship the following month.

SPECIFICATIONS

DISPLACEMENT: 590 tons (535 tonnes)

DIMENSIONS: 252 ft x 30 ft x 6 ft (77 m x 9 m x 1.8 m)

ARMAMENT: Two 9 in (228 mm) smoothbore cannons; one 8 in (203 mm) smoothbore cannon; one 6.4 in (162 mm) rifled cannon

MACHINERY: Steam engine

SPEED: 9 knots

CREW: 65–99

CSS *Selma*

HOG FRAMES
SELMA WAS BUILT AS A PACKET SHIP TO
DELIVER POST. IN REFITTING, SHE WAS
STRENGTHENED WITH HOG FRAMES.

SPEED
SHE REACHED A SPEED OF 9 KNOTS.

PLATING
HER UPPER DECK WAS PLATED WITH
0.375 IN (9.5 MM) OF IRON.

USS *Signal* (1862)

THE *SIGNAL* WAS BUILT AS A WOODEN-HULLED, STERN-WHEEL STEAMER IN 1862 IN WHEELING, VIRGINIA. SHE WAS PURCHASED BY THE NAVY ON SEPTEMBER 22 IN ST. LOUIS, MISSOURI AND CONVERTED TO A TINCLAD. THESE LIGHT DRAFT VESSELS—THE *SIGNAL*'S DRAFT WAS JUST 1 FOOT AND 10 INCHES (558 MM)—WERE THE MOST VERSATILE IN THE WESTERN WATERS.

They performed the important day-to-day work of providing the naval presence that kept waterways under Union control, even where the riverbanks belonged to the Confederates. The tinclads got their name from the ½ to ¾ inch (12.7–19 mm) thick iron plating that protected the power plant and pilot house from small-arms fire. To drive off "bushwhackers," the *Signal* mounted two 30 pounder Parrott rifles, four 24 pounder howitzers, and two 12 pounder Dahlgren rifles. Tinclads could even double as troop transports able to carry up to 200 infantry.

The *Signal* left Corondelet, Missouri on October 22 and headed down the Mississippi River to join in the Vicksburg Campaign. Acting Volunteer Lieutenant John Scott was her commander. One of the biggest threats to Federal vessels plying the Mississippi tributaries was torpedoes, and the *Signal* was part of the action on the Yazoo River on December 12 when the *Cairo* became the first vessel in history to be sunk by a mine.

During 1863, the *Signal* participated in the attack on Fort Hindman, Arkansas in January, made a reconnaissance up the White River in February and supported the Vicksburg Campaign, included as part of Major General William Sherman's diversion to Hayne's Bluff, until the Confederate surrender on July 4. She then served as a dispatch vessel and patrolled the Mississippi to interdict Confederate commerce, especially from the Red River.

Dunn's Bayou Battle

On May 5, 1864, the *Signal* and the *Covington* were escorting the steamer *John Warner* down the Red River when the convoy began receiving heavy fire from Confederate infantry and artillery at Dunn's Bayou below Alexandria, Louisiana. All three ships were badly damaged. The *Signal* was hit 38 times in just four minutes, and her steam pipe was cut. The *John Warner* was forced to surrender, and the *Covington* took the disabled *Signal* in tow and headed upriver until the *Covington*'s rudder became disabled. The *Signal* then anchored while the *Covington* battled the Confederates until she too became disabled and out of ammunition. The crew of the *Covington* set fire to the ship and escaped to Alexandria, but the *Signal*, with 25 killed and 13 wounded, was unable to follow suit. The crew attempted to burn the vessel but she would not catch fire and was captured. The Confederates salvaged the *Signal*'s guns and then sank it as a river obstruction.

SPECIFICATIONS

DISPLACEMENT: 190 tons (172 tonnes)

DIMENSIONS: 150 ft x 30 ft x 1 ft 10 in (46 m x 9 m x 0.55 m)

ARMAMENT: Two 30 pounder Parrott rifles; four 24 pounder howitzers; two 12 pounder Dahlgren rifles

MACHINERY: Steam engine; stern-wheel propelled

SPEED: Unknown

CREW: Unknown

USS *Signal*

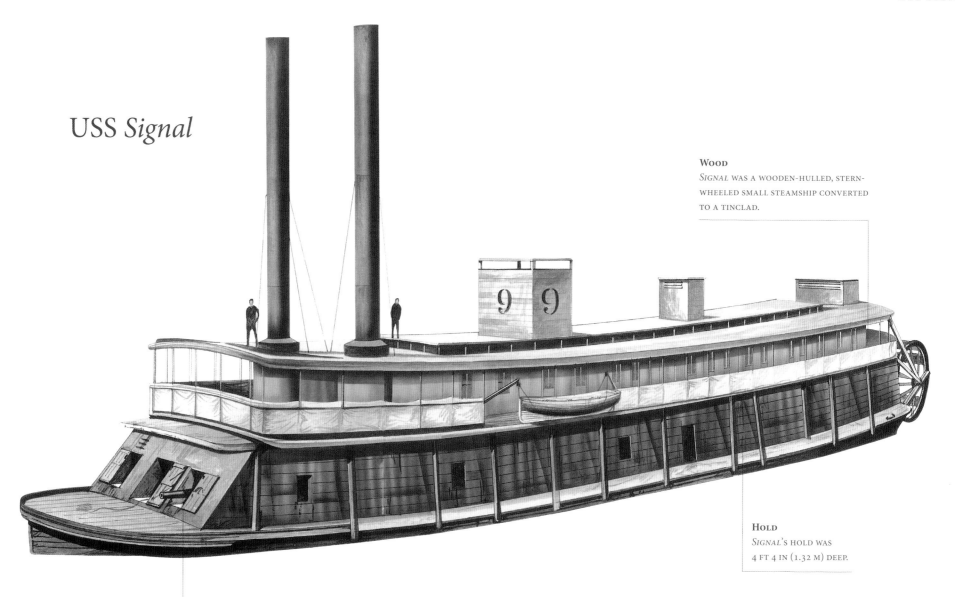

WOOD
SIGNAL WAS A WOODEN-HULLED, STERN-
WHEELED SMALL STEAMSHIP CONVERTED
TO A TINCLAD.

HOLD
SIGNAL'S HOLD WAS
4 FT 4 IN (1.32 M) DEEP.

ARMAMENT
SIGNAL WAS ARMED WITH TWO 30 POUNDER
PARROTT RIFLES, FOUR 24 POUNDER HOWITZERS,
AND TWO 12 POUNDER DAHLGREN RIFLES.

CSS Stonewall Jackson (1862)

THE VESSEL THAT BECAME THE STONEWALL JACKSON BEGAN HER SERVICE AS THE IRONICALLY NAMED *YANKEE*, BUILT IN CINCINNATI, OHIO IN 1849. ON JANUARY 25, 1862, CAPTAIN JAMES MONTGOMERY BEGAN CONVERTING THE *YANKEE* INTO A COTTON-CLAD RAM BY PLACING A 4 INCH (102 MM) OAK SHEATH WITH 1 INCH (25 MM) IRON COVERING ON HER BOW, AND BY INSTALLING DOUBLE PINE BULKHEADS FITTED WITH COMPRESSED COTTON BALES.

The process was completed on March 16, and the *Stonewall Jackson* began her service with the River Defense Fleet. Her armament included two rifled 32 pounders. With Captain George Phillips, a riverboat captain commissioned by the War Department, in command, she was detached from Montgomery's main force and sent to Forts Jackson and St. Philip to assist in the defense of New Orleans. There she became one of several very loosely unified naval assets contributing to the Confederate defense.

When Admiral David Farragut launched his attack on April 24, the steamer *Varuna* outdistanced the other attacking ships and soon found herself isolated upriver. The *Stonewall Jackson* rammed the *Varuna*, which had already been struck by the *Governor Moore*. Captain Beverly Kennon of the *Governor Moore* singles out the *Stonewall Jackson* as the only ship of the River Defense Fleet that took aggressive action. Had the other ships "done their duty simply in firing," laments Kennon, "what might they have accomplished."

River Battle

The ensuing battle has several contradictory accounts, but all agree the *Stonewall Jackson* struck the Federal vessel a second time. Some consider this to be the decisive blow, but historian Chester Hearn and even Kennon credit the *R.J. Breckinridge* with delivering a third ramming that forced the *Varuna* to ground herself on the shore.

The *R.J. Breckinridge* was part of the River Defense Fleet, which may restore some reputation to this organization and deflect some of Kennon's criticism elsewhere. Either way, before the mortally wounded *Varuna* left the battle, she was able to hit the *Stonewall Jackson* with five 8 inch (203 mm) shells. Coming to the *Varuna*'s rescue, the *Oneida* gave chase to the *Stonewall Jackson*, driving her ashore some 4 miles (6.5 km) upriver near Chalmette Battery. Her crew then burned her to prevent capture.

SPECIFICATIONS

DISPLACEMENT: Unknown

DIMENSIONS: Unknown

ARMAMENT: One 32 pounder gun

MACHINERY: Side-wheel steam engine

SPEED: Unknown

CREW: 30

CSS *Stonewall Jackson*

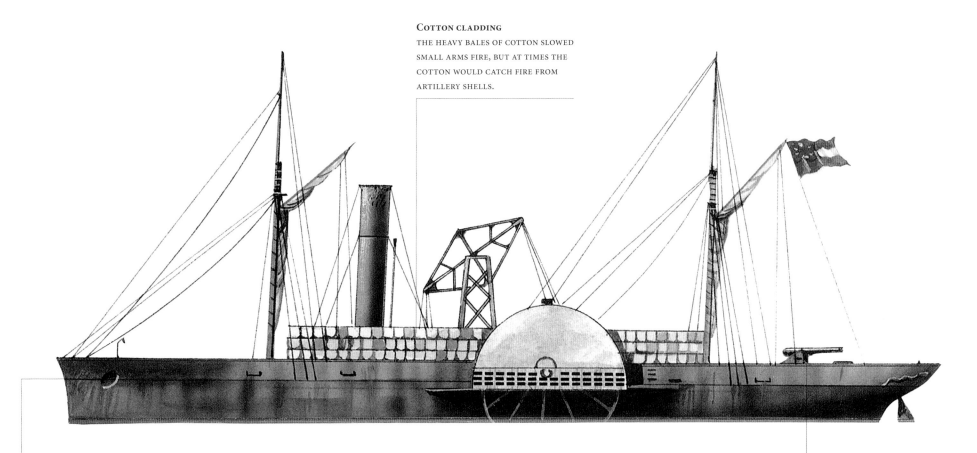

COTTON CLADDING
THE HEAVY BALES OF COTTON SLOWED SMALL ARMS FIRE, BUT AT TIMES THE COTTON WOULD CATCH FIRE FROM ARTILLERY SHELLS.

BOW ARMOR
AT HER BOW SHE HAD 4 IN (100 MM) OAK SHEATH WITH 1 IN (25 MM) IRON COVERING.

ARMAMENT
CSS *STONEWALL JACKSON* WAS ARMED WITH ONE 32 POUNDER GUN.

CSS *Chattahoochee* (1863)

THE *CHATTAHOOCHEE* WAS A 130 FOOT (39 M) LONG GUNBOAT BUILT BETWEEN 1862 AND 1863 IN SAFFOLD, GEORGIA BY A PRIVATE FIRM UNDER CONTRACT BY THE COLUMBUS NAVAL IRON WORKS. SAFFOLD WAS STRATEGICALLY LOCATED 175 MILES (280 KM) SOUTH OF COLUMBUS, GEORGIA AND 140 MILES (224 KM) UPRIVER FROM APALACHICOLA, FLORIDA, AND THE *CHATTAHOOCHEE* WAS THEORETICALLY DESIGNED TO BE BOTH A RIVERBOAT AND OCEAN-SAILING CRAFT.

Once completed, the Confederate Navy intended to steam her downriver, break the Federal blockade, and open the port of Apalachicola for trade. She would also protect the important manufacturing center at Columbus.

The *Chattahoochee* fell far short of these lofty expectations and was plagued by one mishap after another. After many delays reflecting the Confederacy's difficulties in building ships, she was launched in February 1863. On her first day on the river she ran aground, seriously damaging her hull. By the time she was repaired, the Confederate Army had sunk obstructions into the Apalachicola River. While these obstacles may have helped dissuade a Federal attack, they also prevented the *Chattahoochee* from sailing to the sea. Positioned above the obstructions, she became little more than a glorified floating battery.

Disaster struck on May 27, 1863 as the *Chattahoochee* prepared to sail from her anchorage at Blountstown, Florida to attempt to recapture the Confederate schooner *Fashion*. Crew inexperience resulted in a boiler explosion that killed 18, injured others and effectively ended the usefulness of the ship.

Raider Action

On June 10, 1864 she was moved to Columbus for repairs, including the installation of engines and a new boiler. While she was idle, 11 of her officers and 50 crewmen tried unsuccessfully to capture the *Adela*, which was blockading Apalachicola. The Somerset drove off these raiders, capturing six of their seven boats, a large amount of equipment and four of their men.

In April 1865, with Federal forces commanded by Major General James Wilson closing in on Columbus,

the Confederate Navy destroyed the *Chattahoochee* to prevent her capture. A 30 foot (9 m) section of her stern and steam engines were recovered from the Chattahoochee River in 1964, and her remnants are currently on display at the National Civil War Naval Museum in Columbus.

SPECIFICATIONS

DISPLACEMENT: Not known

DIMENSIONS: 130 ft (39 m) x 25 ft (7.6 m) x 8 ft (2.4 m)

ARMAMENT: Four 32 pounder smoothbore cannons; one 32 pounder rifled cannon; one 9 in (228 mm) smoothbore cannon

MACHINERY: Twin screw

SPEED: 12 knots

CREW: 120 officers and crew

CSS *Chattahoochee*

MASTS
UNUSUALLY FOR A RIVERINE GUNBOAT,
THE *CHATTAHOOCHEE* CARRIED THREE
SAILING MASTS.

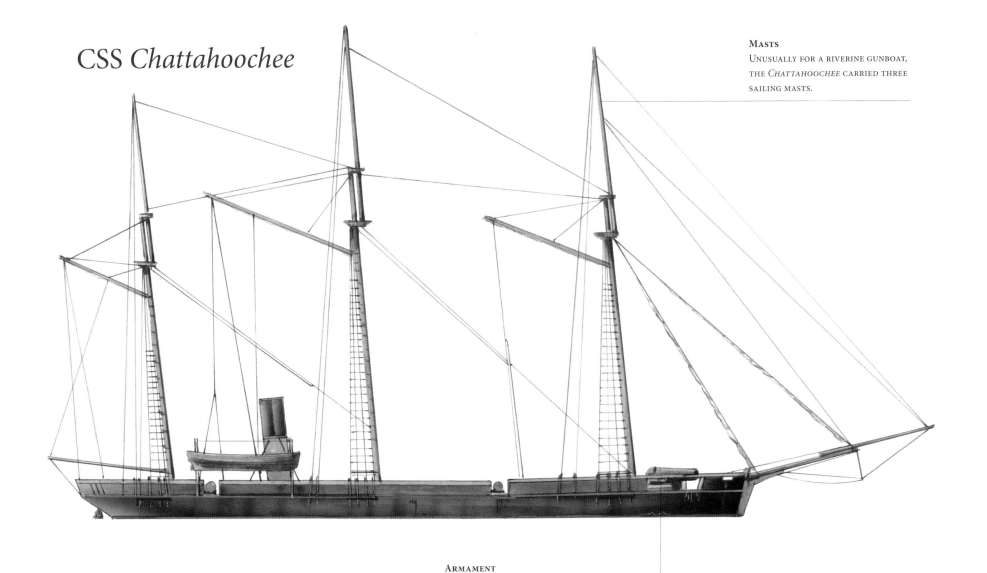

ARMAMENT
HER GUNS INCLUDED FOUR 32 PDR SMOOTHBORE
CANNONS, A 32 PDR RIFLED CANNON, AND ONE
9 IN (228 MM) SMOOTHBORE CANNON.

USS *Fort Jackson* (1863)

THE *FORT JACKSON* WAS A WOODEN, SIDE-WHEEL STEAMER BUILT IN NEW YORK IN 1862. SHE WAS PURCHASED BY THE NAVY ON JULY 20, 1863 AND COMMISSIONED ON AUGUST 18, WITH CAPTAIN HENRY WALKE IN COMMAND. SHE HAD PREVIOUSLY BEEN NAMED THE *KENTUCKY* AND *UNION*.

On September 2, the *Fort Jackson* left New York for Fort Monroe, Virginia and quickly began enforcing the blockade. With the steamer *Connecticut* she intercepted a British arms shipment from Bermuda to Wilmington, North Carolina, but on September 16, while sailing from Bermuda, a boiler burned out and forced her to go to New York for repairs.

Her repairs complete, the *Fort Jackson* was assigned to the North Atlantic Blockading Squadron in December 1863. She took a position off the Cape Fear, and in January 1864 helped destroy the grounded blockade runner *Bendigo* at Folly Inlet. She also had a new commander, Captain Benjamin Sands.

In April, Sands led a raiding party from the *Fort Jackson* across the bar to Masonboro Sound and destroyed a salt works and took a number of prisoners. She captured the blockade runner *Thistle* in June and the *Boston* in July. She also collected cotton bales and bags floating in the water and sent them north. On October 21, she captured the *Wando* attempting to run through the blockade with a cargo of cotton.

Her final duty with the North Atlantic Blockading Squadron was to support both attacks on Fort Fisher. During the first attack she helped bombard Battery Anderson and Battery Gatlin. During the second attack, Captain Sands observed the sailors that went ashore "fall like ten-pins in a bowling alley" during the land assault. Between the two battles she had the grim duty of carrying the dead to Beaufort and the wounded to Hampton Roads.

Texas Blockade

On February 1, 1865, the *Fort Jackson* was transferred to the West Gulf Blockading Squadron. After some repairs in Pensacola, Florida she took up station on the Texas coast. In April she and the *Columbia* captured the schooner *Chaos* off Galveston. On June 2, Lieutenant General Edmund Kirby Smith signed papers surrendering the Confederate Army of the Trans-Mississippi onboard the Fort Jackson in Galveston Bay. The war over, the *Fort Jackson* was decommissioned in New York on August 7 and sold on September 27.

SPECIFICATIONS

DISPLACEMENT: 1,850 tons (1,678 tonnes)

DIMENSIONS: 250 ft x 38 ft 6 in x 18 ft (76 m x 11.73 m x 5.5 m)

ARMAMENT: One 100 pounder rifle; two 30 pounder rifles; eight 9 in (228 mm) smoothbore guns (1864)

MACHINERY: Side-wheel steam engine

SPEED: 14 knots

CREW: Not known

USS *Fort Jackson*

NAME
FORT JACKSON WAS A LARGE,
FAST SHIP FORMERLY NAMED
KENTUCKY AND *UNION*.

ARMAMENT
IN 1864, SHE HAD ONE 100 PDR PARROTT
RIFLE, TWO 30 PDR RIFLES AND EIGHT
9 IN (228 MM) DAHLGREN SMOOTHBORES.

SPEED
A SIDE-WHEEL STEAMER, *FORT JACKSON*
COULD REACH A SPEED OF 14 KNOTS.

USS *Fuchsia* (1863)

THE USS *FUCHSIA* WAS BUILT IN 1863 AS A STEAM TUGBOAT BY FINCOURT IN NEW YORK. SHE WAS PURCHASED BY THE NAVY ON JUNE 16 AND COMMISSIONED IN AUGUST WITH ACTING MASTER W.T. STREET IN COMMAND.

USS FORT HINDMAN

She joined the Potomac Flotilla in reconnaissance and patrol duty on the Potomac, Rappahannock, Piankatank, Tappahannock, Curitoman, and St. Mary's Rivers.

A few incidents serve to illustrate the typical duties performed by the *Fuchsia*. In October 1861 she, with the *Currituck*, apprehended the steamer *Three Brothers*, which the pair found sailing unladen without proper papers. Later that month, the *Fuchsia* sent a landing party ashore from the Rappahannock River to arrest two men known to be blockade runners. The day after that encounter, she took a Virginia soldier prisoner.

After returning from repairs at the Washington Naval Yard in February, on March 7, 1864, the *Fuchsia* traveled up the Piankatank, searching for the Army tugboat *Titan*, which had been captured previously by the Confederates. Finding the tugboat burned to the water's edge,

she sent men to disable the tugboat's boilers, preventing their future use by the Confederates. The *Fuchsia* performed similar service in the same waters until decommissioned in Washington on August 5, 1865. She was sold on September 23, 1865.

USS *Fort Hindman* (1863)

The USS *Fort Hindman* began her career as the side-wheel steamer *James Thompson*. She was purchased March 14, 1863 and quickly renamed the USS *Manitou*. She joined the Mississippi Squadron as a tinclad in April with Acting Volunteer Lieutenant Thomas Selfridge in command. She was renamed the *Fort Hindman* on November 8.

In July 1863, the *Fort Hindman* headed an expedition up the Little Red River, a tributary of the Black River, and captured the ironclad *Louisville*. She continued to patrol the central Mississippi and its

tributaries, to include participating in the Red River Campaign. With water levels lowering and Confederate resistance increasing, the *Fort Hindman* and the rest of Admiral David Porter's fleet found themselves in trouble. On April 27, 1864, the *Fort Hindman*, towing the crippled *Juliet*, ran past the Confederate shore batteries near the junction of the Cane River and the Red. The *Fort Hindman* was struck 19 times by artillery rounds and suffered two fatalities. Surviving the engagement, the *Fort Hindman* made her way down to the rapids above Alexandria on April 27. She passed over the upper falls with the *Osage* and *Neosho* on May 9.

For the duration of the war, the *Fort Hindman* operated in the rivers and bayous of southern Louisiana, occasionally returning to Natchez. She was decommissioned in Mound City, Illinois on August 3, 1865, and sold on August 17.

SPECIFICATIONS

DISPLACEMENT: 240 tons (185 tonnes)

DIMENSIONS: 98 ft 3in x 21 ft 9 in x 8 ft (30 m x 6.42 m x 2.44 m)

ARMAMENT: One 30 pounder rifle; one 24 pounder howitzer (1863)

MACHINERY: Screw-propelled steam engine

SPEED: Not known

CREW: Not known

USS *Fuschia*

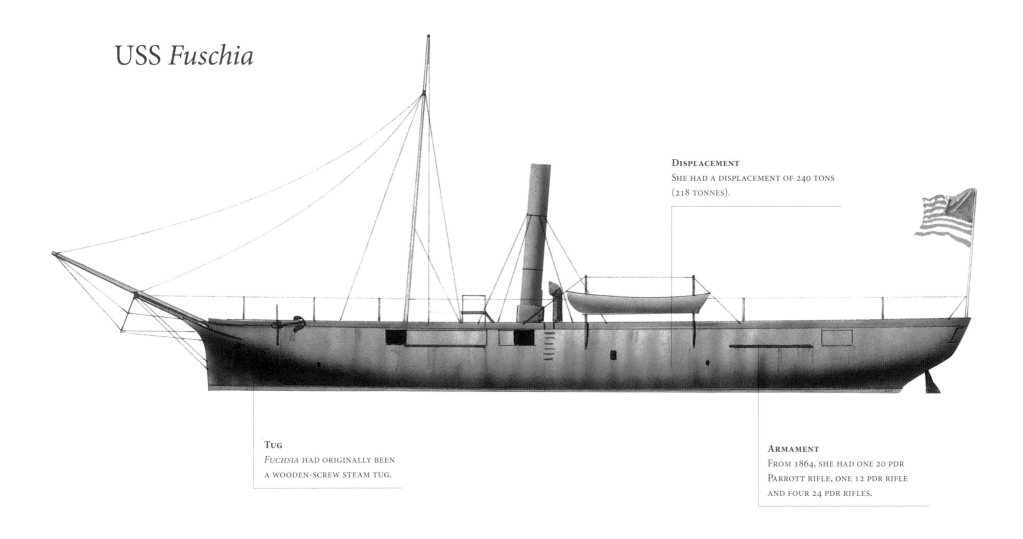

DISPLACEMENT
SHE HAD A DISPLACEMENT OF 240 TONS
(218 TONNES).

TUG
FUCHSIA HAD ORIGINALLY BEEN
A WOODEN-SCREW STEAM TUG.

ARMAMENT
FROM 1864, SHE HAD ONE 20 PDR
PARROTT RIFLE, ONE 12 PDR RIFLE
AND FOUR 24 PDR RIFLES.

USS *Peosta* (1863)

THE *PEOSTA* WAS A ST. JOSEPH, MISSOURI-BASED FERRY BUILT IN 1857 IN CINCINNATI, OHIO. SHE WAS PURCHASED IN DUBUQUE, IOWA IN THE SUMMER OF 1863. CONVERTED TO A LIGHT-DRAUGHT TINCLAD GUNBOAT, SHE RETAINED HER CIVILIAN NAME AND WAS ALSO DESIGNATED *TINCLAD NO. 36*. SHE WAS COMMISSIONED ON OCTOBER 2 WITH LIEUTENANT THOMAS SMITH IN COMMAND.

USS *NYMPH*

The *Peosta* departed Cairo, Illinois on October 28 and arrived in Paducah, Kentucky on November 3. She seldom got away from Paducah except for an occasional trip up the Tennessee River, patrolling as far as Eastport, Mississippi to offer protection to Union shipping and support Army activities.

In the spring of 1864 she helped halt a Confederate land and river offensive against Paducah aimed at recapturing lost defensive positions along the river. More typical of her unremarkable career was her January 10 effort to help the stranded Paw Paw bail out a leak. During the attempt, two of the *Peosta*'s crew fell overboard and drowned. Other inglorious episodes include the April 30 arrest of half a dozen drunken *Peosta* sailors. She was decommissioned on August 7, 1865 and sold at auction 10 days later.

USS *Nymph* (1864)

The *Nymph* was originally the *Cricket No. 3*, a stern-wheel, wooden river steamer built in Cincinnati, Ohio in 1863. She was purchased by the Navy on March 8, 1864, fitted out as a tinclad gunboat, and commissioned in Mound City, Illinois as the *Nymph* on April 11, 1864. She was commanded by Acting Master Patrick Donnelly.

The *Nymph*'s career was a quiet one spent patrolling the Mississippi River and its tributaries to keep those waterways open to Federal supply operations and communications. In December 1864, she played a part in a small retaliatory raid and foraging operation near Williamsport, Louisiana. She is more often remembered as a footnote in the saga of the CSS *Webb*, which in April 1865 was ordered to sea to raid Federal commerce. On April 23, the erstwhile privateer passed unrecognized and unmolested by the *Nymph*'s position

off Lobdell's Stores Landing, Louisiana, but ultimately failed in her attempt to cruise the open sea.

The *Nymph* was decommissioned shortly after this episode on June 28. She was sold at public auction at Mound City on August 17.

SPECIFICATIONS

DISPLACEMENT: 233 tons (211 tonnes)

DIMENSIONS: 151 ft 2 in x 34 ft 3 in x 6 ft (46 m x 10.4 m x 1.83 m)

ARMAMENT: Three 30 pounder Parrott rifles; two 32 pounder rifled guns; two 12 pounder smoothbore guns; six 24 pounder howitzers

MACHINERY: Side-wheel propelled steam engine

SPEED: 5 knots

CREW: Not known

USS *Peosta*

NAME
A WOODEN, SIDE-WHEEL STEAMER, SHE WAS ALSO KNOWN AS *TINCLAD 36*.

HOLD
HER HOLD WAS 5 FT 2 IN (1.57 M) DEEP.

TONNAGE
SHE WEIGHED 204 TONS (185 TONNES).

USS Queen City (1863)

THE *QUEEN CITY* WAS A WOODEN, SIDE-WHEEL STEAMER PURCHASED BY THE NAVY IN CINCINNATI, OHIO FROM SAMUEL WIGGINS ON FEBRUARY 13, 1863. SHE WAS CONVERTED INTO A TINCLAD AND COMMISSIONED ON APRIL 1, 1863 WITH ACTING MASTER JASON GOUDY IN COMMAND.

She was originally armed with two 30 pounder Parrott rifles, as well as two 32 pounder guns and four 24 pounder howitzers. On October 7, she received an additional 12 pounder gun to complete her armament. The *Queen City* is also known as Gunboat No. 26 based on the number assigned to her after Admiral David Porter ordered all "light draft vessels of the Mississippi Squadron will have a number, two feet [60 cm] long, painted neatly in black on the forward part and sides of the pilot house."

The *Queen City* supported Army operations from the Tennessee River through the spring, and then was transferred to the Mississippi River in the summer. There she conducted regular patrols to protect the lines of supply and communications. On October 13, she departed Helena, Arkansas, carrying troops to Friar's Point, Mississippi, where they landed and surrounded the town.

The next morning they seized a large quantity of cotton.

Cavalry Attack

In ensuing months, the *Queen City* continued operations along the rivers of Arkansas. On June 24, she was anchored off Clarendon, Arkansas on the White River near the mouth of the Cache River. Two regiments of Confederate cavalry led by Brigadier General Joseph Shelby and supported by artillery attacked her, and within 20 minutes the ship was riddled with bullets and both engines were disabled.

The captain of the vessel, Acting Master Michael Hickey, was forced to surrender the ship while giving his crew the choice of surrendering with her or trying to escape by swimming to safety. About half of the crew was captured and the rest escaped to the opposite side of the river, where they were picked up later in the day by the *Tyler*.

When the *Tyler* attempted to recover the *Queen City*, the Confederates blew her up. Shelby's raid was the first to result in the destruction of a Union gunboat in Arkansas and it disrupted shipments on the river for a short period. In 1977, the University of Missouri-Columbia located a sunken boat near the site of the action, but was unable to determine if it was the *Queen City*.

SPECIFICATIONS

DISPLACEMENT: 212 tons (192 tonnes)

DIMENSIONS: Not known

ARMAMENT: Two 30 pounder Parrott rifles; two 32 pounder guns; four 24 pounder howitzers; one 12 pounder gun

MACHINERY: Side-wheeled propelled steam engine

SPEED: Not known

CREW: 65

USS *Queen City*

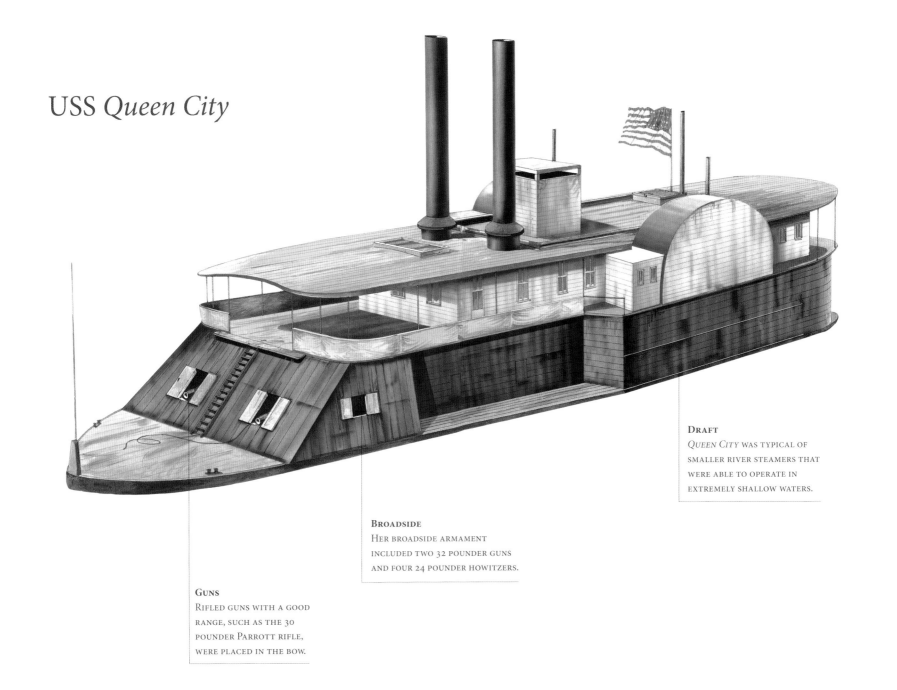

DRAFT
QUEEN CITY WAS TYPICAL OF
SMALLER RIVER STEAMERS THAT
WERE ABLE TO OPERATE IN
EXTREMELY SHALLOW WATERS.

BROADSIDE
HER BROADSIDE ARMAMENT
INCLUDED TWO 32 POUNDER GUNS
AND FOUR 24 POUNDER HOWITZERS.

GUNS
RIFLED GUNS WITH A GOOD
RANGE, SUCH AS THE 30
POUNDER PARROTT RIFLE,
WERE PLACED IN THE BOW.

USS *Iosco* (1864)

THE *IOSCO* WAS A WOODEN, DOUBLE-ENDED, SIDE-WHEEL GUNBOAT, COMMISSIONED AT THE BOSTON
NAVY YARD ON APRIL 26, 1864 WITH COMMANDER A.J. DRAKE IN COMMAND. HER FIRST DUTY WAS
IN THE GULF OF ST. LAWRENCE, WHERE SHE PROTECTED AMERICAN FISHING VESSELS IN THE AREA,
INCLUDING ASSISTING SEVERAL SHIPS ENDANGERED BY FIERCE STORMS.

She was ordered to Hampton Roads on October 2 to join the North Atlantic Blockading Squadron. On November 21, she captured the British schooner *Sybil*, which was attempting to escape to sea from Wilmington, North Carolina with 307 bales of cotton.

The *Iosco* participated in the first attack initiated against Fort Fisher, North Carolina on December 24, 1864. She was part of a massive but indiscriminate naval bombardment in which the Federals fired 21,000 rounds over the course of two days, but which did little damage to Fort Fisher. The *Iosco* did succeed, however, in shooting down the Confederate flag that flew above the Mound Fort, while Confederate return fire carried away the head of the *Iosco*'s foremast.

On the second day of the action at Fort Fisher, the *Iosco* led nine other ships in bombarding the fort and supporting what proved to be a disappointingly tepid land assault. Her boats also dragged the channel for torpedoes.

When this first attack failed, the Federals launched a better coordinated effort on January 13, 1865. In addition to assisting with the landing of troops and providing covering fires, the *Iosco* contributed 44 of her men under acting Ensigns William Jameson and Ulric Feilberg to the land attack. Two were killed and 12 were wounded. These men were part of a naval contingent of 1,600 sailors and 400 marines ordered by Admiral David Porter to participate in the assault with the Army. This naval force was commanded by Lieutenant Commander K.R. Breese and ultimately contributed little to the Federal success.

North Carolina Sounds

The *Iosco* spent the remainder of the war on routine duty in the North Carolina sounds. She was decommissioned on July 28, 1865. Her engines were removed and her hull was turned over to the Bureau of Construction and Repair to be used as a coal hulk in 1868.

SPECIFICATIONS

DISPLACEMENT: 1,173 tons (1,064 tonnes)

DIMENSIONS: 205 ft x 35 ft x 9 ft 6 in (62.5 m x 10.7 m x 2.9 m)

ARMAMENT: Two 100 pounder rifles; four 9 in (228 mm) smoothbores; two 24 pounder howitzers

MACHINERY: Direct-acting inclined engines

SPEED: 13 knots

CREW: 200

USS *Iosco*

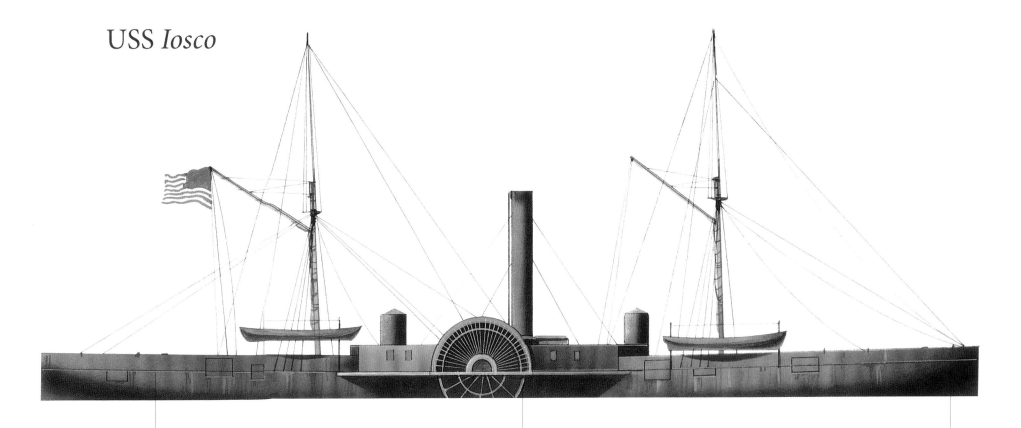

DRAFT
DESIGNED TO BE ABLE TO NAVIGATE INLAND WATERWAYS, *IOSCO* HAD A SHALLOW DRAFT OF 9 FT 6 IN (3 M).

ENGINE
THE BOILERS INCLUDED THE NEW FEATURE OF FORCED DRAFT FROM MECHANICAL BLOWERS.

RUDDER
RESPONDING TO THE NEED TO BE HIGHLY MANEUVERABLE IN TIGHT WATERWAYS, *IOSCO* HAD A RUDDER AT EACH END.

USS *Tallapoosa* (1864)

THE USS *TALLAPOOSA* WAS A *SASSACUS*-CLASS WOODEN-HULLED, DOUBLE-ENDED STEAMER BUILT AT THE NEW YORK NAVY YARD BY C.W. BOOZ. DOUBLE-ENDERS WERE SPECIFICALLY DESIGNED TO OPERATE IN SHALLOW COASTAL WATERS AND RIVERS. THEY WERE EQUIPPED WITH RUDDERS AT EACH END, ALLOWING THEM TO OPERATE IN EITHER DIRECTION. THIS FEATURE WAS CRITICAL IN SHALLOW AND NARROW RIVERS WHERE TURNING AROUND MIGHT BE DIFFICULT.

Displacing 1,173 tons (1,063 tonnes), the *Tallapoosa* was launched on February 17, 1863 and commissioned on September 13, 1864 with Lieutenant Commander Joseph DeHaven in command.

On August 4, the commerce raider CSS *Tallahassee* had slipped through the Union blockade at Wilmington, North Carolina and was creating a panic among Atlantic coast shipping from the Virginia Capes to Nova Scotia. Hurried into service in October, the *Tallapoosa* joined the *Maumee* and *Yantic* in patrolling up and down the coast. Reflecting the crisis the *Tallahassee* had created, Admiral David Porter ordered that if the *Tallahassee* were found, the Federal captains were to "sink her at all hazards." The *Tallapoosa* ended her futile search when she encountered a two-day storm that disabled both her rudders and caused other damage. She finally limped into Boston on the morning of November 7. The *Tallahassee* had long returned to Wilmington on August 26 after having taken 33 Union ships.

East Gulf Blockading Squadron

After being repaired, the *Tallapoosa* went to sea again on December 24, but not before three of her crew had deserted while the ship was in Boston. She sailed for Key West, Florida and duty with the East Gulf Blockading Squadron, where she enjoyed a quiet period of service.

Perhaps her greatest contribution came on January 11, 1865 when she helped with the salvage of material and equipment from the screw frigate *San Jacinto*, which had run aground in the Bahamas. When the war ended, the *Tallapoosa* was in Galveston, Texas. She served in the Gulf Squadron until 1867 when she was laid up at the Washington Navy Yard.

The *Tallapoosa* was reactivated in 1869 as a dispatch vessel and maintained some connection with the Civil War by carrying the legendary war hero Admiral David Farragut on two small voyages. Although she was condemned as unfit for service in 1892, she lives on as part of a memorial to Civil War veterans in Norwalk, Connecticut taht features a 100 pounder Parrott rifle that was once part of her armament.

SPECIFICATIONS

DISPLACEMENT: 1,173 tons (1,063 tonnes)

DIMENSIONS: 205 ft x 35 ft x 6 ft 6 in (62.5 m x 10.7 m x 1.9 m)

ARMAMENT: Two 100 pounder Parrott rifles; four 9 in (228 mm) Dahlgren smoothbores; two 24 pounder howitzers

MACHINERY: Steam engine, side wheel-propelled

SPEED: 11.5 knots

CREW: 190 officers and enlisted

USS *Tallapoosa*

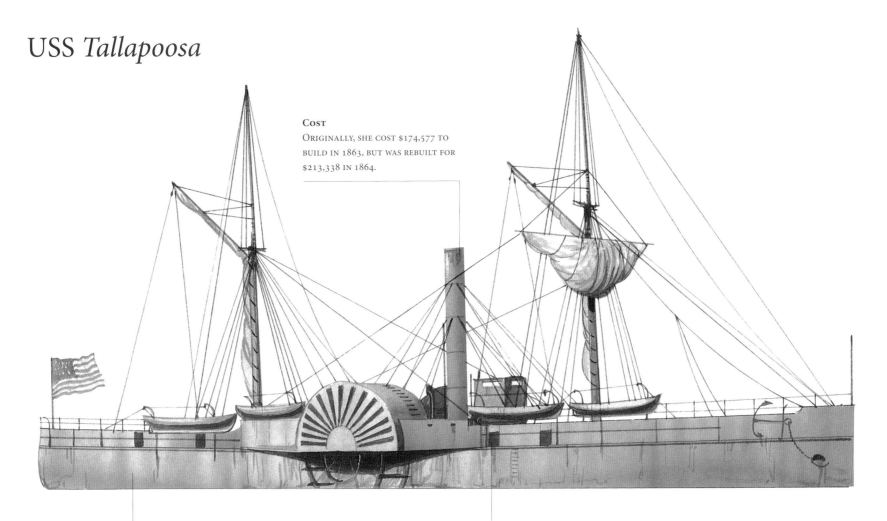

COST
ORIGINALLY, SHE COST $174,577 TO
BUILD IN 1863, BUT WAS REBUILT FOR
$213,338 IN 1864.

PAINT
THE *TALLAPOOSA* WAS PAINTED A LIGHT
GRAY COLOR SIMILAR TO THAT OF
BLOCKADE RUNNERS.

ARMAMENT
IN 1864, THE TALLAPOOSA CARRIED TWO 100 PDR
PARROTT RIFLES, FOUR 9 IN (228 MM) DAHLGREN
SMOOTHBORES, AND TWO 24 PDR HOWITZERS.

USS *Vindicator* (1864)

IN EARLY 1862, CHARLES ELLET CONVINCED THE WAR DEPARTMENT THAT THE ADVENT OF STEAM POWER BROUGHT RENEWED UTILITY TO THE OUTDATED NAVAL TACTIC OF RAMMING. ELLET WAS MADE A COLONEL AND ORDERED TO CREATE A RAM FLEET FOR OPERATION ON THE MISSISSIPPI RIVER AND ITS TRIBUTARIES. THESE VESSELS WERE OLD RIVERBOATS THAT HAD BEEN CONVERTED BY REINFORCING THEIR HULLS AND FILLING THEIR BOWS WITH TIMBER SO THAT THEY COULD SURVIVE DELIBERATE COLLISIONS WITH ENEMY SHIPS.

They existed strictly for combat against other vessels. The *Vindicator* was acquired by the Army for this purpose in 1863 in New Albany, Indiana. Since such vessels carried little or no armament other than their rams, they were of limited utility once the Confederate fleet had ceased to be an immediate threat. Thus the *Vindicator* was transferred to the Navy in 1864 and commissioned on May 24. Lieutenant Commander Thomas Selfridge was her commander.

The *Vindicator* was assigned the 5th District of the Mississippi River Squadron on July 4 and deployed off Natchez, Mississippi later that month. There she performed patrol and reconnaissance duties. With her ram and powerful armament, including a 100 pounder bow Parrott rifle mounted in a wooden casemate, the *Vindicator* was an imposing gunboat. The mere presence and vigilance of her and the other ships of the squadron helped dissuade a planned Confederate crossing of the river on August 22.

Supporting Ground Forces

In early November, the *Vindicator* was transferred to the 6th District. During an expedition up the Yazoo River on November 27, the *Vindicator* and the stern-wheeler *Prairie Bird* transported and covered Union cavalry forces in an attack on Confederate communications in western Mississippi. Declaring the operation "eminently successful," Major General Napoleon Dana reported destroying a railroad bridge over the Big Black River, some 30 miles (48 km) of railroad track, and supplies destined for the Confederate Army. Dana praised the performance of the two gunboats, saying: "The assistance of the vessels of the Sixth Division Mississippi Squadron rendered the expedition a complete success."

The *Vindicator* remained in the 6th District for the duration of the war. Her activities included the lively but unsuccessful pursuit of the ram *William H. Webb* off the mouth of the Red River in Mississippi on April 23 and 24 of 1865. The *Vindicator* was partially dismantled in Mound City, Illinois in July and sold at public auction on November 29.

SPECIFICATIONS

DISPLACEMENT: 750 tons (680 tonnes)

DIMENSIONS: Length and beam unknown; draft 6 ft (1.8 m)

ARMAMENT: Stern ram; one 100 pounder Parrott rifle; two 24 pounder howitzers; one 12 pounder rifle; one heavy 12 pounder gun (1865)

MACHINERY: Side-wheel propelled steam engine

SPEED: 12 knots

CREW: unknown

USS *Vindicator*

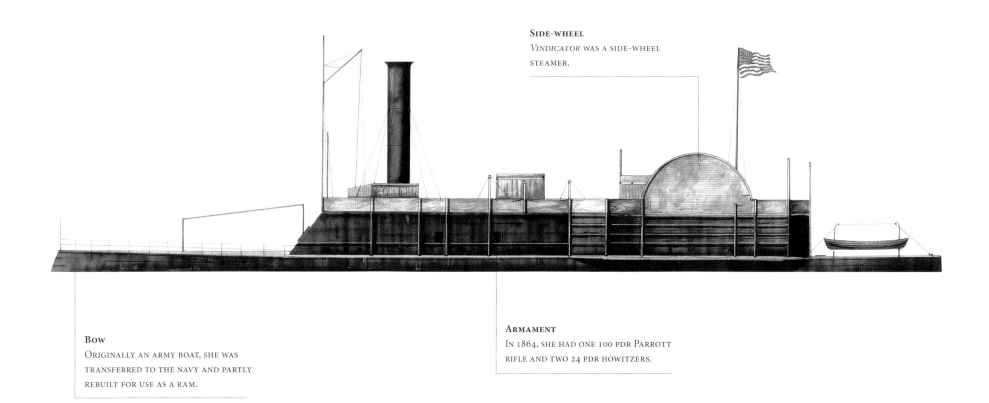

SIDE-WHEEL
VINDICATOR WAS A SIDE-WHEEL
STEAMER.

BOW
ORIGINALLY AN ARMY BOAT, SHE WAS
TRANSFERRED TO THE NAVY AND PARTLY
REBUILT FOR USE AS A RAM.

ARMAMENT
IN 1864, SHE HAD ONE 100 PDR PARROTT
RIFLE AND TWO 24 PDR HOWITZERS.

CSS *Calhoun* (1861)

THE SHIP THAT BECAME THE *CALHOUN* WAS BUILT IN NEW YORK IN 1851 AS THE *CUBA*. SHE WAS COMMISSIONED BY THE CONFEDERATE GOVERNMENT AS A PRIVATEER ON MAY 15, 1861 WITH CAPTAIN JOHN WILSON IN COMMAND. OVER THE NEXT FIVE MONTHS, SHE CAPTURED SIX PRIZES, BUT WITH ONLY FIVE SMALL DECK GUNS, IT BECAME OBVIOUS SHE WAS NO MATCH FOR THE FEDERAL NAVY'S SUPERIOR FIREPOWER.

Given this disadvantage, she was transferred to the Confederate States Navy and placed under the command of Lieutenant. J.H. Carter. Lightly armed but spacious (she could accommodate a crew of 150), the *Calhoun* became the flagship for Commodore George Hollins as he labored against all odds to defend the maritime approaches to New Orleans. The *Calhoun* was present when Hollins successfully attacked the surprisingly complacent Federal fleet at the Head of the Passes into the Mississippi River on October 12, but the lightly armed flagship took no active part in the fight.

On January 23, 1862, the schooner *Samuel Rotan* captured the *Calhoun* in East Bay, formed by the Southwest Pass and Grand Pass fingers of the Mississippi delta. The *Calhoun* had been attempting to slip into the Southwest Pass with a cargo of over 25 tons (22.5 tonnes) of gunpowder, rifles, chemicals and coffee.

The *Calhoun* was then commissioned for Federal service with Lieutenant J.E. De Haven in command. She joined the West Gulf Blockading Squadron on March 19 and patrolled off the Head of the Passes. The *Calhoun* proved adept as a blockader, helping capture 13 ships before May 5 when she steamed up the Mississippi for duty in Lake Ponchartrain. There she captured a steamer, a gunboat, two schooners, and a sloop. Later that year, she captured another sloop in Atchafalaya Bay.

River Fight

On April 14, 1863 the *Calhoun* joined the *Estrella* and the *Arizona* in an attack on the Atchafalaya River, Louisiana. A long-range shot from the *Calhoun* ignited the *Queen of the West*'s cotton and engulfed her in flames. She subsequently grounded and exploded.

On April 20, the *Calhoun* participated in the attack on Fort Butte-a-la-Rose and

in August was ordered to base on Ship Island, where she took four more prizes. During the last two weeks of February 1864, she served as Admiral David Farragut's flagship during the bombardment of Fort Powell from Mobile Bay.

The *Calhoun* was turned over to the United States Marshal in New Orleans on May 6 and sold on June 4 to the U.S. Army.

SPECIFICATIONS

DISPLACEMENT: 509 tons (462 tonnes)

DIMENSIONS: Unknown

ARMAMENT: One 18 pounder gun; two 12 pounder guns; two 6 pounder guns

MACHINERY: Screw-propelled steam engine

SPEED: Unknown

CREW: 85

CSS *Calhoun*

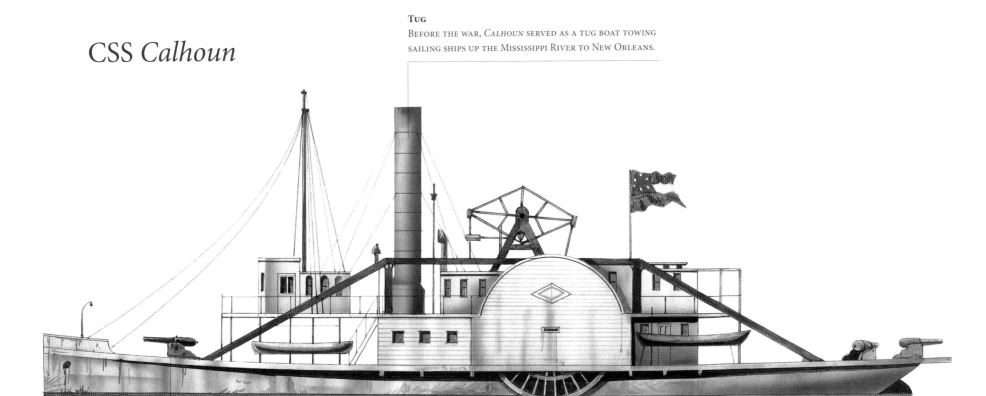

TUG
BEFORE THE WAR, *CALHOUN* SERVED AS A TUG BOAT TOWING SAILING SHIPS UP THE MISSISSIPPI RIVER TO NEW ORLEANS.

ARMAMENT
SHE WAS ARMED WITH ONE 18 POUNDER, TWO 12 POUNDER AND TWO 6 POUNDER GUNS.

STEAMER
CALHOUN WAS A FAST, POWERFUL, LOW-PRESSURE SIDE-WHEEL STEAMER.

USS *Quaker City* *(1861)*

THE *QUAKER CITY* WAS A SIDE-WHEEL STEAMER BUILT IN PHILADELPHIA IN 1854 AND PURCHASED BY THE NAVY ON AUGUST 12, 1861. SHE WAS COMMISSIONED IN NEW YORK ON DECEMBER 14 WITH COMMANDER JAMES FRAILEY IN COMMAND. SHE BECAME ONE OF THE MOST ACTIVE AND EFFECTIVE FEDERAL BLOCKADERS.

Even before being commissioned, she was chartered by the Navy and stationed off the entrance to Chesapeake Bay. She quickly proved her worth. On May 14, 1861, she shared in the capture of the *North Carolina* and on May 25 the bark *Pioneer* in Hampton Roads and the bark *Winifred* off Cape Henry. On May 30, she captured the schooner *Lynchburg* in Chesapeake Bay. On June 4, she took the bark *General Green* off Cape Henry. On June 10, she helped capture the *Amy Warwick* in Hampton Roads. She took the bark *Sally Magee* there on June 26 and shared in taking the schooner *Sally Mears* on July 1. She captured the schooner *Fair Wind* on August 29.

After sailing north for repairs and to pick up her Navy crew, she was dispatched to hunt for the *Sumter*. She captured the *Model* in the Gulf of Mexico on June 30, 1862 and the *Lilla* off Hole-in-Wall, Virginia on July 3. Four days later, she

helped take the *Adela* off the Bahamas, and on July 24 the blockade runner *Orion* at Champeche Bank, south of Key West.

Blockade Fight

On January 31, 1863, she helped repulse an attack by the *Chicora* and the *Palmetto State* on the Federal blockade fleet off Charleston. During this fight, she suffered considerable damage when a shell exploded in her engine room. After repairs, she was soon back in action and took the schooner *Douro* off Wilmington on March 9. She picked up 40 bales of cotton adrift at sea on June 26, 1864 and shared in the capture of the steamer *Elsie* off Charleston on September 5. She participated in the failed first attack on Fort Fisher, North Carolina on December 24.

She then cruised in the Gulf of Mexico, taking the schooner *R.H. Vermilyea* on March 12, 1865, the *Telemico* on March 16, and the *George Burkhart* on March

17. With the war coming to a close, the steamer *Cora* surrendered to her near Brazos Santiago, Texas on March 24 and she chased the *Webb* in its dash to the sea on April 24. The *Quaker City* was decommissioned at the Philadelphia Navy Yard on May 18 and sold at auction on June 20.

SPECIFICATIONS

DISPLACEMENT: 1,600 tons (1,451 tonnes)

DIMENSIONS: 244 ft 8 in x 36 ft x 13 ft (74.6 m x 10.9 m x 3.9 m)

ARMAMENT: One 20 pounder Parrott rifle; eight 32 pounder guns (1863)

MACHINERY: One side-lever engine with an 8 ft (2.4 m) stroke

SPEED: Maximum 13 knots; 10 average

CREW: 99

USS *Quaker City*

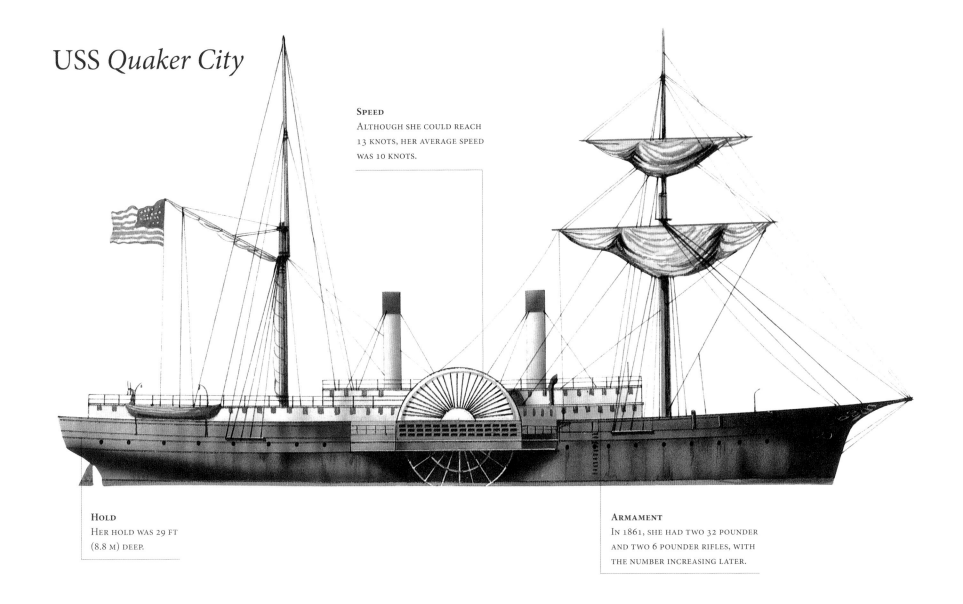

SPEED
ALTHOUGH SHE COULD REACH 13 KNOTS, HER AVERAGE SPEED WAS 10 KNOTS.

HOLD
HER HOLD WAS 29 FT (8.8 M) DEEP.

ARMAMENT
IN 1861, SHE HAD TWO 32 POUNDER AND TWO 6 POUNDER RIFLES, WITH THE NUMBER INCREASING LATER.

CSS *Rattlesnake* (1861)

THE *RATTLESNAKE* FIRST SERVED AS THE *NASHVILLE* AND THEN AS THE *THOMAS L. WRAGG*. AS THE *NASHVILLE*, SHE WAS A MAIL SERVICE SHIP THAT RAN BETWEEN NEW YORK AND CHARLESTON, SOUTH CAROLINA BEFORE THE CIVIL WAR. AFTER THE FALL OF FORT SUMTER, SHE WAS SEIZED AT CHARLESTON AND FITTED OUT AS A CRUISER UNDER THE COMMAND OF LIEUTENANT R.B. PEGRAM.

She ran the blockade on October 21, 1861 and sailed to Southampton, England, becoming the first ship of war to fly the Confederate flag in English waters. On November 19, she captured and burned the sailing merchantman *Harvey Birch* in the English Channel. Returning to the United States, she captured and burned the schooner *Robert Gilfillan* on February 26, 1862. These two prizes were valued at $66,000. She ran the blockade and arrived in Beaufort, North Carolina on February 28. She remained there until mid-March, when she went to Georgetown, South Carolina.

The *Nashville* was sold to a private party and operated as a blockade runner under the name *Thomas L. Wragg*, but her deep draft limited her effectiveness. She was sold again in November and became the privateer *Rattlesnake*. Her silhouette was lowered and she received heavier guns. In February 1863 she sailed for Fort McAllister on the Ogeechee River to prepare to head to sea. The arrival of the *Montauk* caused her to retire on February 27 and she ran aground in Seven Mile Reach a short distance above the fort.

The next day, the *Montauk* engaged her with 11 inch (280 mm) and 15 inch (381 mm) guns at a range of 1,200 yards (1,092 m) while other Federal ships shelled Fort McAllister. The *Rattlesnake* caught on fire and her magazine exploded. By mid-afternoon she had burned to the water's edge.

Salvage Work

The wreck was partially salvaged between 1866 and 1868 and again in 1888. Divers with the Georgia Historical Society salvaged much of the ship's machinery and other items between 1956 and 1959 for the Fort McAllister Museum. During the 1960s and 1970s, the Army Corps of Engineers lowered the wreck to reduce it as a navigational hazard. Private salvagers worked the wreck extensively over the next two decades and tried to claim salvage rights, but the State of Georgia won a lawsuit establishing its claim to the wreck.

SPECIFICATIONS

DISPLACEMENT: 1,221 tons (1,108 tonnes)

DIMENSIONS: 225 ft 6 in x 34 ft 6 in x 21 ft 9 in (68.73 m x 10.52 m x 6.63 m)

ARMAMENT: Two 12 pounder guns (1862)

MACHINERY: Sails and steam engine

SPEED: unknown

CREW: 130

CSS *Rattlesnake*

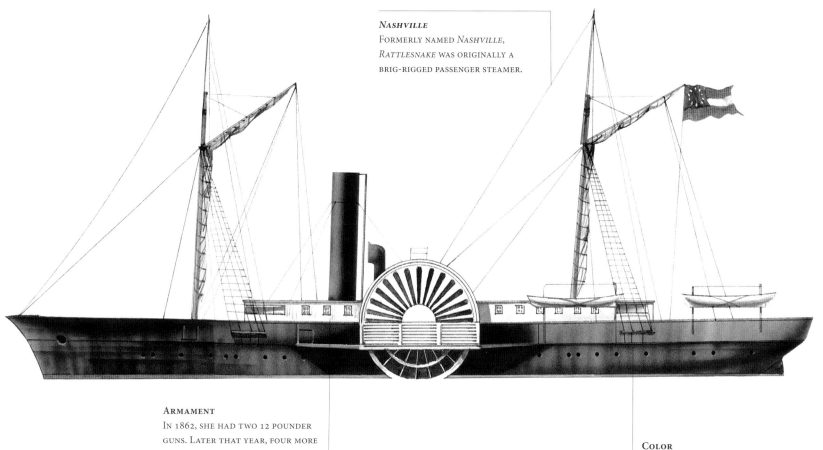

NASHVILLE
FORMERLY NAMED *NASHVILLE*, *RATTLESNAKE* WAS ORIGINALLY A BRIG-RIGGED PASSENGER STEAMER.

ARMAMENT
IN 1862, SHE HAD TWO 12 POUNDER GUNS. LATER THAT YEAR, FOUR MORE GUNS WERE ADDED.

COLOR
SHE WAS PAINTED GRAY TO REDUCE HER VISIBILITY.

CSS *Sumter* (1861)

THE *SUMTER* WAS BUILT IN 1859 AS THE BARK-RIGGED STEAMER *HABANA* FOR MCCONNELL'S NEW ORLEANS & HAVANA LINE. SHE WAS PURCHASED IN NEW ORLEANS IN APRIL 1861 AND CONVERTED TO A CRUISER BY CAPTAIN RAPHAEL SEMMES. SHE WAS COMMISSIONED ON JUNE 3 AND SOON PUT TO SEA AS A COMMERCE RAIDER.

On June 30, the *Sumter* took advantage of the blockader *Brooklyn* having left her station in pursuit of another ship and raced out of Pass a l'Outre. Once the *Brooklyn* noticed the *Sumter*, she gave chase, but the *Sumter* escaped. She then cruised the West Indies and south to Maranhao, Brazil, capturing several prizes. She returned to Martinique, where she was discovered in the act of coaling by the *Iroquois*, whose captain protested to local authorities and prepared to intercept the *Sumter* leaving St. Pierre.

Nine days later the *Sumter* escaped under cover of darkness and reached Cadiz, Spain on January 4, 1862. By then, however, American protests were pressing European authorities to enforce their neutrality laws. The *Sumter* was allowed only to make necessary repairs, and then, without refueling, was forced to go to Gibraltar. With his hands full, Confederate naval agent in Europe James

Bulloch on November 25 ordered James Wilson, an agent of Fraser, Trenholm and Company, to sell the *Sumter*. Lieutenant Robert Chapman succeeded in fulfilling this transaction by finding a British buyer. Although Bulloch feared the *Chippewa* might try to intercept the ship's move to Britain, the residual tensions from the *Trent* Affair dissuaded the United States from interfering with a ship now flying the British flag.

Prize Raider

In a period of just six months, the *Sumter* had taken 18 prizes and diverted Federal resources away from the blockade. She now began a new career as the Liverpool-based blockade runner *Gibraltar*. As such, she ran at least once into Wilmington, North Carolina under Captain E.C. Reid. Still carefully watching the former *Sumter*, the U.S. Consul in Britain protested when Reid departed Liverpool on July 3, 1863,

complaining the *Gibraltar* "is one of the privileged class and not held down like other vessels to strict rules and made to conform to regulations." Reid's cargo included a pair of 22 ton (20 tonne) Blakely guns and other munitions. He returned with a full load of cotton. The last official report of her was on July 10, 1864 when the U.S. Consul at Liverpool recorded, "The pirate *Sumter* (called *Gibraltar*) is laid up at Birkenhead."

SPECIFICATIONS

DISPLACEMENT: 449 tons (407 tonnes)

DIMENSIONS: 184 ft x 30 ft x 12 ft (56 m x 9.1 m x 3.7 m)

ARMAMENT: One 8 in (203 mm) shell gun; four 32 pounders

MACHINERY: Screw steam and sail

SPEED: 10 knots

CREW: 18

CSS *Sumter*

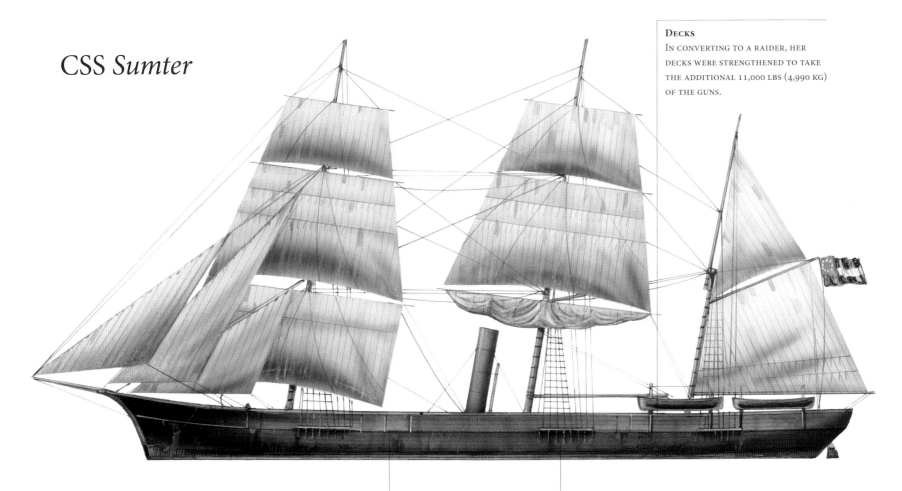

DECKS
IN CONVERTING TO A RAIDER, HER
DECKS WERE STRENGTHENED TO TAKE
THE ADDITIONAL 11,000 LBS (4,990 KG)
OF THE GUNS.

BULWARKS
SECTIONS 12 FT (3.66 M) WIDE WERE
CUT INTO THE BULWARKS AND COULD
BE HINGED BACK, ALLOWING THE DECK
GUNS A WIDE ARC OF FIRE.

MACHINERY
THE ENGINES WERE PARTLY ABOVE THE WATERLINE.
IRON BARS WERE PLACED TO PROTECT THE UPPER
PARTS OF THE ENGINES.

CSS *Alabama* (1862)

THE CSS *ALABAMA* WAS THE MOST FAMOUS AND EFFECTIVE OF THE CONFEDERATE COMMERCE RAIDERS, SINKING, BURNING OR CAPTURING 69 SHIPS VALUED AT $6 MILLION IN HER IMPRESSIVE CAREER. THE *ALABAMA* WAS A 1,050 TON (952 TONNE) SCREW STEAM SLOOP OF WAR BUILT IN BIRKENHEAD, ENGLAND AS PART OF JAMES BULLOCH'S COVERT EFFORTS TO OBTAIN SHIPS FOR THE CONFEDERACY.

John Laird Sons and Company built the ship, and she was launched as the *Enrica*, under the guise of being a merchant ship. She then rendezvoused with supply ships and was outfitted out at sea as a cruiser and commissioned as the *Alabama* on August 24, 1862. Captain Raphael Semmes was her flamboyant and driven captain.

The *Alabama* cruised in the North Atlantic and West Indies throughout 1862, capturing over two dozen Union merchant ships. Most of the prizes were burned with the notable exception of the mail steamer *Ariel*, which was taken off Cuba on December 7 with hundreds of passengers onboard.

On January 11, 1863, Semmes descended on Galveston, Texas, planning to harass a Federal force he thought was assembling there. In reality, Confederate forces had recently recaptured the city, and Semmes took advantage of the changed situation to sink the *Hatteras*. He then sailed the *Alabama* into the South Atlantic, stopping in Cape Town in August, continuing on to the East Indies, and making a call in Singapore in December. Throughout 1863, the *Alabama* seized nearly 40 more merchantmen and created panic in the maritime trade of the United States.

Fight Off Cherbourg

As Semmes pressed the *Alabama*, heavy usage began to take its toll. The ship's speed was slowed, and the *Alabama* only captured a few ships in 1864. Realizing a major overhaul was needed, Semmes brought the *Alabama* to Cherbourg, France on June 11 for repairs. The *Kearsarge* soon arrived off the port, and on June 19 the *Alabama* steamed out to meet the challenge. In an hour of intense combat, the *Kearsarge* sunk the *Alabama*. Most of the Confederates were rescued by the *Kearsarge*, but others, including Semmes, succeeded in escaping to the English yacht *Deerhound*.

The French naval mine hunter *Circe* discovered the *Alabama*'s remains while conducting operational exercises off Cherbourg, France in 1984. Since then, French and American researchers have conducted archaeological investigations of the site.

SPECIFICATIONS

DISPLACEMENT: 1,050 tons (953 tonnes)

DIMENSIONS: 220 ft x 31 ft 8 in x 17 ft 8 in (67 m x 9.65 m x 5.38 m)

ARMAMENT: Six 32 pounder cannons; one 110 pounder cannon; one 68 pounder cannon

MACHINERY: Two 300 hp (224 kW) horizontal steam engines; single-screw propeller; auxiliary sails

SPEED: 13 knots

CREW: 114

CSS *Alabama*

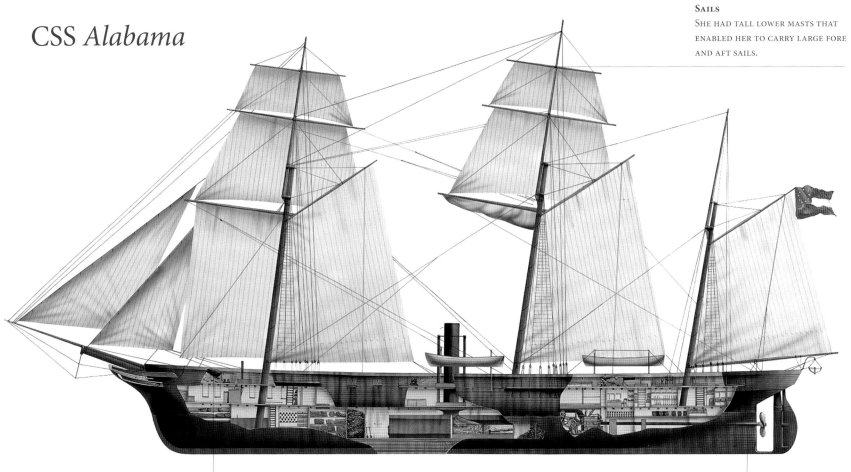

SAILS
SHE HAD TALL LOWER MASTS THAT
ENABLED HER TO CARRY LARGE FORE
AND AFT SAILS.

ARMAMENT
HER ARMAMENT CONSISTED OF SIX 32
POUNDER GUNS, ONE 110 POUNDER GUN,
AND ONE 68 POUNDER GUN.

SCREW
SHE WAS FITTED WITH A LIFTING SCREW, WHICH
COULD BE RAISED IN 15 MINUTES, REDUCING THE
DRAG OF AN IDLING PROPELLER WHEN ONLY SAIL
WAS BEING USED.

CSS *Florida* (1862)

THE *FLORIDA* WAS ONE OF THE CONFEDERATE SHIPS BUILT IN ENGLAND AS THE RESULT OF EFFORTS BY JAMES BULLOCH. SHE WAS A STEAM-SCREW CRUISER OF ABOUT 700 TONS (635 TONNES). SHE WAS BUILT UNDER THE ITALIAN-SOUNDING NAME *ORETO* IN AN EFFORT TO CONVINCE SUSPICIOUS ONLOOKERS SHE WAS BEING BUILT FOR ITALIAN INTERESTS RATHER THAN THE CONFEDERACY.

She sailed in March 1862 for the Bahamas as a merchant ship under the British flag and with a British captain. She carried no guns or other military stores, and the only Confederate presence on board was Acting Master John Low. Upon arrival at Nassau, Low turned the ship over to Lieutenant John Maffitt, who would earn the nickname "Prince of the Privateers."

Still under much international scrutiny, Maffitt fitted her as a naval vessel and commissioned her as the *Florida* in August 1862. He took her first to Cuba and then to Mobile, Alabama, where she completed her outfitting and repaired damage sustained while running the Union blockade.

The *Florida* ran the blockade again on January 16, 1863 and began an eight-month cruise in the Atlantic and West Indies. She captured 22 prizes before going in August 1863 to Brest, France, where she lay in the French government dock. His health broken by yellow fever, Maffitt was forced to relinquish command to Lieutenant Charles Morris.

In February 1864 the *Florida* took to sea again. She bunkered at Barbados, skirted the coast of the United States, and sailed east to Tenerife in the Canary Islands. She took another 11 prizes in total before arriving in Bahia, Brazil in October 1864.

Neutrality Violated

On October 7, she was attacked by the *Wachusett* while anchored in port with her captain and half her crew ashore. Virtually defenseless, she was captured and towed to sea. This act was a violation of Brazilian neutrality, and after the *Florida* was taken to the U.S., a court ordered her returned to Brazil.

On November 28, she was sunk off Newport News, Virginia after a collision with the USAT *Alliance*, a troop ferry. Some observers doubt if this collision was purely accidental. Regardless, the *Florida* was unable to be returned to Brazil.

SPECIFICATIONS

DISPLACEMENT: 700 tons (635 tonnes)

DIMENSIONS: 191 ft x 27 ft 2 in x 13 ft (58 m x 8.28 m x 4.0 m)

ARMAMENT: Six 6 in (152 mm) Blakely rifles; two 7 in (178 mm) Blakely rifles; one 12 pounder gun

MACHINERY: Sails and steam engine

SPEED: 9.5 knots; 12 under canvas

CREW: 146

CSS *Florida*

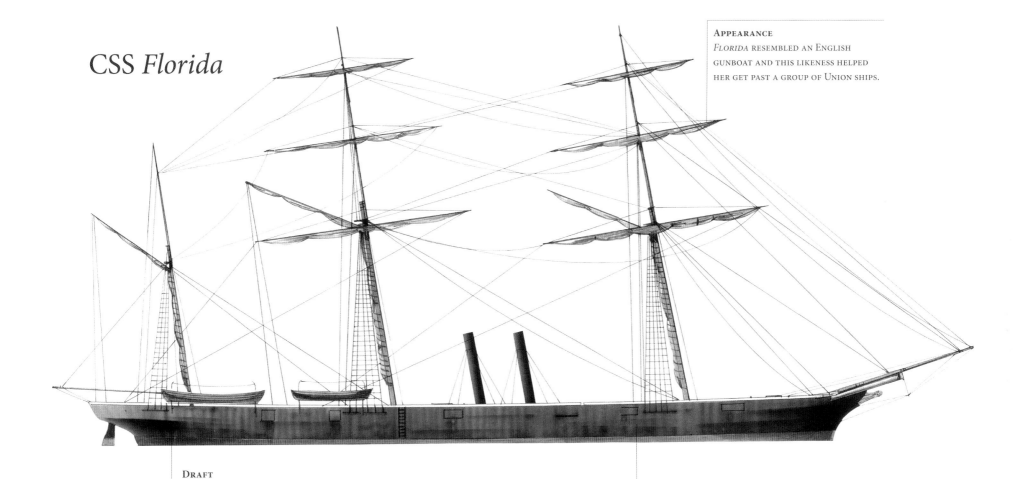

APPEARANCE
FLORIDA RESEMBLED AN ENGLISH
GUNBOAT AND THIS LIKENESS HELPED
HER GET PAST A GROUP OF UNION SHIPS.

DRAFT
HER DEEP 13 FT (3.96 M) DRAFT FORCED
HER TO BE ANCHORED 28 MILES (45 M)
FROM MOBILE, ALABAMA.

ARMAMENT
SHE WAS ARMED WITH TWO 7 IN
(178 MM) BLAKELY RIFLES, SIX 6 IN
(152 MM) BLAKELY RIFLES, AND ONE
12 POUNDER HOWITZER.

CSS *Georgia* (1863)

THE *GEORGIA* WAS BUILT IN 1862 AS THE FAST MERCHANTMAN *JAPAN*. SHE WAS PURCHASED AT DUMBARTON, SCOTLAND IN MARCH 1863 BY COMMANDER MATTHEW MAURY, WHO, LIKE HER CAPTAIN, NEVER SAW THE SHIP. THE PURCHASE WAS BASED ON THE RECOMMENDATION OF CAPTAIN MARVIN JENSEN OF THE ROYAL NETHERLANDS NAVY AND OVER THE OBJECTION OF COMMANDER JAMES BULLOCH, WHO CONSIDERED HER IRON HULL ILL SUITED FOR SUSTAINED CRUISING OPERATIONS AND THAT SHE WOULD HAVE TO MAKE PORT ON A REGULAR BASIS TO HAVE HER HULL CLEANED.

In spite of this deficiency, Maury was apparently willing to settle for the *Japan* because of the difficulty in obtaining contracts for wood-constructed vessels in Britain (where copper bottoms were becoming increasingly popular). Even more debilitating was the fact that the ship's sail rig was designed for auxiliary use only, so she would have to find a neutral port where she could take on coal every 90 days or so.

Atlantic Raiding

The *Georgia* left Greenock, Scotland on April 1 and rendezvoused with the steamer *Alar* off Ushant, France. She took on guns, ordnance and other stores, and raised the Confederate flag on April 9 with William Maury, a distant cousin of Matthew Maury, in command. Maury had succeeded in acquiring the ship and getting her to sea in record time. That said, however, the *Georgia*

was certainly not of the same quality as the vessel's procured by Bulloch.

The *Georgia* took nine prizes on a cruise that crisscrossed the Atlantic. She ended up in Cherbourg, France on October 28. While undergoing repairs there, Maury protested the *Georgia*'s many deficiencies and asked to be relieved of command. He was replaced by Lieutenant William Evans, and it was decided that her armament would be shifted to the *Rappahannock*, but this transfer was never affected. Instead, the *Georgia* was moved to an anchorage 3 miles (5 km) below Bordeaux where she was effectively decommissioned. She was under close Federal surveillance in France and the mounting international pressure coupled with her poor performance resulted in the decision to sell her.

On May 2, 1864 she was taken to Liverpool and sold on June 1 over U.S. protests. She put to sea on August 11

only to be captured by the *Niagara* off Portugal four days later. She was then sent to Boston, Massachusetts, where she was condemned and sold as a prize of the United States.

SPECIFICATIONS

DISPLACEMENT: 700 tons (635 tonnes)

DIMENSIONS: 212 ft x 27 ft x 13 ft 9 in (65 m x 8.2 m x 4.19 m)

ARMAMENT: Two 100 pounder cannons; two 24 pounder cannons; one 32 pounder cannon

MACHINERY: Two steeples with a diameter of 54 in (1372 mm) and a 4-stroke engine

SPEED: Not known

CREW: Not known

CSS *Georgia*

DESIGN
GEORGIA WAS DESIGNED AS A FAST-SCREW, BRIG-RIGGED, MERCHANT STEAMER.

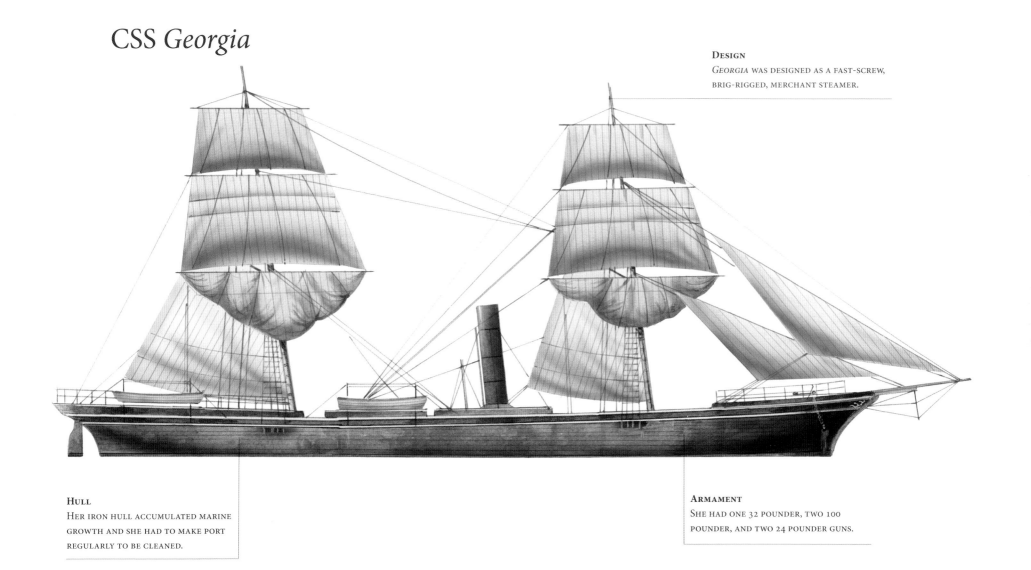

HULL
HER IRON HULL ACCUMULATED MARINE GROWTH AND SHE HAD TO MAKE PORT REGULARLY TO BE CLEANED.

ARMAMENT
SHE HAD ONE 32 POUNDER, TWO 100 POUNDER, AND TWO 24 POUNDER GUNS.

CSS *Rappahannock* (1863)

THE *RAPPAHANNOCK* WAS ORIGINALLY A STEAM SLOOP-OF-WAR NAMED *VICTOR* BUILT IN THE THAMES RIVER IN 1857 FOR THE BRITISH GOVERNMENT. IN SPITE OF HER IMPRESSIVE APPEARANCE, SHE HAD MANY DEFECTS. NONETHELESS, COMMANDER MATTHEW MAURY PURCHASED HER ON NOVEMBER 13, 1863 AND LIEUTENANT CHARLES FAUNTLEROY WAS PLACED IN COMMAND.

CSS *PAMPERO*

One recent scholar describes her as a "mechanical nightmare," and indeed in passing out of the Thames estuary her bearings burned out and she had to be sent to Calais for an immediate refit. There, French authorities initially wanted to detain her, but ultimately decided to let her depart but with only a crew of 35 rather than the 100 officers and men she had arrived with.

The *Rappahannock* had a wooden hull and other characteristics that seemingly better equipped her as a cruiser than the *Georgia*, which was another of Maury's marginal acquisitions. Indeed, at one point, Maury intended to shift the *Georgia*'s armament to the *Rappahannock*, but this transfer was never affected and she became little more than a floating depot. The ship Fauntleroy called "The Confederate White Elephant" never got to sea under the Confederate flag and was turned over to the United States at the close of the war.

CSS *Pampero* (1863)

The *Pampero* was a composite wood and iron steamship built for the Confederacy as a commerce raider at the James and George Thomson Shipyard in Glasgow, Scotland in 1863. She was similar in design to the *Alabama*. Lieutenant George Sinclair superintended the construction for the Confederacy, and she is often referred to as "Sinclair's ship." She was also known as the *Canton*.

The multiple names were part of an effort to conceal her true identity from British and American authorities bent on enforcing British neutrality laws, an effort that gained increased energy after the Federal victory at Antietam and the subsequent issuance of the Emancipation Proclamation that did much to curb British support for the Confederacy. The *Pampero* was launched in the Clyde River on about November 3, but was detained around November 30 before she could be commissioned under the intended name *Texas*.

SPECIFICATIONS

DISPLACEMENT: 857 tons (777 tonnes)

DIMENSIONS: 200 ft x 30 ft 4 in x 14 ft 6 in (61 m x 9.25 m x 4.42 m)

ARMAMENT: One 7 in (178 mm) 110 pounder breechloader; one 40 pounder breechloader; four 20 pounder breechloaders

MACHINERY: Two-cylinder, horizontal, single-expansion, single-screw steam engine

SPEED: 11.6 knots

CREW: 100

CSS *Rappahannock*

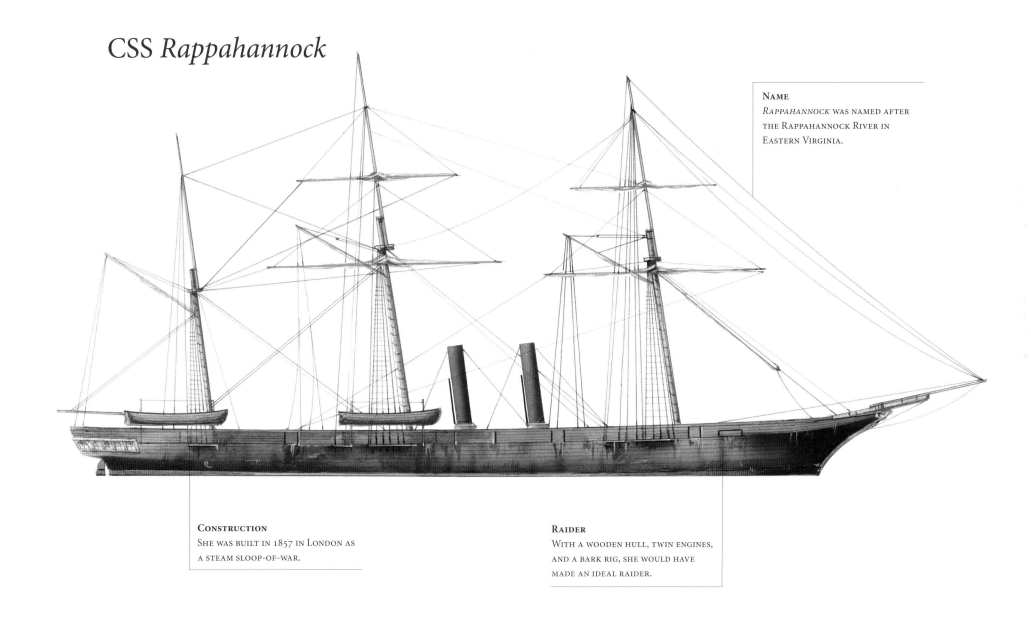

NAME

RAPPAHANNOCK WAS NAMED AFTER THE RAPPAHANNOCK RIVER IN EASTERN VIRGINIA.

CONSTRUCTION

SHE WAS BUILT IN 1857 IN LONDON AS A STEAM SLOOP-OF-WAR.

RAIDER

WITH A WOODEN HULL, TWIN ENGINES, AND A BARK RIG, SHE WOULD HAVE MADE AN IDEAL RAIDER.

CSS *Chickamauga* (1864)

THE *CHICKAMAUGA* WAS ORIGINALLY THE BLOCKADE RUNNER *EDITH*. SHE WAS PURCHASED BY THE CONFEDERATE NAVY IN WILMINGTON, NORTH CAROLINA IN 1864. ALTHOUGH THE ARMY SOUGHT TO RETAIN HER IN PLACE FOR USE AS A TROOP AND SUPPLY TRANSPORT, SHE PUT TO SEA ON OCTOBER 28 AS A COMMERCE RAIDER.

Her captain, Lieutenant John Wilkinson, was at first skeptical, noting, "She was more substantially built than most of the blockade runners, and was very swift, but altogether unfit for a cruiser, as she could only keep to sea while her supply of coal lasted." Nonetheless, she had an impressive, albeit short, career.

The *Chickamauga* bagged six prizes in the first five days after she ran the blockade at Wilmington. She took two more before November 5 when a frantic Secretary of the Navy Gideon Welles ordered nine warships to find the *Chickamauga* and other cruisers that were wreaking havoc on the Atlantic coast. Before the Federal trap could close, the *Chickamauga* escaped to St. George, Bermuda. There, however, 65 of Wilkinson's crew deserted and local officials refused to help the captain recover his men.

Considerably shorthanded, Wilkinson headed back to Wilmington, and when his pilot became disoriented in the heavy fog, Wilkinson himself brought the *Chickamauga* through the blockade on November 19. He paused above Fort Fisher and, thinking they had found a stranded blockade runner, Federal ships descended upon her. Wilkinson fired his own guns and, with the help of supporting fires from Fort Fisher, brought the *Chickamauga* safely into the Cape Fear River.

New Identity

During the first attack on Fort Fisher on December 24–25, some of the *Chickamauga*'s crew manned a battery of Brooke rifled cannons that had been salvaged from the sunken gunboat *Roanoke* and were unfamiliar to the fort's artillerymen. The ship also transported ammunition during the fight. Between the two battles, she fired on Federal soldiers who had intercepted the Confederate supply ship *Isaac Welles* at Craig's Landing. The *Chickamauga*'s guns dispersed the enemy, but sank the friendly ship as well. The *Chickamauga* was also present for the second battle on January 15, 1865, and periodically shelled Federal troops in their assembly areas and during the attack. After the defeat, the Confederate forces abandoned Wilmington on February 21. The *Chickamauga* retreated up the Cape Fear River to Indian Wells where her crew burned her.

SPECIFICATIONS

DISPLACEMENT: 586 tons (532 tonnes)

DIMENSIONS: Not known

ARMAMENT: One 12 pounder gun; one 32 pounder gun; one 64 pounder gun

MACHINERY: Steam engines

SPEED: Not known

CREW: 120

CSS *Chickamauga*

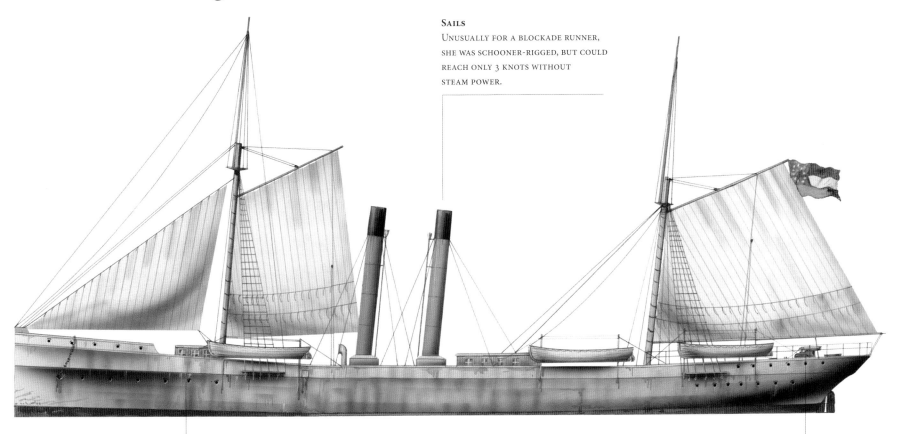

SAILS
UNUSUALLY FOR A BLOCKADE RUNNER, SHE WAS SCHOONER-RIGGED, BUT COULD REACH ONLY 3 KNOTS WITHOUT STEAM POWER.

DISPLACEMENT
SHE DISPLACED 586 TONS (532 TONNES).

GUNS
SHE HAD ONE 12 POUNDER, ONE 32 POUNDER, AND ONE 64 POUNDER AMIDSHIP.

CSS *Shenandoah* (1864)

THE *SHENANDOAH* WAS A 1,160 TON (1,052 TONNE) SCREW-STEAM CRUISER PURCHASED IN BRITAIN BY CONFEDERATE NAVAL AGENT JAMES BULLOCH. THE SHIP WAS LAUNCHED OUT OF GLASGOW, SCOTLAND IN AUGUST 1863 AS THE CIVILIAN STEAMER *SEA KING* AND THEN SECRETLY PURCHASED BY THE CONFEDERACY IN SEPTEMBER 1864. SHE PUT TO SEA IN OCTOBER 1864, UNDER THE COVER STORY THAT SHE WAS HEADED FOR INDIA ON A COMMERCIAL VOYAGE.

Instead, the *Sea King* rendezvoused at sea off Madeira with another ship bearing Confederate Navy officers, a partial crew, and the heavy guns and other equipment needed to refit her as a warship. Lieutenant James Waddell supervised this work and became the ship's commander when she was commissioned as the *Shenandoah* on October 19, 1864.

Waddell sailed the *Shenandoah* through the south Atlantic and into the Indian Ocean. By the end of the year, he had captured nine U.S. flagged merchant vessels, sinking or burning all but two. In late January 1865, the *Shenandoah* arrived in Melbourne, Australia, where she underwent repairs, took on provisions, and added 40 crew members. After spending three weeks in port, the *Shenandoah* returned to sea.

Waddell initially planned to attack the American South Pacific whaling fleet, but could not find sufficient targets. Instead, he headed for the North Pacific, and in early April he seized four Federal merchant ships in the Eastern Carolines. He resupplied his ship from the captured stocks and was cruising northwards when the Civil War ended. Unaware of the Confederacy's collapse, Waddell continued his mission. Between June 22 and 28, the *Shenandoah* captured two dozen more vessels. Waddell then plotted a course for San Francisco, California, which he believed would be weakly defended.

Surrender to the British

On August 2, Waddell encountered a British ship that had left San Francisco less than two weeks before. This crew informed Waddell that the war was over. Waddell then disarmed his ship and set sail for England. The *Shenandoah* rounded Cape Horn in mid-September and arrived in Liverpool in early November. Only then did Waddell haul down the Confederate ensign and turn the *Shenandoah* over to the Royal Navy.

During her storied career, the *Shenandoah* captured or destroyed 36 vessels valued at $1,400,000. She was the only Confederate Navy ship to circumnavigate the globe. In 1866, the *Shenandoah* was sold to the Sultan of Zanzibar and renamed *El Majidi*.

SPECIFICATIONS

DISPLACEMENT: 1,160 tons (1,052 tonnes)

DIMENSIONS: 230 ft x 32.5 ft x 20 ft (70 m x 9.9 m x 6.25 m)

ARMAMENT: Four 8 in (203 mm) smoothbores; two 32 pounders; two 12 pounder Whitworth rifled cannons

MACHINERY: 14 ft (4.3 m) diameter, bronze propeller engine

SPEED: 9 knots under steam

CREW: 109

CSS *Shenandoah*

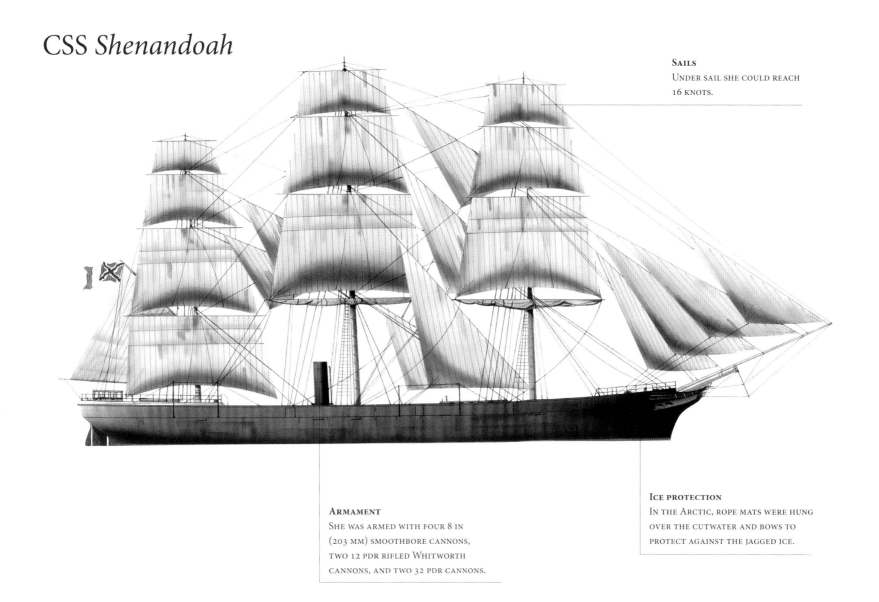

SAILS
UNDER SAIL SHE COULD REACH
16 KNOTS.

ARMAMENT
SHE WAS ARMED WITH FOUR 8 IN
(203 MM) SMOOTHBORE CANNONS,
TWO 12 PDR RIFLED WHITWORTH
CANNONS, AND TWO 32 PDR CANNONS.

ICE PROTECTION
IN THE ARCTIC, ROPE MATS WERE HUNG
OVER THE CUTWATER AND BOWS TO
PROTECT AGAINST THE JAGGED ICE.

CSS *Tallahassee* (1864)

THE *TALLAHASSEE* WAS ORIGINALLY THE BLOCKADE RUNNER *ATALANTA* (OR *ATLANTA*) BUILT BY THE J. & W. DUDGEON COMPANY OF MILLWALL, ENGLAND IN 1863. SHE HAD PASSED THROUGH THE BLOCKADE AT WILMINGTON, NORTH CAROLINA SEVERAL TIMES BEFORE SHE CAUGHT THE EYE OF JOHN TAYLOR WOOD WHO RECOMMENDED HER TO SECRETARY OF THE NAVY STEPHEN MALLORY AS A POTENTIAL COMMERCE RAIDER.

Mallory authorized her purchase, and she was outfitted with cannon and a crew of about 100 sailors drawn from Confederate gunboats on the James River and from North Carolina. She was renamed the *Tallahassee* on July 20, 1864 with Wood as her captain.

Wood took the ship through the blockade on August 6 and began a 19-day raid that struck panic in Federal shipping off the Atlantic coast as far north as Halifax, Nova Scotia. Taylor particularly targeted the waters off New York City, hoping to arouse Democratic and anti-war sentiment that had already manifested itself there in a bloody draft riot.

Insurance underwriters began pressing Secretary of the Navy Gideon Welles to protect their interests. "Will you please have the necessary measures taken, if not already done, to secure [the *Tallahassee*'s] capture" begged John Jones, president of the Board of Underwriters in New York. By August 15, Welles had dispatched a total of 16 vessels to pursue the *Tallahassee* but she eluded capture in the vastness of the ocean. Unable to receive the friendly welcome he had hoped for from authorities in Halifax, Wood was forced to return to Wilmington on August 26 for coal. On his brief but spectacular cruise, he had destroyed 26 vessels and captured seven others.

New Identity

In spite of the *Tallahassee*'s success, there was a vocal group in North Carolina that felt her activities as a commerce raider attracted unwelcome Federal attention to Wilmington and resulted in a tightening of the blockade there and an increased likelihood of attack. Bowing to these concerns, the *Tallahassee* was renamed the *Olustee* and placed under the command of Lieutenant William Ward, the former executive officer. She ran through the blockade off Wilmington again on October 29, taking some damage from Federal fire as she did. She captured and destroyed six ships off the Capes of Delaware before having to return for coal.

The *Olustee* next was renamed the *Chameleon* with Lieutenant John Wilkinson in command. She ran through the blockade on December 24 and went to Bermuda. Having taken on a cargo of supplies, Wilkinson found it impossible to reenter a Confederate port and instead headed for Liverpool, England, where he arrived on April 9, 1865. There, the *Chameleon* was seized by British authorities, but later awarded to the U.S. Government after a suit.

SPECIFICATIONS

DISPLACEMENT: About 500 tons (454 tonnes)

DIMENSIONS: 220 ft x 24 ft x 14 ft (67 m x 7.3 m x 4.3 m)

ARMAMENT: One 84 pounder gun; two 24 pounders; two 32 pounders

MACHINERY: Two 100 hp (74.5 kW) steam engines; two screws; mast and sails

SPEED: 17 knots

CREW: 120

CSS *Tallahassee*

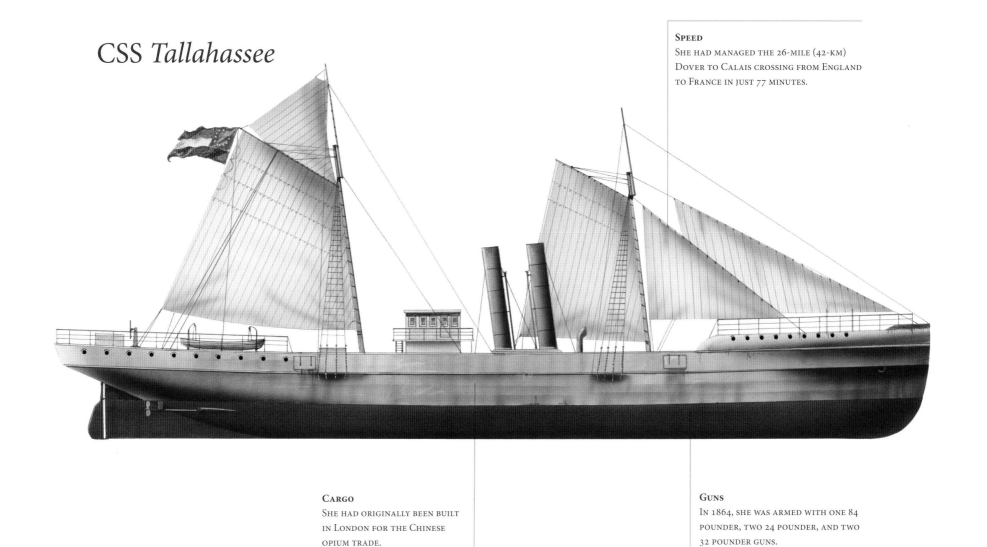

SPEED
SHE HAD MANAGED THE 26-MILE (42-KM) DOVER TO CALAIS CROSSING FROM ENGLAND TO FRANCE IN JUST 77 MINUTES.

CARGO
SHE HAD ORIGINALLY BEEN BUILT IN LONDON FOR THE CHINESE OPIUM TRADE.

GUNS
IN 1864, SHE WAS ARMED WITH ONE 84 POUNDER, TWO 24 POUNDER, AND TWO 32 POUNDER GUNS.

USS *Susquehanna* (1850)

THE *SUSQUEHANNA* WAS COMMISSIONED ON DECEMBER 24, 1850 WITH CAPTAIN JOHN AULICK IN COMMAND. HER PRE-CIVIL WAR SERVICE INCLUDED BEING PART OF COMMODORE MATTHEW PERRY'S EXPEDITION TO TOKYO BAY IN 1853. AT THE OUTBREAK OF THE CIVIL WAR SHE WAS AT LA SPEZIA, ITALY. SHE DEPARTED THERE AND REACHED BOSTON ON JUNE 6, 1861, WAS ASSIGNED TO THE ATLANTIC BLOCKADING SQUADRON, AND SAILED FOR HAMPTON ROADS.

In August, the *Susquehanna* participated in the attack at Hatteras Inlet, North Carolina. She captured two British schooners, the *Argonaut* and the *Prince Alfred*, and two Confederate schooners, the *San Juan* and the *Baltimore*, in September. She then helped Admiral Samuel Du Pont capture Port Royal, South Carolina in November. The *Susquehanna* then operated primarily on blockade duty off Charleston, where she took the British schooner *Coquette* on April 3, 1862.

On April 27, the *Susquehanna* was ordered to Hampton Roads to strengthen the North Atlantic Blockading Squadron in support of Major General George McClellan's Peninsula Campaign. On May 8, she was part of the bombardment of the Confederate positions at Sewell's Point, Virginia. Later that month, she was assigned to the West Gulf Blockading Squadron. On her way to that new station,

she captured the schooner *Princeton* on June 11. On June 29, she and the *Kanawha* seized the British steamer *Ann* trying to get into Mobile Bay. The *Susquehanna* continued to operate in the Gulf of Mexico until ordered to New York for repairs in the spring of 1863. En route, she captured the schooner *Alabama* off the Florida coast on April 18.

Bravery Award

The *Susquehanna* was recommissioned on July 20, 1864 and assigned to the North Atlantic Blockading Squadron, where she participated in both attacks on Fort Fisher, North Carolina. During the second attack, Landsman Henry Webster, a member of her crew, was awarded the Medal of Honor. His citation reads in part, "When enemy fire halted the attempt by his landing party to enter the fort and more than two-thirds of the men fell back along the open beach, Landsman

Webster voluntarily remained with one of his wounded officers, under fire, until aid could be obtained to bring him to the rear."

After the end of the Civil War, the *Susquehanna* served as the flagship of the North Atlantic Squadron and in the West Indies Squadron. She was decommissioned at the New York Navy Yard on January 14, 1868 and sold for scrap in 1883.

SPECIFICATIONS

DISPLACEMENT: 3,824 tons (3,469 tonnes)

DIMENSIONS: 257 ft x 45 ft x 20 ft 6 in (78 m x 14 m x 6.25 m)

ARMAMENT: Twelve 8 in (203 mm) guns; six 32 pounder guns (1851)

MACHINERY: Two inclined, direct-acting engines driving side-wheels

SPEED: 12.5 knots maximum

CREW: 300

USS *Susquehanna*

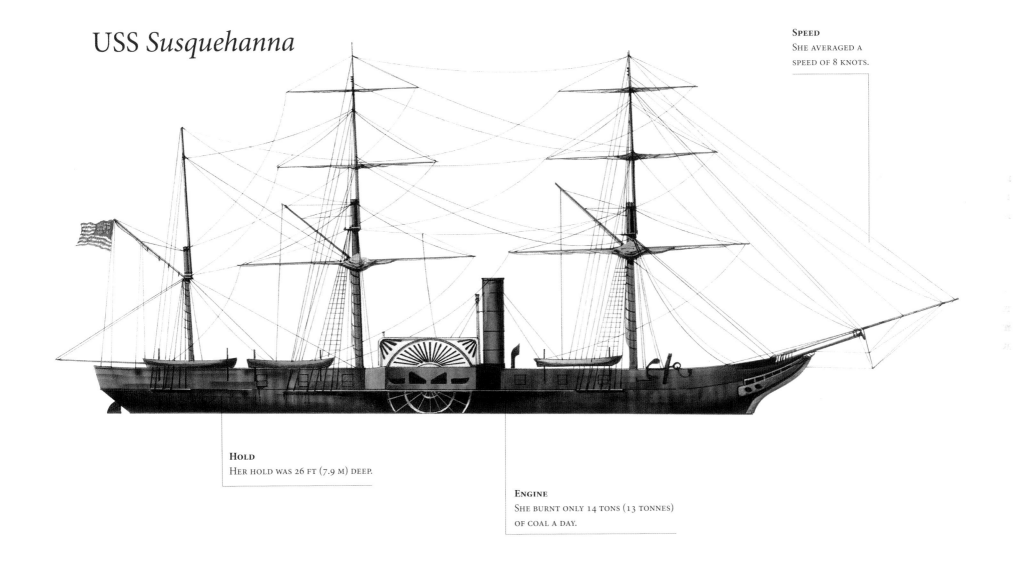

HOLD
HER HOLD WAS 26 FT (7.9 M) DEEP.

ENGINE
SHE BURNT ONLY 14 TONS (13 TONNES)
OF COAL A DAY.

USS *San Jacinto* (1851)

THE *SAN JACINTO* BEGAN ITS CAREER AS ONE OF THE NAVY'S EARLY SCREW WARSHIPS SOMETIME AROUND 1851. BEFORE THE CIVIL WAR BEGAN SHE WAS ON DUTY ON THE WEST COAST OF AFRICA, HELPING SUPPRESS THE SLAVE TRADE. ON AUGUST 8, 1860, SHE CAPTURED THE BRIG *STORM KING* OFF THE MOUTH OF THE CONGO RIVER, TURNING ITS CARGO OF 616 AFRICANS BOUND FOR SLAVERY OVER TO THE U.S. AUTHORITIES IN MONROVIA.

On August 27, 1861, Captain Charles Wilkes took command of the *San Jacinto*. While heading back to the United States, she joined in the search for the Confederate cruiser *Sumter*, which had been attacking Union shipping in the Atlantic. Wilkes was unable to find the *Sumter*, but when he stopped at Cienfuegos, Cuba, for coal, he learned that James Mason and John Slidell, Confederate envoys to England and France, had run the blockade at Charleston, South Carolina on October 12 aboard the *Theodora* and were now in Havana awaiting transportation to Europe.

"*Trent* Affair"

Wilkes was unable to intercept the *Theodora* before she departed Cuba, but learned that Mason and Slidell were still at Havana, intending to sail for St. Thomas a week later aboard the English mail packet *Trent* for the next leg of their journey. Wilkes moved to a choke point from which he could intercept the *Trent* and waited. The *Trent* set sail on November 7 and the next day, Wilkes fired two shots across her bow and sent a boarding party to seize Mason and Slidell. He then allowed the *Trent* to continue on her way and took his two captives to Boston.

Although Wilkes had acted without orders, he was immediately hailed as a hero in most circles in the North. However, he also created an international incident because the British considered his act to be a blatant violation of their neutrality and freedom of the seas, as well as an insult to them as a great power. The ensuing "*Trent* Affair" created a crisis that nearly brought Europe into the war.

The remainder of the Civil War career of the *San Jacinto* was active, but by no means as famous as the *Trent* Affair. She spent her time on blockade duty or chasing commerce raiders and often served as flagship. She was twice quarantined as a result of yellow fever outbreaks on board and spent several periods undergoing repairs. On January 1, 1865, she struck a reef near Great Abaco Island and filled with water. Her guns were saved, but efforts to salvage the ship were unsuccessful.

SPECIFICATIONS

DISPLACEMENT: 2,150 tons (1,950 tonnes)

DIMENSIONS: 234 ft x 37 ft 9 in x 16 ft 6 in (71 m x 11.51 m x 5.03 m)

ARMAMENT: One 11 in (279 mm) smoothbore; ten 9 in (228 mm) smoothbores

MACHINERY: Steam engine; screw propeller

SPEED: Not known

CREW: 235

ENGINES
THE SPACE ALLOCATED TO THE ENGINES
WAS TOO SMALL AND INCREASED
MAINTENANCE PROBLEMS.

USS *San Jacinto*

PROPELLER
THE USE OF A PONDEROUS 7 TON
(6 TONNE) SCREW PROPELLER WAS
FORCED UPON THE DESIGNER TO
AVOID A PATENT CLASH.

ARMAMENT
IN 1862, SHE WAS ARMED WITH ONE 11
IN (279 MM) Dahlgren SMOOTHBORE
AND TEN 9 IN (228 MM) SMOOTHBORES.

USS *Powhatan* (1852)

THE *POWHATAN* WAS LAUNCHED ON FEBRUARY 14, 1850 BY THE NORFOLK NAVY YARD AND COMMISSIONED ON SEPTEMBER 2, 1852 WITH CAPTAIN WILLIAM MERVINE IN COMMAND. SHE HAD AN ACTIVE CAREER BEFORE THE CIVIL WAR, INCLUDING SERVING AS COMMODORE MATTHEW PERRY'S FLAGSHIP WHEN HE SIGNED THE COMMERCIAL TREATY WITH JAPAN AT TOKYO BAY ON MARCH 31, 1854.

At the onset of the Civil War she returned home from Vera Cruz and was originally slated to be part of an expedition to relieve Major Robert Anderson's besieged command at Fort Sumter, South Carolina. She was diverted from this mission, a decision that delayed the other ships as they waited for her rendezvous and left the relief force weakened by her loss of firepower. Instead, the *Powhatan* was dispatched to Fort Pickens, Florida which, like Fort Sumter, had remained occupied by Federal forces after Florida seceded from the Union.

With Lieutenant David Porter in command, the *Powhatan* arrived off Pensacola on April 20. The aggressive Porter wanted to force the harbor and engage the inner Confederate works, but Army Captain Montgomery Meigs, who had arrived a day before, counseled caution. A frustrated Porter guided the *Powhatan* into a position of guard duty to search incoming vessels while he waited for the situation to develop.

Mobile Blockade

Once the Federals secured their position at Fort Pickens, the *Powhatan* went with Porter to establish the blockade off Mobile and Mississippi. She captured the schooner *Mary Clinton* on May 29 and retook the schooner *Abby Bradford* on August 15. From late August to October, she was part of the unsuccessful pursuit of the *Sumter* throughout much of the West Indies.

The *Powhatan* operated off Charleston, South Carolina from October 1862 to August 1863, capturing the schooner *Major E. Willis* on April 19 and the sloop *C. Routereau* on May 16. She then returned to the West Indies from November 1863 to September 1864 as the flagship of Admiral James Lardner.

She participated in both the December 24–25, 1864 and the January 13–15, 1865 attacks on Fort Fisher, North Carolina.

The *Powhatan* continued to have an active career after the Civil War, including service as Admiral John Dahlgren's flagship of the Home Squadron. She was decommissioned in 1886.

SPECIFICATIONS

DISPLACEMENT: 3,765 tons (3,416 tonnes)

DIMENSIONS: 253 ft 8 in x 45 ft x 18ft 6 in (77.32 m x 14 m x 5.64 m)

ARMAMENT: One 11 in (279 mm) smoothbore; ten 9 in (228 mm) smoothbores; four 12 pounder guns

MACHINERY: Two inclined, direct-acting engines driving side-wheels

SPEED: 11 knots

CREW: 300

USS *Powhatan*

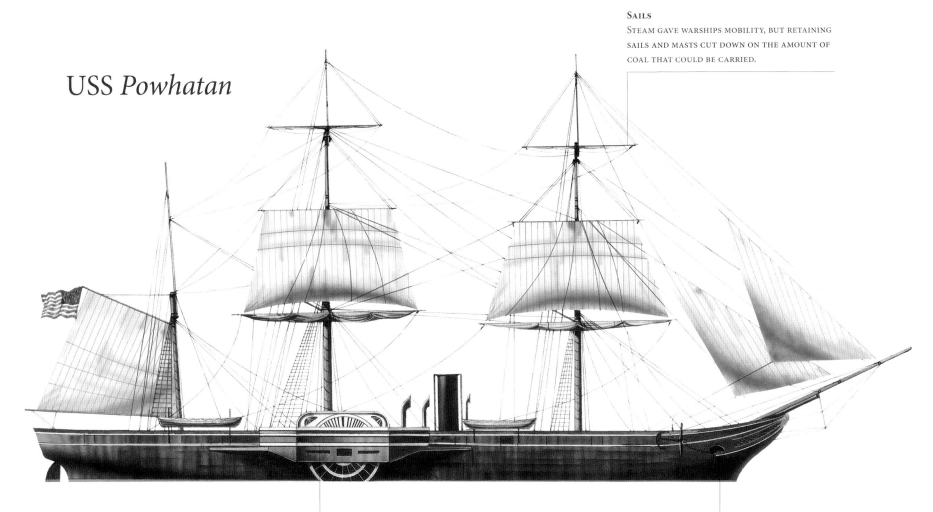

SAILS
STEAM GAVE WARSHIPS MOBILITY, BUT RETAINING SAILS AND MASTS CUT DOWN ON THE AMOUNT OF COAL THAT COULD BE CARRIED.

PADDLES
AT HER PADDLE BOXES SHE WAS 69 FT 6 IN (21 M) WIDE.

ARMAMENT
IN 1861, SHE HAD ONE 11 IN (279 MM) DAHLGREN SMOOTHBORE AND TEN 9 IN (228 MM) DAHLGREN SMOOTHBORES, PLUS SMALLER ARMAMENTS.

USS *Brooklyn* *(1859)*

THE *BROOKLYN* WAS COMMISSIONED ON JANUARY 26, 1859 WITH CAPTAIN DAVID FARRAGUT IN COMMAND. SHE WAS ACTIVE IN SUPPORTING AMERICAN INTERESTS IN MEXICO BEFORE THE OUTBREAK OF THE CIVIL WAR. ON OCTOBER 20, 1860, CAPTAIN WILLIAM WALKER RELIEVED FARRAGUT AS COMMANDER.

In February, the *Brooklyn* helped Federal forces retain Fort Pickens, Florida and then sailed west along the gulf coast to establish the blockade of the Mississippi Passes. She assisted in capturing a number of ships off Pass a l'Outre and Southwest Pass, but the commerce raider Sumter succeeded in escaping past her on June 30. In need of repairs, the *Brooklyn* sailed north late in the autumn and was decommissioned at the Philadelphia Navy Yard.

She was recommissioned on December 19 with Captain Thomas Craven in command. On February 2, 1862, she was back at Pass a l'Outre, where, on February 19, she captured the steamer *Magnolia*, which was attempting to slip out to sea with 1,200 bales of cotton. She played an active role when Farragut attacked New Orleans on April 24 and survived fire from the Confederate forts and attacks by the ram *Manassas* and a fire raft. Eight of her men were killed and 21 wounded in the battle. She required a patch of heavy planking some 24 feet (7.3 m) long to cover a long tear in her hull sustained from her collision with the *Manassas*.

Attack on Donaldsville

The *Brooklyn* was obstructed by friendly ships and was unable to pass Vicksburg when Farragut ascended the Mississippi on his second mission on June 28. On July 2, Captain Henry Bell relieved Craven in command, and in August, the *Brooklyn* took part in the attack on Donaldsonville, Louisiana. She then steamed to Pensacola for more permanent repairs to the damage she had suffered at New Orleans. Those repairs complete, she spent the rest of 1862 on blockade duty off Mobile Bay.

Farragut dispatched Bell to Galveston, Texas in January 1863 after the Confederates recaptured that key port and the *Brooklyn* helped reestablish the blockade there, although Galveston remained in Confederate hands. On August 10, she sailed to the New York Navy Yard for repairs and was recommissioned on April 14, 1864 with Captain James Alden in command. She rejoined the squadron off Mobile Bay and participated in Farragut's attack there on August 5, suffering 54 men killed and 43 wounded in a fierce battle.

The *Brooklyn* departed Mobile Bay on September 6 and headed for Hampton Roads for service in the North Atlantic Blockading Squadron. She participated in both attacks on Fort Fisher, North Carolina and was decommissioned at the New York Navy Yard on January 31, 1865.

SPECIFICATIONS

DISPLACEMENT: 2,532 tons (2,297 tonnes)

DIMENSIONS: 233 ft x 43 ft x 16 ft 3 in (71 m x 13 m x 4.95 m)

ARMAMENT: One 10 in (254 mm) smoothbore gun; one 30 pounder Parrott rifle; twenty 9 in (228 mm) Dahlgren smoothbore guns (1861)

MACHINERY: Two horizontal condensing cross-head engines driving a single screw

SPEED: 11.5 knots

CREW: 335

USS *Brooklyn*

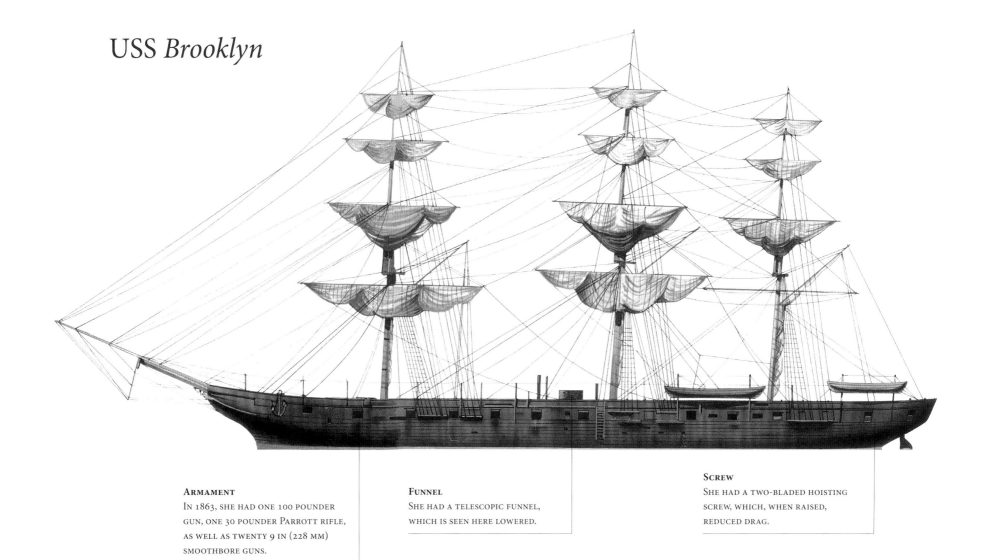

ARMAMENT
IN 1863, SHE HAD ONE 100 POUNDER
GUN, ONE 30 POUNDER PARROTT RIFLE,
AS WELL AS TWENTY 9 IN (228 MM)
SMOOTHBORE GUNS.

FUNNEL
SHE HAD A TELESCOPIC FUNNEL,
WHICH IS SEEN HERE LOWERED.

SCREW
SHE HAD A TWO-BLADED HOISTING
SCREW, WHICH, WHEN RAISED,
REDUCED DRAG.

USS *Hartford* (1859)

THE *HARTFORD* WAS LAUNCHED ON NOVEMBER 22, 1858 AND COMMISSIONED ON MAY 27, 1859 WITH CAPTAIN CHARLES LOWNDES IN COMMAND. SHE WAS ON DUTY IN THE FAR EAST AT THE OUTBREAK OF THE CIVIL WAR AND WAS ORDERED HOME, WHERE SHE BECAME THE FLAGSHIP OF ADMIRAL DAVID FARRAGUT, COMMANDER OF THE WEST GULF BLOCKADING SQUADRON.

Farragut was aboard the *Hartford* for his spectacular victory at New Orleans on April 24, 1861, dodging an attack by the ironclad *Manassas*. He then proceeded up the Mississippi in an effort to take the Confederate stronghold at Vicksburg, but found such a venture would not be possible without a cooperating Army force.

He returned downriver, and on March 14, 1863 he attempted to run a fleet of seven ships past the formidable Confederate position at Port Hudson, Louisiana. Only the *Hartford* and the *Albatross* succeeded, enabling them to block the mouth of the Red River, but the garrison of Port Hudson stubbornly held on. The *Hartford* and her sister ships then began patrolling between Port Hudson and Vicksburg to help isolate the trans-Mississippi from the rest of the Confederacy.

With the Federal victory at Vicksburg on July 4, 1863, Farragut turned his attention to Mobile Bay. When he attacked there on August 5, 1864, his lead vessel, the *Tecumseh*, struck a torpedo and went down swiftly, threatening to unravel Farragut's plan. Remarkably spry for a 63-year-old, Farragut had climbed the rigging of the *Hartford*'s mainmast to ascertain the situation. Farragut knew the battle had reached its crisis point, and he knew what he had to do. "I shall lead," he said famously. "Damn the torpedoes! Full speed ahead." With that, the *Hartford*, with the *Metacomet* lashed alongside, turned sharply to the port and led the Federal attack through the minefield into Mobile Bay.

Hard-Earned Victory

When the ironclad *Tennessee* made one last desperate run against the Federal fleet, the *Lackawanna* accidentally rammed the *Hartford*, momentarily endangering Farragut himself, before the *Tennessee* was forced to surrender. Farragut considered Mobile Bay "one of the hardest-earned victories of my life," and reported the *Hartford* as "greatly cut up."

The *Hartford* sailed to New York on December 13 and was decommissioned for repairs a week later. After these were complete, she continued to serve long after the Civil War in the Pacific and elsewhere until she was placed out of commission on August 20, 1926.

SPECIFICATIONS

DISPLACEMENT: 2,900 tons (2,631 tonnes)

DIMENSIONS: 225 ft x 44 ft x 17 ft 2 in (69 m x 13 m x 5.23 m)

ARMAMENT: Twenty 9 in (228 mm) smoothbores; two 20 pounder rifles; two 12 pounder rifles

MACHINERY: Two horizontal, condensing, double-piston engines driving a single screw

SPEED: 13.5 knots

CREW: 310

USS *Hartford*

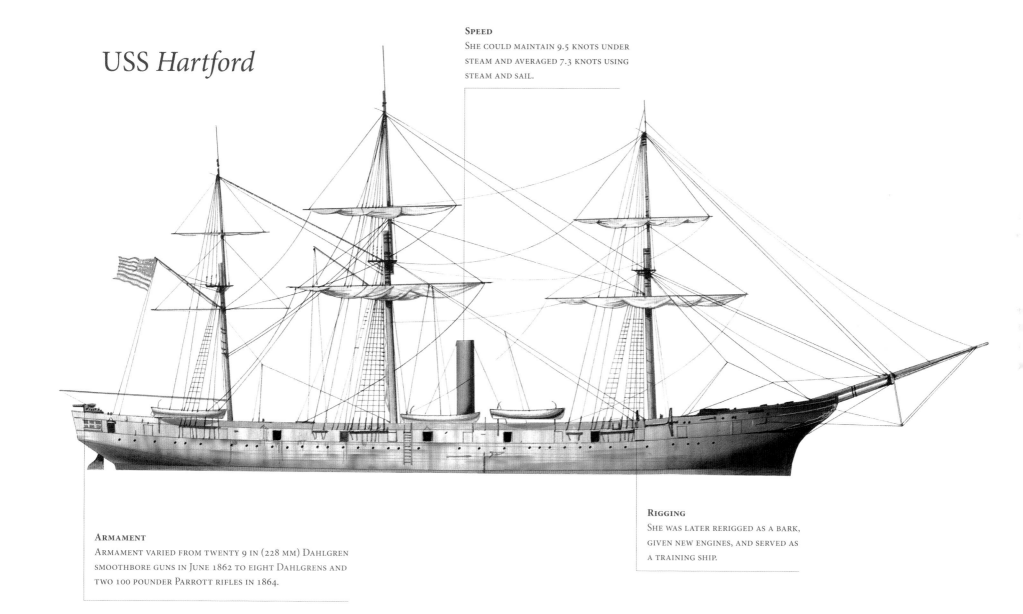

RIGGING
SHE WAS LATER RERIGGED AS A BARK,
GIVEN NEW ENGINES, AND SERVED AS
A TRAINING SHIP.

ARMAMENT
ARMAMENT VARIED FROM TWENTY 9 IN (228 MM) DAHLGREN
SMOOTHBORE GUNS IN JUNE 1862 TO EIGHT DAHLGRENS AND
TWO 100 POUNDER PARROTT RIFLES IN 1864.

USS *Iroquois* (1859)

THE *IROQUOIS* WAS COMMISSIONED ON NOVEMBER 24, 1859 WITH COMMANDER J.S. PALMER IN COMMAND. BEFORE THE CIVIL WAR, SHE OPERATED IN THE MEDITERRANEAN IN AN EFFORT TO STABILIZE ITALY. SHE ARRIVED IN NEW YORK ON JUNE 15, 1861 AND WAS IMMEDIATELY SENT TO THE CARIBBEAN TO SEARCH FOR CONFEDERATE COMMERCE RAIDERS.

At Martinique she found CSS *Sumter* anchored in the harbor. But the Confederate ship, with the assistance of the French authorities, slipped out on 23 November to resume attacks on Union shipping. *Iroquois* continued her patrol in the Caribbean, stopping British sloop *Rinaldo*, which was carrying Confederate ministers; they were allowed to proceed under serveillance.

The *Iroquois* participated in the April 24, 1862 attack on New Orleans, and then advanced up the Mississippi River, where she received the surrender of Baton Rouge on May 8. With the *Oneida*, she took possession of Natchez on May 13. She passed the powerful Vicksburg batteries on June 28, surviving the action virtually unscathed. The *Iroquois* remained in the Vicksburg area until late July, helping in the bombardments and preparations for expeditions into the surrounding marshlands. After she returned to blockade duty in the Gulf of Mexico, she experienced boiler trouble. She arrived in New York on October 2 for repairs.

Blockade Duty

Recommissioned on January 8, 1863 with Commander Henry Roland now in command, the *Iroquois* joined the North Atlantic Blockading Squadron off North Carolina. There she captured the blockade runner *Merrimack* on July 24 and helped in the capture of the *Kate* 12 days later. After several more months of blockade duty, she steamed to Baltimore for repairs.

The *Iroquois* was recommissioned on March 31, 1864 with Commander C.R.P. Rodgers in command. She steamed to the Mediterranean to protect American commerce and took part in the search for the raider *Shenandoah,* arriving Singapore in May 1865 after a long voyage around South America and across the Pacific. She was decommissioned on October 6, 1865.

SPECIFICATIONS

DISPLACEMENT: 1,488 tons (1,350 tonnes)

DIMENSIONS: 198 ft 11 in x 33 ft 10 in x 13 ft 10 in (60.63 m x 10.31 m x 4.22 m)

ARMAMENT: One 50 pounder Dahlgren rifle; two 11 in (279 mm) Dahlgren smoothbore guns; four 32 pounder guns

MACHINERY: Two horizontal steeple engines driving a single screw

SPEED: 11.5 knots

CREW: 123

USS *Iroquois*

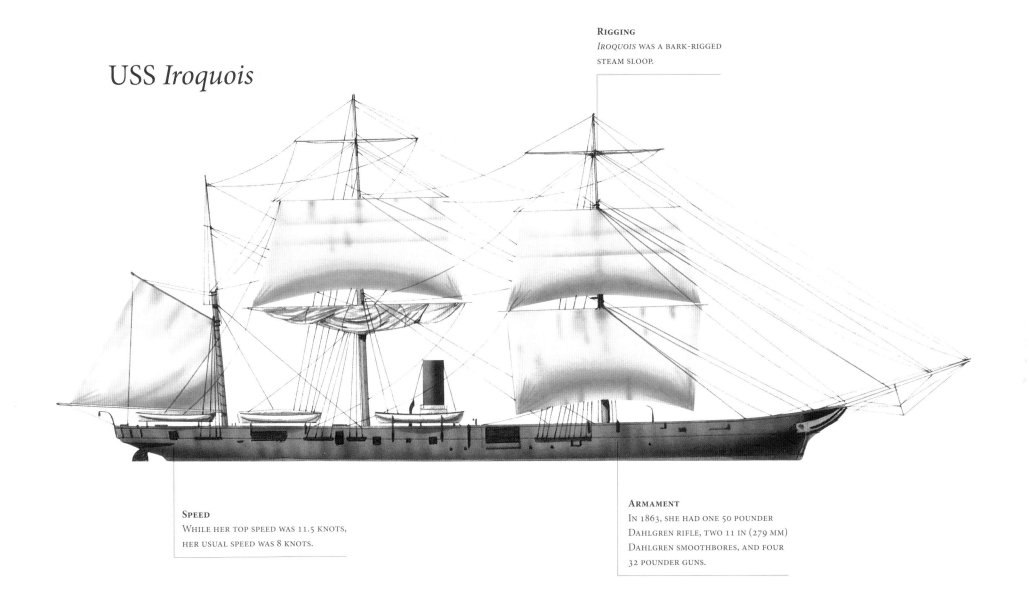

RIGGING
Iroquois WAS A BARK-RIGGED
STEAM SLOOP.

SPEED
WHILE HER TOP SPEED WAS 11.5 KNOTS,
HER USUAL SPEED WAS 8 KNOTS.

ARMAMENT
IN 1863, SHE HAD ONE 50 POUNDER
DAHLGREN RIFLE, TWO 11 IN (279 MM)
DAHLGREN SMOOTHBORES, AND FOUR
32 POUNDER GUNS.

USS *Richmond* (1860)

THE *RICHMOND* WAS A WOODEN STEAM SLOOP OF WAR, LAUNCHED ON JANUARY 26, 1860 WITH CAPTAIN D.N. INGRAHAM IN COMMAND. HER FIRST CIVIL WAR SERVICE WAS PART OF THE UNSUCCESSFUL SEARCH FOR THE *SUMTER*. SHE THEN JOINED THE GULF BLOCKADING SQUADRON AND WAS ON DUTY AT THE HEAD OF THE PASSES AT THE MOUTH OF THE MISSISSIPPI RIVER ON OCTOBER 12, 1861 WHEN SHE AND HER SISTER SHIPS WERE SCATTERED BY A SURPRISE CONFEDERATE ATTACK.

The *Manassas* rammed the *Richmond*, tearing a hole in her side. She was sent for repairs at the New York Navy Yard, but was back at New Orleans in time for Admiral David Farragut's successful attack there on April 24, 1862.

Sailing up the Mississippi, the *Richmond* took part in the actions at Baton Rouge, Natchez and Vicksburg. She unsuccessfully pursued the ram *Arkansas* when she ran past the Federal fleet at Vicksburg on July 15. The *Richmond* was among the part of Farragut's fleet that was unable to pass the Confederate fortifications at Port Hudson, Louisiana on March 13, 1863. Her executive officer, Commander Andrew Cummings, was mortally wounded in the effort and the *Richmond* was hit by a 42 pounder shell, which ruptured her steam lines, filling the engine room and berth deck with live steam.

After Vicksburg surrendered on July 4, the *Richmond* and other ships below Port Hudson helped the Army take possession of the Confederate strong point there, completely opening the Mississippi. On July 30, the *Richmond* headed to the New York Navy Yard for a much-needed overhaul. Her repairs complete, on October 12, 1863 she sailed south to join the blockade off Mobile, Alabama. She participated in Farragut's attack there on August 5, 1864. She suffered no casualties in the action and only slight damage, and contributed to the bombardment that compelled Fort Morgan to surrender on August 23.

Guard Duty

The *Richmond* was on duty at the Southeast Pass of the Mississippi River on April 23, 1865 when the ram *Webb* dashed downriver from the Red River in an attempt to reach the open sea. From her position guarding the estuary leading to the Gulf of Mexico, the *Richmond* helped force the *Webb* ashore. The *Richmond* departed New Orleans on June 27 and was decommissioned in Boston on July 14.

SPECIFICATIONS

DISPLACEMENT: 2,700 tons (2,449 tonnes)

DIMENSIONS: 225 ft x 42.6 ft x 17 ft 5 in (69 m x 13.0 m x 5.32 m)

ARMAMENT: One 80 pounder Dahlgren rifle; twenty 9 in (228 mm) smoothbore guns; one 30 pounder Parrott rifle

MACHINERY: Single, direct-acting engine driving a single screw

SPEED: 9.5 knots

CREW: 260

USS *Richmond*

ARMAMENT

IN EARLY 1863, SHE HAD ONE 80 POUNDER DAHLGREN RIFLE, TWENTY 9 IN (228 MM) DAHLGREN SMOOTHBORES, AND ONE 30 POUNDER PARROTT RIFLE.

DRAFT

HER DEEP DRAFT OF 17 FT 5 IN (5.32 M) RESTRICTED HER USE ON INSHORE WATERWAYS.

USS *Kearsarge* (1862)

THE *KEARSARGE* WAS COMMISSIONED ON JANUARY 24, 1862 WITH CAPTAIN CHARLES PICKERING IN COMMAND. SHE SOON SAILED FOR GIBRALTAR, WHERE SHE WAS ONE OF SEVERAL SHIPS THAT BLOCKADED THE *SUMTER* UNTIL THE CONFEDERATES WERE COMPELLED TO SELL HER. HOWEVER, RAPHAEL SEMMES, THE CAPTAIN OF THE *SUMTER*, SOON COMMISSIONED THE RAIDER *ALABAMA* AND THE STAGE WAS SET FOR THE EPIC SHOWDOWN BETWEEN THAT SHIP AND THE *KEARSARGE*.

The *Kearsarge*, now commanded by Captain John Winslow, found the *Alabama* in port at Cherbourg, France on June 14, 1864. She waited at the harbor's entrance until June 19 when the *Alabama* sailed out of the harbor. Mindful of French neutrality, Winslow allowed the *Alabama* to clear the country's territorial waters before he turned to meet the Confederate ship. Indeed, the French ironclad *Couronne* was on hand to ensure that French territory was respected.

Cruisers Clash

The *Alabama* opened fire first while the *Kearsarge* closed. The two ships then steamed in a circular pattern on opposite courses, each looking for an advantage. It was an unequal contest with the *Kearsarge* well protected by chain cables covering her vital sections, and the *Alabama* suffering from deteriorated powder and shells. However, the *Alabama*'s most serious problem was poor gunnery. Most of her shots sailed harmlessly over the *Kearsarge*, hit her rigging, or hit high on her hull. After an hour of combat, the *Kearsarge* sank the *Alabama*. Most of the Confederates were rescued by the *Kearsarge*, but 41 others, including Semmes, escaped to the English yacht *Deerhound*. One of the battle's enduring controversies is whether or not this support of the Confederate cause from the *Deerhound* had been prearranged.

Part of the romanticism of the battle between the *Kearsarge* and the *Alabama* is that it marked the end of an era for wooden ships. It was the last major sea battle between major powers fielding first-line wooden ships.

The *Kearsarge* next steamed along the French coast in an unsuccessful search for the *Florida*. She then headed to the Caribbean before reporting to Boston for repairs. She was recommissioned on April 1, 1865 and sailed on for the coast of Spain in an unsuccessful attempt to intercept the *Stonewall*.

The *Kearsarge* continued her distinguished career after the Civil War until she was wrecked on Roncador Reef off Central America on February 2, 1894.

SPECIFICATIONS

DISPLACEMENT: 1,550 tons (1,406 tonnes)

DIMENSIONS: 198 ft 6 in x 33 ft 10 in x 14 ft 3 in (60.4 m x 10.26 m x 4.34 m)

ARMAMENT: Two 11 in (279 mm) smoothbores; one 28 pounder rifle; four 32 pounder guns

MACHINERY: Horizontal, back-acting engine driving a single screw

SPEED: 11 knots

CREW: 160

USS *Kearsarge*

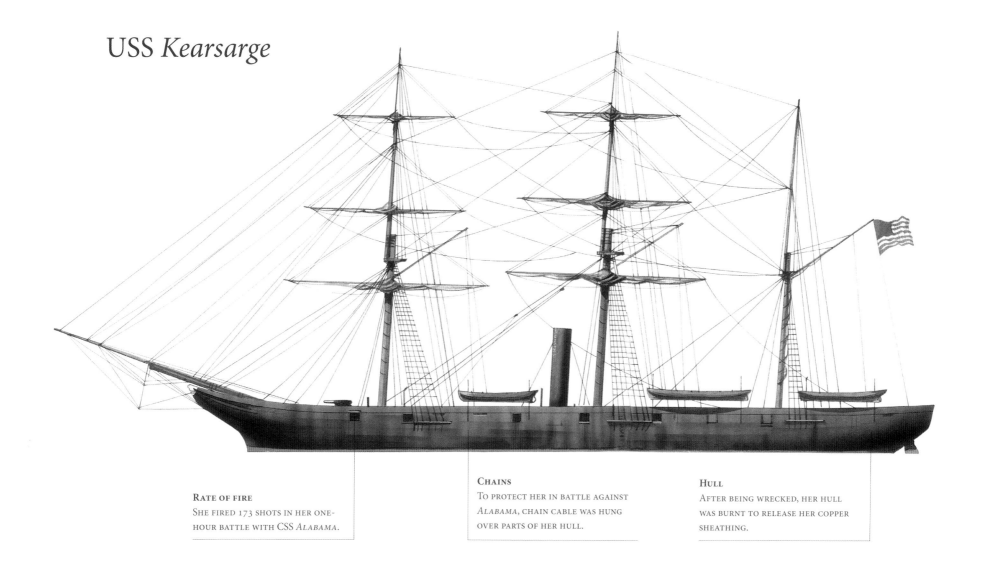

RATE OF FIRE
SHE FIRED 173 SHOTS IN HER ONE-HOUR BATTLE WITH CSS *ALABAMA*.

CHAINS
TO PROTECT HER IN BATTLE AGAINST *ALABAMA*, CHAIN CABLE WAS HUNG OVER PARTS OF HER HULL.

HULL
AFTER BEING WRECKED, HER HULL WAS BURNT TO RELEASE HER COPPER SHEATHING.

USS *Vanderbilt* (1862)

THE *VANDERBILT* WAS BUILT AS A TRANSATLANTIC PASSENGER AND MAIL STEAMER IN 1856 AND 1857 AND SERVED AS THE FLAGSHIP OF COMMODORE CORNELIUS VANDERBILT'S NORTH ATLANTIC MAIL STEAMSHIP LINE. VANDERBILT OFFERED HER TO THE ARMY SHORTLY AFTER THE START OF THE CIVIL WAR AND SUGGESTED FILLING THE BOW OF THE VESSEL WITH CONCRETE AND REINFORCING IT WITH IRON PLATING FOR USE AS A RAM.

This plan was not adopted, and she was transferred to the Navy on March 24, 1862 and fitted with a heavy battery of 15 guns at the New York Navy Yard. She left New York on November 10 and briefly searched for the commerce raider *Alabama* before putting into Hampton Roads on January 17, 1863.

Shortly thereafter, the *Vanderbilt* received orders to embark on what became a year-long cruise in search of the *Alabama*. These travels took her to the West Indies, the eastern coast of South America, Cape of Good Hope, St. Helena, Cape Verde, the Canary Islands, Spain, and Portugal. During the West Indies portion of her deployment, she served as the flagship of Commodore Charles Wilkes' Flying Squadron.

On February 25, 1863, the *Vanderbilt* captured the blockade-running British steamer *Peterhoff* off of St. Thomas, Virgin Islands. A dispute between the British and American governments over the mail the *Peterhoff* was carrying was eventually resolved when President Abraham Lincoln ordered the mail returned to the British. The *Vanderbilt* also captured the British blockade runner *Gertrude*, taken off Eleuthera Island in the Bahamas on April 16 and the British bark *Saxon*, seized at Angra Peguena, Africa, on October 30. However, the *Alabama* continued to elude the search, and the *Vanderbilt* returned to New York in January 1864 for repairs.

Attack on Fort Fisher

In September, the *Vanderbilt* left New York and cruised off Halifax, Nova Scotia, searching for blockade runners. After taking no prizes, she deployed with the blockade off Wilmington, North Carolina in November. There she participated in both attacks on Fort Fisher. The *Vanderbilt* returned to New York in late January 1865, remaining there until March 24

when she left to transport soldiers to the Gulf of Mexico. She then went to Charleston, South Carolina, where she picked up the uncompleted Confederate ram *Columbia* and towed her to Norfolk in May. She next towed the *Onondaga* from Norfolk to New York in June and began service as a receiving ship at the Portsmouth (New Hampshire) Navy Yard. After the war she was in and out of service until she was sold in 1873.

SPECIFICATIONS

DISPLACEMENT: 3,360 tons (3,048 tonnes)

DIMENSIONS: 331 ft x 47 ft 6 in x 19 ft (101 m x 14.48 m x 5.8 m)

ARMAMENT: Two 100 pounder rifles; twelve 9 in (228 mm) Dahlgren smoothbores

MACHINERY: One single-beam engine with a 12 ft (3.6 m) stroke

SPEED: 14 knots

CREW: Not known

USS *Vanderbilt*

STEAMER
VANDERBILT WAS AN EXPERIENCED
TRANSATLANTIC STEAMER THAT COULD
REACH SPEEDS OF UP TO 14 KNOTS.

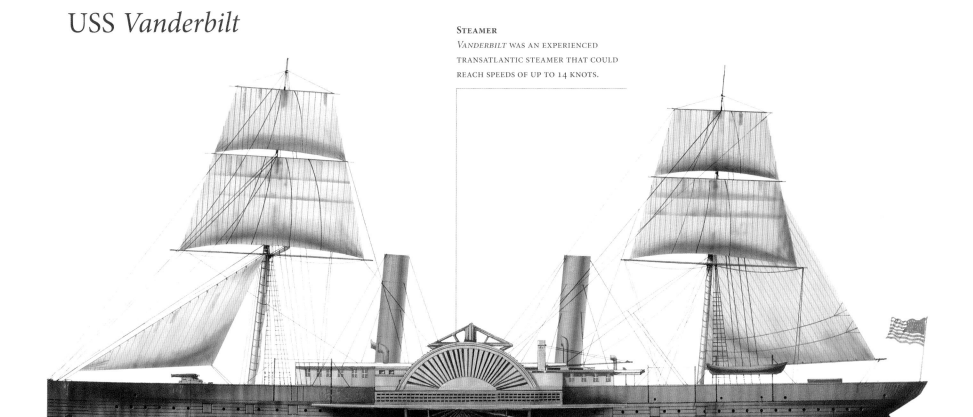

ARMAMENT
IN NOVEMBER 1862, SHE HAD TWO 100
POUNDER RIFLES AND TWELVE 9 IN
(228 MM) SMOOTHBORE GUNS.

EQUIPMENT
WHILE A PASSENGER LINER, SHE WAS ONE
OF THE MOST COMFORTABLE SHIPS OF
THE ATLANTIC.

USS *Wampanoag* (1863)

IN 1863, THE SECRETARY OF THE NAVY POINTED OUT THAT BESIDE THE NEED FOR TURRETED VESSELS AND LARGE ARMORED WARSHIPS FOR BOTH COASTAL PATROLS AND OCEAN-GOING CONFLICTS, THERE WAS A PRESSING NEED FOR A GROUP OF HIGH-SPEED CRUISERS CONTRUCTED OF WOOD THAT COULD SWEEP THE SEA AND HUNT DOWN ENEMY MERCHANT CRAFT AND WARSHIPS.

To counter the threat to Federal commerce posed by the raiders *Alabama* and *Florida*, the U.S. Congress authorized construction of a new class of screw frigates as part of the naval procurement bill of 1863. These vessels were intended to have the speed necessary to track down the elusive Confederate ships. The *Wampanoag* was the lead ship of this new class of supercruisers.

The resulting group of ships were not all of the same design, but when *Wampanoag* was complete, she was an outstanding landmark in US naval and engineering development. Other ships in the class included the *Idaho*, *Chattanooga*, *Madawaska*, *Ammonoosuc*, and *Neshimany*.

Wampanoag and her consorts caused great unease in England at a time when diplomatic relations were strained, and fears were expressed over the safety of English merchant vessels. The British Admiralty in turn set to work building a new and more powerful class of cruiser, the result of which was the *Inconstant* in 1868.

Design Limitations

The design of the *Wampanoag* contained numerous features unprecedented in American naval construction. To increase her speed, her hull was unusually long and tapered relative to her beam, giving her a very sleek appearance. Her machinery featured a geared steam engine in which slow-moving machinery was coupled to fast-moving propulsion gear.

Despite the high speed of most of the ships in the class, the type was generally considered a failure. Too much had been sacrificed for speed; the weight of the machinery took nearly 30 percent of the displacement, and too little room was left for coal, crew, stores, and so forth.

The long, narrow hull also limited their ability to fire ahead.

Debate generated by her controversial features delayed construction and prevented her from being completed in time to serve in the Civil War. In 1869, a naval commission condemned the vessel, finding particular fault with her narrow breadth relative to her length.

SPECIFICATIONS

DISPLACEMENT: 4,215 tons (3,823 tonnes)

DIMENSIONS: 355 ft x 45 ft 2 in x 19 ft 10 in (108.2 m x 13.7 m x 6 m)

ARMAMENT: Ten 9 in (228 mm) Dahlgren smoothbore guns; three 60 pounder Parrott rifles

MACHINERY: Two horizontal, geared, back-acting engines driving a single screw

SPEED: 17.5 knots

CREW: 375

USS *Wampanoag*

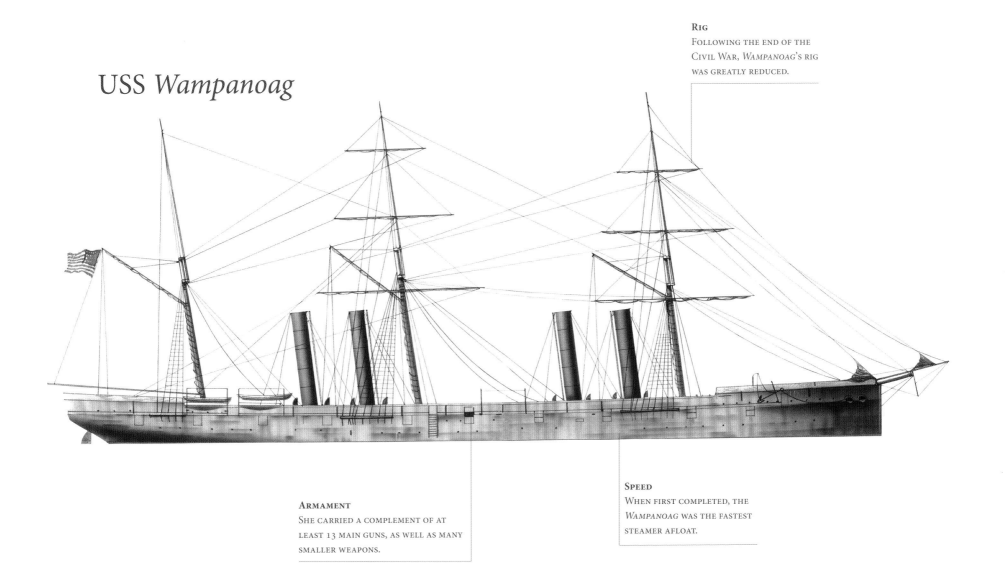

RIG
FOLLOWING THE END OF THE
CIVIL WAR, *WAMPANOAG'S* RIG
WAS GREATLY REDUCED.

ARMAMENT
SHE CARRIED A COMPLEMENT OF AT
LEAST 13 MAIN GUNS, AS WELL AS MANY
SMALLER WEAPONS.

SPEED
WHEN FIRST COMPLETED, THE
WAMPANOAG WAS THE FASTEST
STEAMER AFLOAT.

Teaser (1861)

THE *TEASER* WAS A WOODEN-HULLED, SCREW TUGBOAT PURCHASED BY THE STATE OF VIRGINIA IN APRIL 1861. SHE WAS COMMISSIONED IN THE VIRGINIA STATE NAVY WITH LIEUTENANT J.H. ROCHELLE IN COMMAND. WHEN VIRGINIA SECEDED, THE *TEASER* BECAME PART OF THE CONFEDERATE NAVY AND CONTINUED TO OPERATE IN VIRGINIA WATERS. UNDER LIEUTENANT W.A. WEBB SHE ACTED AS TENDER TO THE *VIRGINIA* DURING THE BATTLE OF HAMPTON ROADS ON MARCH 8–9, 1862.

During the Seven Days' Battles, the *Teaser* served as an "aircraft carrier" for balloonist Lieutenant Colonel Edward Porter Alexander. Tethered to the deck of the *Teaser*, Alexander ascended in the balloon *Gazelle* to observe Federal movements. On July 4, while observing near Malvern Hill, the *Teaser* ran aground on a mud bank in the middle of the James River. The *Maratanza* came upon the struggling ship and captured her after a brief battle. The episode ended the fledgling Confederate balloon activity and led Brigadier General William Booth Taliaferro to lament that the capture of the *Gazelle* represented "the last silk dress in the Confederacy. This capture was the meanest trick of the war and one I have never forgiven."

Later that summer, the *Teaser* was taken into the Federal Navy and assigned to the Potomac Flotilla, where she helped patrol from Alexandria, Virginia south to Point Lookout, Maryland. She spent most of her career intercepting efforts to move contraband between Virginia and Maryland. Such duty was interrupted occasionally by supporting such operations as Major General Ambrose Burnside's Fredericksburg Campaign in December 1862.

Landing Force

In April 1863, the *Teaser* left the Potomac for duty with Admiral Samuel Lee's North Atlantic Blockading Squadron at Hampton Roads. On an expedition up the Nansemond River west of Norfolk she ran aground and damaged her machinery. By mid-summer, she was back in service on the Potomac, patrolling for smugglers. She saw more action on January 5, 1864 when her commander, acting Ensign Philip Sheridan, led a landing force at Nomini, Virginia that captured a lighter and destroyed a skiff while dispersing the Confederate force attached to them. She also saw combat in April as part of an expedition up the St. Mary's River. She spent the rest of the war patrolling the Potomac and was decommissioned at the Washington Navy Yard on June 2 and sold at public auction.

SPECIFICATIONS

DISPLACEMENT: 64 tons (58 tonnes)

DIMENSIONS: 80 ft x 18 ft x 4 ft (24.4 m x 5.5 m x 1.2 m)

ARMAMENT: One 32 pounder gun; one 12 pounder rifle

MACHINERY: Steam engine

SPEED: Not known

CREW: 25

Teaser

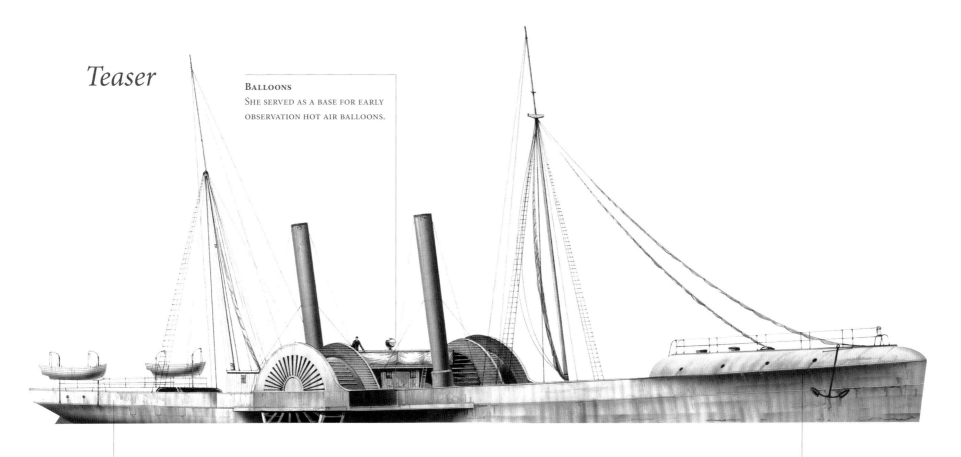

BALLOONS
SHE SERVED AS A BASE FOR EARLY
OBSERVATION HOT AIR BALLOONS.

MINES
TEASER ALSO SERVED AS A MINELAYER.

ARMAMENT
SHE WAS ARMED WITH ONE 32
POUNDER GUN AND ONE 12 POUNDER
RIFLE IN THE BOW.

205

CSS *A.D. Vance* [Advance] (1863)

THE *A.D. VANCE* WAS ORIGINALLY THE SIDE-WHEEL STEAMER *LORD CLYDE*, BUILT IN 1862 IN GREENOCK, SCOTLAND. UNDER THE SPONSORSHIP OF GOVERNOR ZEBULON VANCE, SHE WAS BOUGHT BY THE STATE OF NORTH CAROLINA FOR $175,000. SHE WAS PLACED UNDER THE COMMAND OF JOANNES WYLIE, WHO BROUGHT HER TO WILMINGTON ON JUNE 28, 1863 WITH A CARGO OF DRY GOODS, SHOES, AND COTTON CARDS.

The *A.D. Vance* was an effective blockade runner, but one that operated under state control. This arrangement created some competition between the North Carolina and the central Confederate government, a condition that Governor Vance encouraged on other fronts as well. Still, the greatest competition in the area of blockade running was not between the state and the central government, but from private blockade runners who made huge profits delivering high-demand luxury items that did little to further the war effort.

The *A.D. Vance* made 20 successful voyages before she was captured on September 10, 1864 by the *Santiago de Cuba* at sea northeast of Wilmington, attempting to carry a cargo of cotton to Europe. Governor Vance blamed her capture on the use of low-grade North Carolina bituminous coal and accused Secretary of the Navy Stephen Mallory of giving the more effective smokeless anthracite to the *Tallahassee* at the *A.D. Vance*'s expense. "Why a State struggling for the common good, to clothe and provide for its troops in the public service," Vance complained, "should meet with no more favor than a blockade gambler passes my comprehension."

Swift Purchase

The U.S. Navy quickly purchased the *A.D. Vance* from the prize court, and she was commissioned on October 28 with Lieutenant Commander J.H. Upshur in command. Her name was also slightly modified to the *Advance*.

The *Advance* joined the North Atlantic Blockading Squadron in patrolling off the North Carolina coast at Wilmington. She took part in the first attack on Fort Fisher, North Carolina, but was more active during the second attack in which she covered the landings and then used her boats to bring stores and ammunition ashore.

After the victory, her boats were used to carry prisoners out to transports. She spent the next two months transferring passengers, messages and mail among the ships of the squadron, before sailing to New York on March 14 and being briefly put out of commission. On April 22, her name was changed to the *Frolic* and she was assigned to the newly formed European Squadron. She was finally decommissioned in 1877.

SPECIFICATIONS

DISPLACEMENT: 880 tons (798 tonnes)

DIMENSIONS: 230 ft x 26 ft x 11 ft 8 in (70 m x 7.9 m x 3.56 m)

ARMAMENT: Four 24 pounder smoothbore howitzers; one 20 pounder rifled howitzer

MACHINERY: Side-wheel propelled steam engine

SPEED: 12 knots

CREW: 107

CSS *A.D. Vance [Advance]*

RIGGING
SHE WAS A SCHOONER-RIGGED SIDE-WHEEL STEAMER.

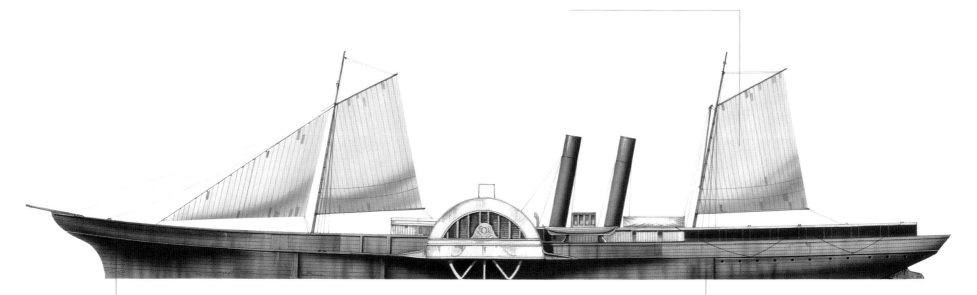

ARMAMENT
SHE WAS ARMED WITH FOUR 24 POUNDER SMOOTHBORE HOWITZERS AND ONE 20 POUNDER RIFLED HOWITZER.

BLOCKADE RUNNER
HAVING BEEN A BLOCKADE RUNNER FOR THE CONFEDERATES, WHEN CAPTURED BY THE UNION, HER ROLE CHANGED TO CATCHING BLOCKADE RUNNERS.

Hope (1864)

BLOCKADE RUNNING BECAME INCREASINGLY CRITICAL TO THE CONFEDERACY AS THE WAR DRAGGED ON, AND IN 1864 THE SIDE-WHEELERS *HOPE* AND *COLONEL LAMB* BEGAN SHORT-LIVED CAREERS TRYING TO FILL THIS NEED. BOTH WERE NEARLY 280 FEET (85 M) IN LENGTH WITH A REGISTERED TONNAGE OF 1,003 TONS (910 TONNES), ALMOST THREE TIMES THE CAPACITY OF MOST RUNNERS.

USS *SALVOR*

The *Hope* was ready by July and the *Colonel Lamb* two months later. With the Federal blockade tightening, the *Hope* did not last long. Captained by William Hammer, she arrived at Wilmington in late July with a cargo that included two 150 pounder Armstrong cannons and two 12 pounder Whitworth guns. Hammer quickly planned another trip and the *Hope* was captured by the *Eolus* on October 22 after a 65 mile (105 km) chase. The *Hope* was sold in prize court to a private interest and renamed the *Savannah* on January 11, 1865.

USS *Salvor*

The *Salvor* was built as the *M.S. Perry* and then purchased in 1859 by James McKay for use as a wrecker in Florida. McKay had emigrated to the United States from Thurso, Scotland and ended up in Tampa after stops in St. Louis, Missouri,

and Mobile, Alabama. He had made substantial profits from business ventures prior to arriving in Tampa, and he soon established himself as a local entrepreneur and personality. Finding insufficient work for the *Salvor* as a wrecker, the enterprising McKay began a business supplying cattle to the U.S. officers stationed at Tortugas, a base about 75 miles (120 km) west of Key West. Major William French, the commanding officer at Key West, reported dryly that "the blockade stopped that," and French seized the vessel for use by the quartermaster's department.

McKay was paid more than $1,000 for this use of the *Salvor* for a period of three months, during which she suffered damage to her boilers from the saltwater and was deemed unfit to go to sea. The vessel was returned to McKay on the condition he not use her in any way to support the Confederacy or take her to

a port under their control. He then took her to Havana for repairs, and, as events would soon demonstrate, a new career as a blockade runner.

On October 14, 1861, the *Keystone State* found the *Salvor* attempting to run the blockade while flying a British flag about 20 miles (32 km) south of Tortugas. The *Keystone State* captured the ship with her "cargo of assorted merchandise, principally coffee and cigars" and sent her to a prize court where she was sold on March 1, 1862. McKay, who vigorously protested his innocence as a victim of circumstances, was imprisoned at Fort Lafayette, New York until he was ordered released on March 8.

SPECIFICATIONS

DISPLACEMENT: 1,003 tons (910 tonnes)

DIMENSIONS: 281 ft 6 in x 35 ft x 8ft (85.8 m x 10.7 m x 2.4 m)

ARMAMENT: Not known

MACHINERY: Slow pressure, vertical, direct-acting engines

SPEED: 8 knots

CREW: Not known

Hope

PADDLE BOXES
CANVAS WOULD BE DRAPED
AROUND THE PADDLE BOXES
TO DEADEN THE SOUND OF
THE WHEELS.

QUARTERS
THE LIVING QUARTERS WERE BENEATH
THE PILOT HOUSE AND ABOVE THE
ENGINES AND BOILERS.

ENGINE
THE ENGINE WAS
COMPACTLY HOUSED.

CARGO SPACE
THERE WAS EXTENSIVE CARGO SPACE
FORE AND AFT OF THE BOILERS.

Stag *(1864)*

To run the blockade, the indefatigable Confederate agent in Europe, Commander James Bulloch, envisioned overwhelming the Federal Navy with fast, shallow-draft ships. The first four vessels he pursued with this purpose in mind were the *Owl*, *Bat*, *Stag*, and *Deer*. The latter two were slightly smaller than the others and were earmarked for the shallow waters off Texas and Florida.

They drew only 5 feet (1.5 m) of water with a load of 750 bales of cotton, coal and other supplies.

The *Stag* was a steel paddle-steamer Bulloch contracted with Jones, Quiggin and Company, who then subcontracted construction at Liverpool to Bowder, Chaffer and Company. She was transferred to the Confederacy upon receipt of payment in cotton. She sailed from the Mersey River in August 1864 under British Captain J.M. Burroughs. She arrived at Wilmington, North Carolina on December 4 from Bermuda, and Lieutenant Richard Gayle of the Confederate Navy replaced Burroughs as commander. There is some confusion between this *Stag* and another vessel built at Glasgow as the *Stag* that ran the blockade into Charleston, South Carolina in September 1864 and was then renamed the *Kate Green*.

During the first bombardment of Fort Fisher, the *Stag* escaped as a warship from Old Inlet bound for Nassau. She returned with a load of arms, blankets, shoes, and other materials and attempted to run the blockade at Wilmington on January 20, 1865. By then a second attack had succeeded in taking Fort Fisher, and the area was securely in Federal control.

Champagne Reception

The *Stag* and the *Charlotte* unwittingly responded to signal lights from the Federal fleet and unsuspectingly anchored near the Malvern in the Cape Fear River. When she realized her mistake, the *Stag* threw some of her papers overboard and tried to flee. She had received three shots from the blockaders and was easily captured along with the *Charlotte*.

On board the Charlotte were five English passengers, one of whom was an English army officer. They told their captors they had made the trip "on a lark," and were celebrating their safe arrival with champagne when their vessel was boarded.

The *Stag* was sent to prize court in Boston, where she was sold to a private interest and renamed the *Zenobia*.

SPECIFICATIONS

DISPLACEMENT: Not known

DIMENSIONS: 230 ft x 26 ft x 7 ft 6 in (70 m x 7.92 m x 2.3 m)

ARMAMENT: Not known

MACHINERY: Side-wheel steamer

SPEED: 16 knots

CREW: Unknown

Stag

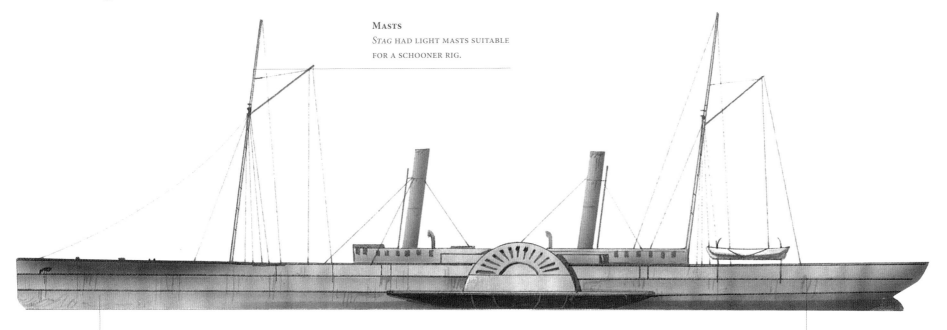

MASTS
Stag had light masts suitable for a schooner rig.

SPEED
The *Stag* was fast among blockade runners, with a typical speed of 16 knots.

SHALLOW DRAFT
Like all blockade runners, the *Stag* had a shallow draft for increased speed.

CSS *Pioneer* (1862)

IN MARCH 1862, ROBERT BARROW, JAMES MCCLINTOCK, AND BAXTER WATSON APPLIED FOR A LETTER
OF MARQUE AT NEW ORLEANS FOR A SUBMARINE NAMED *PIONEER*. THE CRAFT WAS MADE FROM
¼ INCH (6 MM) RIVETED IRON PLATES THAT HAD BEEN CUT FROM OLD BOILERS AND WAS PROPELLED
BY A CRANK SHAFT. SHE WAS DESIGNED TO CARRY TWO MEN.

In a post-Civil War interview, McClintock described the *Pioneer* as being 30 feet (9 m) long with a 10 foot (3 m) cylindrical midship section. Tapered conical ends extended from the cylindrical section, resulting in a cigar shape. She had a conning tower with manholes in the top and small windows of circular glass in her sides. She was armed by a clockwork torpedo, carried on top of the submarine, and intended to be screwed into the bottom of the enemy ship by gimlet-pointed screws of tempered steel. J.K. Scott was the commander.

The application for letter of marque for the *Pioneer* requested "authority to cruise the high seas, bay, rivers, estuaries, etc., in the name of the Government, and aid said Government by the destruction or capture of any and all vessels opposed to or at war with the said Confederate States, and to aid in repelling its enemies."

After the war, McClintock claimed the *Pioneer* had made several descents in Lake Pontchartrain and destroyed a small schooner and several rafts during experiments. However, she was never tested in combat because she was scuttled to prevent her falling into Federal hands when Admiral David Farragut captured New Orleans in May 1862.

Pioneer II

Horace Hunley was one of the guarantors for the *Pioneer* and, after her loss, he, McClintock and Watson went to Mobile, Alabama to continue their experiments with submarines. A new submarine commonly called the *Pioneer II* resulted from this effort. Designed for five men and mounting a spar torpedo, this submarine sank off Fort Morgan in Mobile Bay in mid-February 1863.

The remains of the *Pioneer* were once considered to be those of a submarine on display at the Louisiana State Museum in New Orleans. However, the museum now believes its submarine and the *Pioneer* are not the same vessel. The identity of the museum's submarine remains unknown.

SPECIFICATIONS

DIMENSIONS: 30 ft x 10 ft (9 m x 3 m)

ARMAMENT: One clockwork torpedo

SPEED: Unknown

CREW: 2–3

CSS *Pioneer*

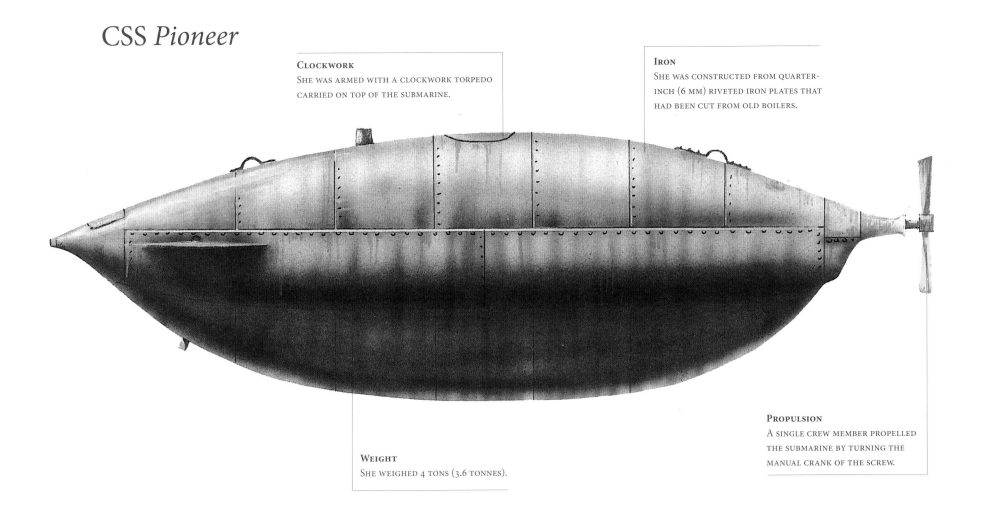

CLOCKWORK
SHE WAS ARMED WITH A CLOCKWORK TORPEDO CARRIED ON TOP OF THE SUBMARINE.

IRON
SHE WAS CONSTRUCTED FROM QUARTER-INCH (6 MM) RIVETED IRON PLATES THAT HAD BEEN CUT FROM OLD BOILERS.

WEIGHT
SHE WEIGHED 4 TONS (3.6 TONNES).

PROPULSION
A SINGLE CREW MEMBER PROPELLED THE SUBMARINE BY TURNING THE MANUAL CRANK OF THE SCREW.

CSS *David* (1863)

AN EARLY SEMI-SUBMERSIBLE, *DAVID* WAS DESIGNED TO OPERATE LOW IN THE WATER AS A SURFACE VESSEL. SHE WAS A CIGAR-SHAPED BOAT THAT CARRIED AN EXPLOSIVE CHARGE ON THE END OF A SPAR PROJECTING FORWARD FROM HER BOW. SHE WAS DESIGNED BY DR. ST. JULIAN RAVENEL AND BUILT AT STONEY LANDING ON THE COOPER RIVER.

Although built as a private venture, she was put under the control of the Confederate Navy. The *David* made at least three attacks against Federal vessels.

The first attack occurred on the night of October 5, 1863. Under the command of Lieutenant W.T. Glassell, the *David* slipped into Charleston Harbor and approached undetected until she was within 50 yards (45 m) of the *New Ironsides*. When the *New Ironsides* hailed the *David*, Glassell replied with a shotgun blast and attacked, detonating the torpedo under the starboard side of the ironclad. The explosion showered the *David* with a column of water that extinguished her boiler fires.

With her engine dead, the *David* was subjected to small arms fire from the *New Ironsides*. Thinking the *David* was sinking, Glassell and two others abandoned her, but the pilot, W. Cannon,

who could not swim, remained onboard. Seeing the *David* was still afloat, Assistant Engineer J.H. Tomb swam back to the craft and climbed on board. Tomb was able to rebuild the fires and get the *David*'s engine working again. Cannon piloted the *David* up the channel to safety, but Glassell and Seaman J. Sullivan, the *David*'s fireman, were captured.

Attack on the *Memphis*

Other attacks may have occurred over the next four months, but the next one clearly documented is the *David*'s March 6, 1864 attack on the *Memphis* in the North Edisto River, South Carolina. The *David* twice struck the ship with her torpedo, but both attacks were ineffective. The *Memphis* responded with her heavy guns, sending the *David* retreating upriver to safety. The *Memphis* was not damaged in the attack. The *David*'s final confirmed action was an April 18 attack on the

Wabash. This effort was thwarted by alert lookouts and neither vessel suffered any damage.

The term "David" was used to refer to any of the several vessels that resembled the *David*. Several of these vessels were captured by Federal forces by the end of the war, and the *David* may have been among them. However, her exact fate remains unknown.

SPECIFICATIONS

DIMENSIONS: 50 ft x 6 ft x 5 ft (15 m x 1.8 m x 1.5 m)

ARMAMENT: One 134 lb (60 kg) gunpowder charge

SPEED: Not known

CREW: 4

CSS *David*

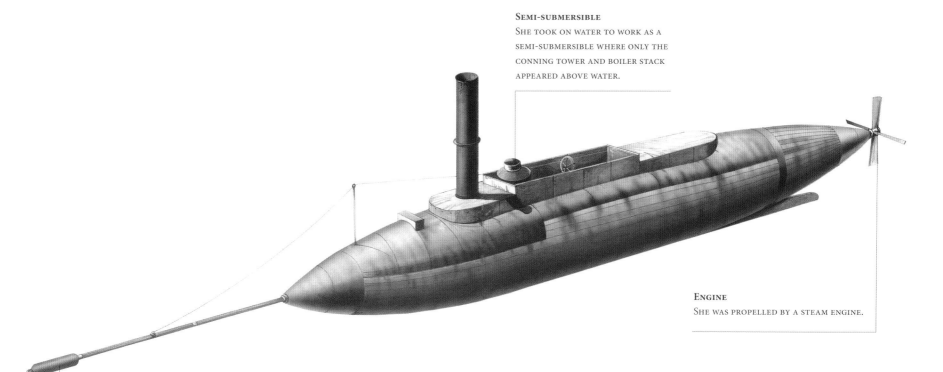

SEMI-SUBMERSIBLE
SHE TOOK ON WATER TO WORK AS A
SEMI-SUBMERSIBLE WHERE ONLY THE
CONNING TOWER AND BOILER STACK
APPEARED ABOVE WATER.

ENGINE
SHE WAS PROPELLED BY A STEAM ENGINE.

ARMAMENT
SHE CARRIED A SINGLE 134 LB (60 KG)
EXPLOSIVE GUNPOWDER CHARGE ON
THE END OF THE SPAR.

CSS *Hunley* (1863)

THE *HUNLEY* WAS A SUBMARINE PRIVATELY BUILT IN THE SPRING OF 1863 IN THE MACHINE SHOP OF PARK AND LYONS AT MOBILE, ALABAMA UNDER THE DIRECTION OF LIEUTENANTS WILLIAM ALEXANDER AND GEORGE DIXON, TWO CONFEDERATE ARMY ENGINEERS. SHE WAS BASED ON PLANS FURNISHED BY HORACE HUNLEY, JAMES MCCLINTOCK, AND BAXTER WATSON, WHO HAD EARLIER WORKED ON THE *PIONEER*.

After successful trials in Mobile Bay, General Pierre Gustave Toutant Beauregard, in command of the defenses of Charleston, called for her to be transported there in hopes of destroying some of the Federal ships blockading the harbor. By August 15, she arrived in Charleston on board two railroad flat cars.

The *Hunley* was 40 feet (12 m) long, 3.5 feet (1 m) wide and 4 feet (1.2 m) deep. Her main hull was made out of a boiler, cut lengthwise with a 12 inch (305 mm) wide longitudinal strip added to it to increase her height. A pointed bow and stern attached to the boiler gave the *Hunley* a cigar-shape.

She was designed for a crew of nine: one man to steer and the other eight to power the vessel by hand-turning a crankshaft that moved the propeller. In spite of sinking twice and drowning 13 men, including Hunley, an intrepid third crew of volunteers stepped forward. On the night of February 17, 1864, this crew approached the 1,934 ton (1,754 tonne) screw Federal sloop *Housatonic*. The Housatonic spotted the *Hunley* and engaged her with small arms and tried to escape, but it was too late. The *Hunley* exploded her 130 pounder spar torpedo, and the *Housatonic* became the first ship in the history of naval warfare to be sunk by a submarine. The blast, however, likely damaged the *Hunley* as well, and she sank while returning to shore. Her entire crew was lost.

Wreckage Raised

The wreckage of the *Hunley* was discovered off of Sullivan's Island in 1995 and recovered in 2000. She is currently on display at the Warren Lasch Conservation Center on the old Navy Base in North Charleston. In 1999, the remains of four members of the *Hunley*'s first crew were found in a forgotten Confederate cemetery during renovations at the Johnson Hagood football stadium at The Citadel. The remains of the eight crewmen who were recovered when the *Hunley* was raised were buried in Magnolia Cemetery in Charleston in 2004 with full military honors.

SPECIFICATIONS

DIMENSIONS: 40 ft x 3 ft 6 in x 4 ft (12.2 m x 4 m x 1.2 m)

ARMAMENT: One spar torpedo

SPEED: 2.5 knots

CREW: 1 officer, 7 enlisted

CSS *Hunley*

LIGHT
LIGHT WAS PROVIDED BY A CANDLE. THIS ALSO INDICATED
IF AIR SUPPLY WAS LOW.

HULL
THE MAIN PART OF THE HULL WAS
FASHIONED FROM A CYLINDRICAL
STEAM BOILER.

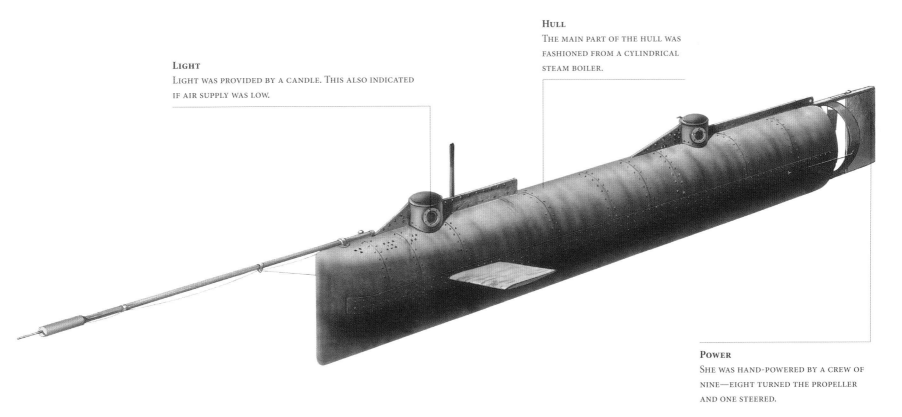

POWER
SHE WAS HAND-POWERED BY A CREW OF
NINE—EIGHT TURNED THE PROPELLER
AND ONE STEERED.

USS *Intelligent Whale* (1863)

CIVIL WAR SUBMARINING IS MOST ASSOCIATED WITH THE CONFEDERACY WHO NEEDED THE ASYMMETRIC THREAT TO COUNTER THE FEDERAL BLOCKADE. HOWEVER, BOTH ADMIRALS SAMUEL DU PONT AND JOHN DAHLGREN, WHO COMMANDED THE BLOCKADE EFFORT AT CHARLESTON, EXPRESSED SOME INTEREST IN THE UNION DEVELOPING A SUBMARINE CAPABILITY. THERE WERE TWO ATTEMPTS IN THIS DIRECTION: THE *ALLIGATOR* AND THE *INTELLIGENT WHALE*.

The *Alligator* was the first effort and was envisioned as a means of countering the threat posed by reports of the Confederate's ongoing conversion of the *Merrimack* to an ironclad. A contract was signed on November 1, 1861, with the urgency of the situation specifying completion of the vessel in just 40 days. This ambitious time line proved unrealistic, and the Navy was not able to accept the vessel until June 13, 1862.

She was dispatched to support Major General George McClellan's Peninsula Campaign, but Commander John Rodgers could find no suitable task for her and, fearing she might fall into enemy hands, he requested permission to send the *Alligator* back to Hampton Roads. She ended up at the Washington Navy Yard for more tests that were generally denounced as failures. Nonetheless, Du Pont felt she may be of use to him at Charleston, and on March 31, 1863 she began being towed there. She ran into bad weather on April 2 and sank.

Bulbous Raider

The next Federal submarine effort was the *Intelligent Whale*, built at Newark, New Jersey by the American Submarine Company according to a design developed by Scovel Merriam. The vessel could be submerged by filling compartments with water, and then expelling the water by pumps and compressed air. Her bulbous shape allowed her to accommodate a crew of 13, but only six were required to operate her. She contained enough air to stay submerged for up to 10 hours and could make a speed of about four knots.

Litigation and difficulty in finding crews delayed progress and prevented the *Intelligent Whale* from being employed in the Civil War. She was tested in April 1866 by Brigadier General Thomas William Sweeny, who submerged the submarine, exited her in a diving suit, planted an explosive charge on a target scow, and reentered the submarine. After the *Intelligent Whale* moved a safe distance away, Sweeny exploded the charge by a lanyard and destroyed the scow.

In spite of this successful demonstration, the *Intelligent Whale* gained the reputation of being the "Disastrous Jonah," sinking three times and drowning her crews. The Navy ultimately abandoned the project, and the *Intelligent Whale* is now on display at the National Guard Militia Museum of New Jersey in Sea Girt, New Jersey.

SPECIFICATIONS

DIMENSIONS: 28 ft 8 in x 7 ft x 9 ft
(8.74 m x 2.1 m x 2.7 m)

ARMAMENT: Not applicable

SPEED: 4 knots

CREW: 6–13

USS *Intelligent Whale*

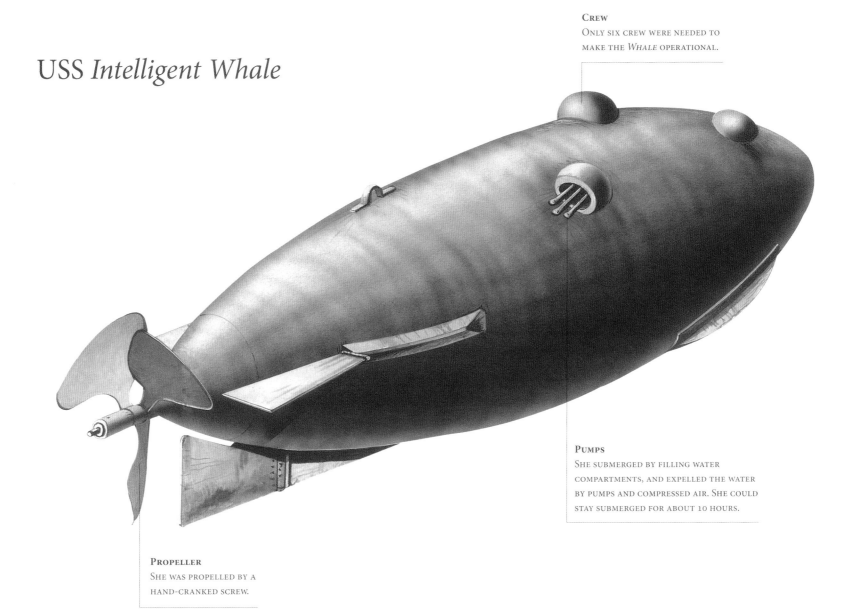

CREW
ONLY SIX CREW WERE NEEDED TO
MAKE THE *WHALE* OPERATIONAL.

PUMPS
SHE SUBMERGED BY FILLING WATER
COMPARTMENTS, AND EXPELLED THE WATER
BY PUMPS AND COMPRESSED AIR. SHE COULD
STAY SUBMERGED FOR ABOUT 10 HOURS.

PROPELLER
SHE WAS PROPELLED BY A
HAND-CRANKED SCREW.

Select Bibliography

Anderson, Bern. *By Sea and By River: A Naval History of the Civil War*. Westport: Greenwood Press, 1962.

Bailey, Ronald. *Forward to Richmond: McClellan's Peninsular Campaign*. Alexandria, VA: Time-Life, 1983.

Browning, Robert. *Success Is All That Was Expected: The South Atlantic Blockading Squadron during the Civil War*. Washington, DC: Brassey's, Inc, 2002.

Campbell, R. Thomas. *Fire & Thunder: Exploits of the Confederate Navy*. Shippenburg, PA: Burd Street Press, 1997.

Dougherty, Kevin. *Encyclopedia of the Confederacy*. San Diego, CA: Thunder Bay Press, 2010.

Dougherty, Kevin. *Strangling the Confederacy*. Havertown, PA: Casemate, 2010.

Dougherty, Kevin. *The Peninsula Campaign of 1862: A Military Analysis*. Jackson: The University Press of Mississippi, 2005.

Duffy, James. *Lincoln's Admiral: The Civil War Campaigns of David Farragut*. NY: John Wiley & Sons, Inc, 1997.

Gaines, W. Craig. *Encyclopedia of Civil War Shipwrecks*. Baton Rouge: Louisiana State University Press, 2008.

Gosnell, H. Allen. *Guns on the Western Waters: The Story of River Gunboats in the Civil War*. Baton Rouge: Louisiana State University Press, 1993.

Gragg, Rod. *Confederate Goliath*. NY: Harper Perennial, 1992.

Hearn, Chester. *The Capture of New Orleans*. Baton Rouge: Louisiana State University, 1995.

Konstam, Angus and Tony Bryan. *Confederate Ironclad 1861–65*. Oxford, UK: Osprey Publishing, 2001.

Konstam, Angus and Tony Bryan. *Confederate Submarines and Torpedo Vessels 1861–65*. Oxford, UK: Osprey Publishing, 2004.

Konstam, Angus and Tony Bryan. *Union River Ironclad 1861–65*. Oxford, UK: Osprey Publishing, 2002.

Musicant, Ivan. *Divided Waters: The Naval History of the Civil War*. Edison, NJ: Castle Books, 1995.

Porter, David. *Naval History of the Civil War*. Secaucus, NJ: Castle, 1984.

Quarstein, John. *The Battle of the Ironclads*. Charleston, SC: Arcadia, 1999.

Sauers, Richard. *The Burnside Expedition in North Carolina*. Dayton, OH: Morningside House, 1996.

Sears, Stephen. *To the Gates of Richmond: The Peninsular Campaign*. New York, NY: Ticknor and Fields, 1992.

Smith, Myron. *Tinclads in the Civil War: Union Light-draught Gunboat Operations on Western Waters, 1862–1865*. Jefferson, NC: McFarland, 2009.

Still, William. *Iron Afloat: The Story of the Confederate Armorclads*. Nashville, TN: Vanderbilt University Press, 1971.

Time-Life Books, editors. *The Blockade: Runners and Raiders*. Alexandria, VA: Time-Life Books, 1983.

Tucker, Spencer. *A Short History of the Civil War at Sea*. Wilmington, DE: Scholarly Resources Inc, 2002.

Tucker, Spencer. *Blue & Gray Navies: The Civil War Afloat*. Annapolis, Maryland: Naval Institute Press, 2006.

Van Doren Stern, Philip. *The Confederate Navy: A Pictorial History*. Garden City, NJ: Doubleday & Company, 1962.

Weddle, Kevin. *Lincoln's Tragic Admiral: The Life of Samuel Francis Du Pont*. Charlottesville: University of Virginia Press, 2005.

West, Richard. *Mr. Lincoln's Navy*. New York, NY: Longmans, Green and Company, 1957.

Glossary of Terms used in Specifications

Direct-acting: Engines that apply their power directly to the crankshaft via the piston rod.

Howitzer: A short cannon used to fire projectiles at medium muzzle velocities. Howitzers are often loaded with high-explosive (HE) ammunition for close range impact.

Pounder (pdr): A gun designed to fire a shell weighing a specified number of pounds.

Rifled gun: A barrel that has had grooves cut into it, in order to impart spin on the projectile on its long axis. This in turn acts as a stabilizing force, making the projectile more accurate at longer ranges.

Single screw: A ship with a single propeller.

Smoothbore: A gun without rifling.

Twin screw: Having two propellers, one on either side of the keel, usually revolving in opposite directions.

Walking-beam: A type of steam engine where a pivoted beam is vibrated by a vertical steam cylinder at one end, so transmitting motion.

Ships Index

General Index